Doing Sociology

Doing Sociology

Case Studies in Sociological Practice

EDITED BY
JAMMIE PRICE
ROGER A. STRAUS
JEFFREY R. BREESE

LEXINGTON BOOKS
A division of
ROWMAN & LITTLEFIELD PUBLISHERS, INC.
Lanham • Boulder • New York • Toronto • Plymouth, UK

Published by Lexington Books
A division of Rowman & Littlefield Publishers, Inc.
A wholly owned subsidiary of The Rowman & Littlefield Publishing Group, Inc.
4501 Forbes Boulevard, Suite 200, Lanham, Maryland 20706
http://www.lexingtonbooks.com

Estover Road, Plymouth PL6 7PY, United Kingdom

British Library Cataloguing in Publication Information Available

Library of Congress Cataloging-in-Publication Data
Doing sociology : case studies in sociological practice / edited by Jammie Price, Roger Straus, Jeffrey R. Breese.
   p. cm.
 Includes bibliographical references and index.
 ISBN 978-0-7391-3394-1 (hardcover : alk. paper) — ISBN 978-0-7391-3395-8 (pbk. : alk. paper) — ISBN 978-0-7391-3978-3 (ebook)
 1. Sociology—Case studies. 2. Sociology. I. Price, Jammie. II. Straus, Roger A. (Roger Austin), 1948– III. Breese, Jeffrey R., 1964–
 HM585.D65 2009
 301—dc22

                                                                    2009014055

Printed in the United States of America

Contents

Preface

Roger A. Straus, Certified Clinical Sociologist, Portland

In many ways, sociology has long been the Rodney Dangerfield of the social sciences, referring to the late American comedian best known for his catch phrase, "I don't get no respect." Students flock to psychology programs, counseling programs, social work programs, even anthropology programs—and why is that?

I suspect it is because they (or their parents) think that graduates with that major can get a "real job." Of course, there are always faculty positions to be had by sociologists and others, but how often do you see a classified ad "sociologist wanted?" You can't find "sociologist" in the Yellow Pages, as John F. Glass,[1] who cofounded the Clinical Sociology Association with me (and a host of others) so crisply put it (2001).

And why is that? Funny you should ask. I think part of the answer is that we've historically been so concerned to get sociology recognized as a "real" social science that we've been a bit embarrassed about all those sociological practitioners who work outside the academic realm. While this division between "pure" sociology and "practical" sociology is as old as our discipline (Fritz and Clark 1989), nobody ever told me about it. It seems that we keep forgetting and rediscovering this exciting part of our history over and over again.

I was, for example, astonished to find a thick volume, *The Uses of Sociology* (Lazarsfeld, Sewell and Wilensky, 1967) at a used bookstore one day. It was a compilation of papers presented at the previous years American Sociological Association meetings devoted to what we are now calling sociological practice. Nobody ever told me about that when I was in graduate school the following decade. I didn't know that many sociologists were graduating from schools like

Columbia University and finding positions in the "outside world." It was a kind of secret.

But we finally "came out of the closet" in the late 1970s and formed the organizations that have evolved into the Association for Applied and Clinical Sociology and the Sociological Practice and Public Sociology section within the American Sociological Association. And we're not going back. Rather, we have been developing teaching and training programs in applied and clinical sociology that attract an ever-increasing number of students even while so many traditional sociology programs go begging. And we've been finding more and more ways to go from "thinking about sociology" to "doing sociology." This volume attests to that. We're strong, we're proud—and I have to say it—we're fun. There is something deeply satisfying about taking our theories and methods and applying them to the "real world."

Another reason is that other social science disciplines like psychology and anthropology have been far less reticent to publicize and promote their practical applications and value. And sociology has, to be blunt, freely given away our concepts and methods to virtually all comers. Have you ever heard of focus groups? Survey research? Guess what discipline invented or at least developed them? Hint: that wasn't done by MBAs or psychologists. Those are "our" babies.

As the American Sociological Association puts it in its brochure, *Sociology: A World of Opportunities*, "the diversity of sociological careers ranges much further than what you might find under 'S' in the Sunday newspaper employment ads. Many jobs outside of academia do not necessarily carry the specific title of *sociologist*." Yet they are being done by sociologists, in the United States and elsewhere. It's time to claim back our own—and we're doing that.

Around the time I received my Ph.D. I started doing a form of sociological counseling. When I presented papers on this at national and regional meetings, it was amazing how many others literally came out of the woodwork, often looked around nervously, and told me that they, too, were doing clinical sociology. After a brief interlude teaching, I answered an ad for sociologists interested in becoming market research analysts. For approximately twenty years now, I've been a professional market researcher—and I'm continually astonished to discover how many of my peers hold sociology degrees. They just don't talk about it because we're not widely recognized by the business world. And practitioners have not been supported by organized sociology. But that's changing.

As you will see in this volume, we're out there. Doing sociology—not just analyzing sociology or talking about social issues, we're actively engaged in practicing what we preach. The authors of these chapters span generations. We're university professors, community college faculty, sociologists working in state and federal government, even, like myself, sociologists in private practice. What we're doing ranges from the application of statistics and survey methodology to using qualitative, ethnographic and field methods to help communities solve real problems. From applied research to straightforward clinical practice.

Our intention has been to have this volume complement a traditional textbook, to make it as easy as possible for an instructor to assign a reading from our book to supplement the large text. We want it to be useable both at the lower and upper division levels, perhaps even in graduate courses on sociological practice. We have designed it to be potentially used in the Introductory course, in Social Problems, Applied, or Junior or Senior Seminar, or Internship courses. That is, to be flexible. To that end, these fourteen chapters have been laid out to marry with an Introduction to Sociology textbook. You'll find an introductory chapter, chapters on ethics, theory, methods, deviance, crime, community, education . . . and more.

At the same time, each of the chapters is by intention and design a *personal* statement, in and of itself a case study illustrating how the author or authors practice sociology. In their own words and their own style—we deliberately have not imposed a "style sheet" on our contributors. We have asked them to tell their stories from their own perspectives, each in their own style.

As my coeditor Jammie Price puts it, we want readers to come away from this book and say that it was readable. Accessible. That they understood what sociologists DO outside of teaching in universities. That we are engaged in communities. That you can DO something with Sociology. Not just blow smoke.

We begin with not just one but two chapters introducing applied, clinical, and public sociology. Chapter One shows you how we bring a sociological perspective to the many things we do under these three "umbrellas." The next chapter goes further to lay out some of the roles we play in doing sociology, then shows you how we are enacting those roles around the world.

Our third chapter explains how sociological practitioners differ from others who might work in similar roles and on similar problems, through our background and application of sociological theory to whatever we are doing. Next, we provide a fascinating example of how this has been done in a context far removed from the usual safe, academic setting by a clinical sociologist working with substance abusers in a court-mandated treatment program for felony probationers.

From there, it seemed only natural to turn to the topic of applying sociology to issues of crime and criminal justice. Chapter Five describes work at the juncture of clinical sociology, applied sociology and public sociology, doing collaborative research to facilitate and improve community policing and crime prevention. The next chapter offers a glimpse into what is traditionally considered applied sociology—evaluation research—here using it to evaluate and improve drug courts.

Another area of great interest to sociologists and sociology has been education and the educational system. Chapter Seven discusses how a project originally designed to evaluate the achievement of specific, formal goals and objectives in the Kentucky higher education system was expanded, though a sociological perspective, to take into account the ability of the system to develop the capacity to sustain those goals.

From here, we turn to a set of chapters discussing ways in which sociological practitioners work with communities, another major interest of sociologists. First, we present the results of a project designed to marry community research with social change, through a sociologically informed assessment of the needs and assets of an inner city neighborhood. Then we move to a fascinating project in which the consultants created evaluation tools designed to foster development of housing and other environments meeting the needs of our aging population.

Just in case the foregoing chapters have implied that all those who do sociology have somehow joined or at least work within "the system," our tenth chapter illustrates how some of us apply what is commonly termed a "critical sociology" perspective to their practice. This chapter applies post-modernist critical theory to the understanding of several intentional communities and lessons learned regarding how they have managed to persist in the face of opposition from the conventional culture and society surrounding them. These include, for example, a multiracial community that took root in the rural Deep South of the 1940s.

Making an almost 180 degree turn, we then consider how sociological practitioners can expand our opportunities by taking advantage of federal funding opportunities offered by the National Institutes of Health. From there, it seems only natural to explore the role of applied sociologists working in government settings—in this case, doing evaluation research for the State of California. Chapter Twelve shows how the survey methodology competencies developed by so many of us in our graduate programs can be turned to practical use—and how, as sociologists, we can transform and enhance those methodologies beyond a rote or "cookbook" approach.

That discussion nicely sets the stage for a case example in which one of the editors and her colleagues utilized survey methodology to evaluate preparedness of health care providers to provide emergency services for children across the State of North Carolina. While health care, of course, is a major concern of sociologists, that project had an additional goal of developing a survey process and design that would maximize response rates, which are always problematic because busy medical professionals are continually barraged by requests to participate in research (including by those who, like myself, conduct market research and can offer the provider cash honoraria that cannot be matched by those doing research for public agencies). That is, not only to get the information but to apply sociology in order to enhance the quality of that information.

Our last chapter then tackles the issue of ethics and values in applied socio-logical research. It specifically focuses on the development of human research protections, how these have been designed in the context of federally funded biomedical and behavioral research, and the issues they have come to present to the sociological practitioner in obtaining approval for her or his research activi-ties. As one who is waiting for data from a study that was interrupted by the vacillation of an Institutional Review Board with respect to approving a simple questionnaire, I can attest to the importance of being aware of and understand-ing these considerations!

This volume is designed as a successor, or possibly supplement, to my earlier text, *Using Sociology*. While the earlier book focuses more on the principles of and possibilities for sociological practice from the perspective of distinguished experts in the field, what you hold in your hand is something different—con-crete, living examples of sociological practice by individuals who are, as the title implies, actually *Doing Sociology*.

Works Cited

Amercian Sociology Association, n.d. *Sociology: A World of Opportunities*. www.asanet. org/cs/root/leftnav/careers_and_jobs/sociology_a_world_of_opportunities.

Fritz, Jan M. and Elizabeth J. Clark. 1989. "Overview of the Field: Definitions and His-tory." *Sociological Practice* 7: 9–14.

Glass, John F. 2001. "The Founding of the Clinical Sociology Association: A Personal Narrative." *Sociological Practice* 3, no. 1: 75–85.

Lazarsfeld, Paul F., William H. Sewell, and Harold L. Wilensky, eds. 1967. *The Uses of Sociology*. New York: Basic Books.

Straus, Roger A., ed. 2002. *Using Sociology: An Introduction from the Applied and Clinical Perspectives*. 3rd Edition. Lanham, MD: Rowman & Littlefield.

Note

1. This is not the same John Glass who contributes Chapter Four of this volume. While both are clinical sociologists and my friends, I can attest that they are very differ-ent people!

CHAPTER 1

An Introduction to Doing Sociology

APPLIED, CLINICAL, AND PUBLIC SOCIOLOGY

Stephen F. Steele, Anne Arundel Community College, Maryland
Jeffrey R. Breese, Rockhurst University

Sociology is a discipline of study, which focuses on human group life, communities, and societies. Sociology can also be considered a way of viewing human behavior that focuses on the patterns of relationships among individuals rather than solely the individuals themselves. This distinguishes sociology from the field of psychology. The sociological perspective offers a way to view facts, conditions, and people, and a way to perceive and understand the world around us.

In a very real sense, all sociology is applied. C. Wright Mills (1959) described the "sociological imagination" as a way of understanding the complex relationship between individual lives and the larger social world in which they live. For Mills, the personal troubles experienced by individuals are always connected to and impacted by larger public issues. Building on this notion, all of social life is a potential outlet for the study and application of sociological principles and ideas. Sociologists study a wide range of institutions (from families to political structures and the economic development of nations), and the unique nature of how these various institutions interrelate and impact each other. The applications of sociology are evident everywhere. Sociologists engage in all types of work as they study the conditions, people, and issues of society. Public opinion polling, market analysis, community needs assessments, policy analysis, and the study of social problems, are often the domain of sociologists. Understanding crime rates, population shifts and growth, and trends in the media are all more fully understood through the sociological perspective.

The focus of this book, unlike others offering an overview of the field of sociology, is the applicability and usefulness of sociology to many social issues, dilemmas, and trends in society. We will focus on those who practice sociology as part of their profession, the applied, clinical, and public sociologists. Sociology can be, and often is, used to gain a more basic understanding of fundamental aspects of social phenomena. However, sociology can also be applied with the goal of making practical, real world applications to individuals and organizations. Applied sociology tends to have a "client centered" focus where some group, agency, or corporation is drawing upon the essential skills of the sociologist in a community based setting, where an actual or "real world" issue is in need of being resolved or considered. Taking this even further, clinical sociologists are often asked to be part of a team where the goal is to alter a problematic social relationship or to restructure some social institution. Here, the sociologist as a consultant is brought on board to assist a corporation in the midst of significant change or maybe asked by therapists to research a new form of group therapy for their client. Other clinical sociologists themselves do therapy, community development or other work as change agents (Glassner and Freedman, 1979; Straus, 2002).

Sociology is also in many ways a public enterprise. As Herbert J. Gans (1999) said, "a public sociologist is a public intellectual who applies sociological ideas and findings to social issues about which sociology has something to say" (265). The focus of this book is to help you understand how sociologists do this, and each chapter is written by sociologists who have engaged in practicing sociology. This book will demonstrate how sociologists are "taking sociology to publics beyond the university, engaging them in dialogue about public issues that have been studied by sociologists" (Burawoy, 2005, 71). Applied, clinical, and public sociologists participate in grassroots organizing, community-based non-profits, government agencies, policy think tanks, and research organizations. They do consulting work, research proposal writing, administer programs, census research, market analysis, environmental impact studies, and work in the fields of criminal justice, education, health care, government, among others. Their stories will be told in the pages of this book and how they came to understand and do these various jobs will be better understood by you as move from chapter to chapter.

A Fundamental Dimension of Sociology: Change

The type and speed of social change have been central to sociology since its beginning. Sociologists have always tried to understand how and why society changes. Countless theories have been considered and concepts rendered for understanding of change. Most *Introduction to Sociology* courses include applications of the sociological imagination by identifying variables that influence outcomes and then extending that logic to imagine the labyrinth of social forces that produce the status quo. By extension, the sociological imagination is of little use unless we can use it to create new and improved social realities.

This focus on change holds with practicing sociologists. We are engaged in evaluating, assessing, implementing, promoting, measuring social behavior, all of which imply change, or, in some cases, resisting change. Plans to seek solutions to problems intrinsically suggest that change will occur. Practicing sociologists have a professional obligation to make sure that the research and observations that they conduct will produce a change that impacts an organization or society or even a human interaction in an appropriate way. Further, practicing sociologists have an obligation to make clients aware of all the potential outcomes that a social and organizational change might make. Each substantive chapter in this book will walk the reader through how the author(s) addressed a social issue with a community partner or client. Hence, every chapter focuses on change.

Fundamental Perspectives of Sociology: Tools

Practicing sociologists build things. They create reality, they intervene in it, they make change and they challenge others to improve the social condition. But doing this is not possible without tools. For us there are fundamentally four kinds of tools: perspectives, theories, concepts, and methods. We're sure many sociologists only think of research methods as tools. But, we hope we can make a case for things conceptual as well as methodological to be tools just the same.

PERSPECTIVE AS A TOOL

We've all had the experience in which we look at something and think that it's one thing and then when turned 90° we may find out that it might be quite something else. The way we look at things—the paradigms we bring with us when we enter a social reality—have a major impact on what we see. Fundamentally sociologists focus on the situations, and the characteristics of those situations, in which action occurs. We spend our time trying to understand how situations are organized and ordered and how these situations lead to dynamic boxes in which social actors find themselves. Over decades of study, sociologists improve upon theories, and are better able to explain how people will behave in certain situations. Some will go so far as to predict how people will act in certain situations, given the strength of the theory and research. But overall, when explaining why social phenomena, such as homelessness, alcoholism, or terrorism occur, sociologists share an emphasis on the characteristics of the social situation. That is the sociological perspective.

While the sociological perspective is certainly not the center of the universe when it comes to problem solving, our perspective does shed new light on problems. Sociologists are aware that their perspective, while valuable and dynamic, is certainly not the only one. Taken with perspectives on the individual, environmental biology, and the natural sciences, we may come to realize that human action is much more complex. We're not surprised when someone tells us that invoking the sociological perspective "is just plain something they hadn't ever thought of." The sociological perspective encourages us to get outside of ourselves and walk in other's shoes, to see the world as other's see it. This process is known as "taking the role of the other."

THEORIES AS TOOLS

We've all heard people talk about the dichotomy between theory and practice. This is so often stated as if these things were completely unrelated. Truly in academic settings the distinction between theory and practice is an ideological battleground. This is unfortunate. On one hand this battle does provide for synthesis and change in the way we see and do things. We practicing sociologists say, "let them fight it out." Our plan is to use these theories as tools. Instead of being beholden to some ideological view of whether Karl Marx was right or someone else was right, or whether this or that one theoretical perspective really does explain what's going on, practicing sociologists are looking for a good tool to address an issue. Can we skillfully impose a perspective or a structure (such as a theory) on a situation that may seem chaotic to the persons in it? Will the perspective or the theory provide an explanation of the situation? If yes, this ability strengthens our sense-making capabilities and makes it possible for us to add valuable professional skills to the social setting. For example, getting a CEO to see problems in his organization as system problems or as simply symbolically created may be an important breakthrough in solving these problems. Fascinatingly, a synthesis among major social theories may be the best way to solve a problem. If one is wed to a single approach we risk failing to use the entire toolbox to solve the problem.

CONCEPTS AS TOOLS

Concepts are ideas that help us make sense of the world. Since sensemaking is so critical in understanding a problem or situation, being able to express social settings effectively in terms and concepts is a powerful tool. Using concepts as tools is a double edged sword. On one hand, concepts provide a shorthand way of quickly making sense of very complex situations. On the other hand, these very concepts may need to be translated in a variety of ways by the sociological practitioner so that that situation can make sense to our clients. Being able to see and express any social situation as, say, "a social construction of reality" can be a powerful wrench or, at times, a "road block" to effective communication.

METHODS AS TOOLS

In his classic work *Fads and Foibles in Modern Sociology and Related Sciences* Sorokin (1956) points out—and we're paraphrasing—that sociology at that time was a very poor photograph of the status quo. Even in the 21st century, Sorokin's point remains. The methods of measuring and the processes for knowing human interaction then, and perhaps now, move slowly behind reality. Practicing sociologists are not interested in a battle over quantitative versus qualitative methods. Rather the question really is, "Which tools produce the most accurate understanding of social reality in whatever condition we may find ourselves?" For a practicing sociologist, whether applied, clinical, or public, the more tools one understands and over which one has mastery the better off he or she is. So, the broader wider and deeper the practicing sociologists tool kit is, the better.

Importantly, a practicing sociologist must not be limited to tools produced only in their own discipline. So many wonderful and imaginative tools originate in a variety of fields, that we weaken our mastery by failing to accept them. Furthermore, one must realize that sociology is far too narrow a discipline to deal with the problems that face a global society. No longer can we use excuses that suggest that we are exclusively social scientists and hence need not know other scientific, religious, or cultural domains. No one is surprised when a discussion of the 21st century drifts to a conversation of information overload. The technological ability to produce information and noise in our world is excessive. Practicing sociologists contribute an ability to make sense of this information overload with its massive infusions of information and data. As Thomas Friedman indicates in *The World Is Flat*, "pattern discernment" jobs are at the forefront in the 21st century. They should put sociologists at the head of the pack with the developed skills of sensemaking.

One final point: Practicing sociologists are solution centered. This is important because our role is not just to know what is going on but help construct solutions and interventions to promote better or more effective human interaction. Striving for client-centered solutions to a problem requires a distinct perspective that sets practicing sociologists apart from other sociologists.

Works Cited

Burawoy, Michael. 2005. "The Return of the Repressed: Recovering the Public Face of U.S. Sociology, One Hundred Years On." *The ANNALS of the American Academy of Political and Social Science* 600: 68–85.

Friedman, Thomas. 2007. *World Is Flat 3.0: A Brief History of the Twenty-first Century.* London: Picador.

Gans, Herbert J. 1999. *Making Sense of America: Sociological Analyses and Essays.* Lanham, MD: Rowman & Littlefield.

Glassner, Barry and Jonathan Freedman. 1979. *Clinical Sociology.* New York: Longmans.

Mills, C. Wright. [1959] 2000. *The Sociological Imagination. 40th Anniversary Edition: New Afterword by Todd Gitlin.* New York: Oxford University Press.

Sorokin, Piritim A. 1956. *Fads and Foibles in Modern Sociology and Related Sciences.* Chicago: Henry Regnery.

Straus, Roger, ed. 2002. *Using Sociology: An Introduction from the Applied and Clinical Perspectives.* Lanham, MD: Rowman & Littlefield.

CHAPTER 2

Doing Sociology Worldwide

Gene Shackman, The Global Social Change Research Project
Xun Wang, University of Wisconsin at Parkside
Ya-Lin Liu, The Global Social Change Research Project
Jammie Price, Appalachian State University

As sociologists, we are interested in applying our sociological knowledge to improving society's conditions and people's lives. But how do sociologists do this? In general, we play three different roles in doing sociology. First, we conduct research to systematically analyze social conditions and possible solutions to problems in the conditions. Second, we develop models, theories, and perspectives to further help us understand how the social conditions might be changed for the better. Third, we facilitate improving the social conditions as policy makers and activists (see Table 2.1).

Probably our most common role is conducting research, searching for possible causes of problems, and evaluating possible solutions. For example, a review of a number of sociological associations indicates that their main focus is research, which we will discuss later in the paper. Similarly, in the United States, about 75% of sociologists are in academic institutions (National Science Foundation, 2006). Less commonly, doing sociology might include direct intervention, including things like improving access to clean water or training people on how to advocate for their rights.

In this chapter, we focus primarily on this third role, direct interventions by sociologists around the world. We would like to explore how our efforts could collectively work together in helping to change the world for the better.

The chapter includes three parts. First, we briefly describe the current world social, political, and economic conditions. This is the context in which sociologists are working. A description of the world sets the stage for a description of the work of the sociologists described in this chapter. In the second section, we

Table 2.1. Roles of Sociologists

Areas	Specific Tasks
Describe social conditions	Conduct research Surveys Census Observations Use existing data Develop systematical interpretations to help people understand how to improve social conditions
Understand and improve social conditions	Models Theories Perspectives
Facilitate and improve social conditions	Develop intervention to change social conditions in people's lives Policies Training programs Activists

describe several sociological associations worldwide. How sociologists work is very much influenced by the general condition of sociology in the country. The more sociology and sociological methods are accepted, the more options the sociologists have in conducting their projects. In the third section, we introduce some sociologists who are currently involved with direct interventions aimed at changing people's lives. We start with describing the general sociological conditions of various countries, based on information from the sociologists, or from other sources. The above sociological conditions can serve as indicators of what kinds of sociological activities or practices are possible. Last, we describe what the sociologists are actually doing, as they apply sociology throughout the world; what kinds of activities they do and how they do it.

We hope that, by reading this chapter, people can develop a better understanding about what sociologists do, around the world. People can then see how and where sociology may be useful in understanding, explaining, and helping to change the world.

Current Global Conditions and Trends: A Sociological View

There are a number of major trends in the world concerning population, health (represented by infant mortality rate [IMR]), economics, and politics (represented by freedom).

Table 2.2.   Population

	N	Mid-year population, 1960 (millions)	Mid-year population, 1980 (millions)	Mid-year population, 2001 (millions)	Annual Average Growth Rate 60–80	Annual Average Growth Rate 80–01
All	223	3,039	4,456	6,157	2.33%	1.82%
Less Developed Countries	167	2,129	3,375	4,968	2.93%	2.25%
More Developed Countries	6	910	1,081	1,189	0.94%	0.48%
Ratio of LDC to MDC populations		2.3	3.1	4.2		

Source: U.S. Census Bureau, International Database, www.census.gov/ipc/www/idb/. Also presented in Table 5 from Shackman, Gene, Xun Wang and Ya-Lin Liu. 2002. Brief review of world demographic trends. Available at http://gsociology.icaap.org/report/demsum.html.

First, the population in the Less Developed Countries (LDCs) is becoming an increasingly large proportion of world population, growing from 70% in 1960 to 81% in 2001 (Table 2). However, population growth is declining, in both the LDCs and More Developed Countries (MDCs). Second, IMR declined significantly between 1960 and 2001, for the world, and for both LDCs and for MDCs (Table 3). While both LDCs and MDCs, on average, made dramatic improvements, gains for LDCs were much slower than were gains among the MDCs. Third, in the last several decades, gross domestic product (GDP) per capita increased in both developing and developed countries (Table 4). GDP—the market value of all goods and services produced in a given year—is one of the measures used to describe a country's economy. In general, GDP per capita increased about the same in both developed and developing countries. Finally, in the last several decades, there has only been moderate growth in freedom, and

Table 2.3.   Infant Mortality Rates (infant deaths per 1,000 births)

	1980	2001
More Developed Countries (*N* = 30)	13	6
Less Developed Countries (*N* = 83)	102	61
World	89	54

Source: U.S. Census Bureau, International Database, www.census.gov/ipc/www/idb/. Also presented in Table 6 from Shackman, Gene, Xun Wang and Ya-Lin Liu. 2002. Brief review of world demographic trends. Available at http://gsociology.icaap.org/report/demsum.html.

Table 2.4.   GDP Per Capita (in thousands of dollars)

	1980	2000
More Developed Countries	$18,491	$28,168
Less Developed Countries	$961	$1,491
World	$3,973	$5,229

Source: International Macroeconomic Data, www.ers.usda.gov/Data/Macroeconomics/. Also presented at Shackman, Gene, Ya-Lin Liu and Xun Wang. 2005. Brief review of world economic trends. Available at http://gsociology.icaap.org/report/econ/econsum.html.

in 2000, about 43% of people in LDCs still lived in countries that were not free (Table 5).

However, the general trends of improving living conditions described above don't apply to every country. For example, five countries (three in Africa) recently had increases of IMR greater than 10 percentage points (Shackman, Wang and Liu, 2002). Also, seven countries had GDP per capita declines of more than 40 percent, and four of these countries were in the Middle East (Shackman, Liu and Wang, 2005). Finally, twelve countries experienced a large decline in freedom, and seven of these were in Asia (Shackman, Liu and Wang, 2004).

In sum, there were large gains in many aspects of society. On the other hand, there were also many countries that did not share in these gains. It would seem reasonable to use sociology to understand why some of the countries did not improve, and what could be done about it. This is the rationale behind a project developed by the chapter authors called the Global Social Change Research Project (Shackman, Liu and Wang, 2008). The project provides a set of reports showing global social, political, economic, and demographic trends, hopefully in formats that are easy for everyone to read. The Global Social Change Research

Table 2.5.   Percent of People Living in Countries That Are Free

	1980	2000
More Developed Countries	88%	99%
Less Developed Countries	27%	32%
Percent of People Living in Countries That Are Not Free		
More Developed Countries	7%	0%
Less Developed Countries	45%	43%

Source: Freedom House ratings available at www.freedomhouse.org/template.cfm?page=1. Combined with U.S. Census Bureau's population data from the International Data Base. Also presented at Shackman, Gene, Ya-Lin Liu and Xun Wang. 2004. Brief review of world political trends. Available at http://gsociology.icaap.org/report/polsum.html.

Project provides a sociological point of view of where the world is, where it is going, and how it might get there. The project facilitates others who may want to apply sociology to address various social problems, either globally or locally.

Doing Sociology at Institutional Levels

There are a number of international, regional, national, and topic specific sociological associations (see Table 2.6). In this section, we briefly review information from these organizations. We also briefly describe several sociologists working at major institutions. Through these reviews, we demonstrate what sociologists are doing worldwide at the institutional level, which, as mentioned above provides indicators of the varying conditions throughout the world in which sociology can be applied.

The major theme of most sociological associations is to promote sociology, sociological knowledge, and research, and also to develop networks for sociological researchers. For example, the International Sociological Association supports activities to: "(a) secure and develop institutional and personal contacts between sociologists and other social scientists throughout the world; (b) encourage the international dissemination and exchange of information on developments in sociological knowledge; and (c) facilitate and promote international research and training" (ISA, 2008). Most other associations have similar statements.

A few associations specifically have goals of promoting sociological interventions in public affairs. For example, the Association for Applied and Clinical Sociology has a goal to "promote the use of applied and clinical sociology in local, regional, state, national, and international settings" (AACS, 2008). A few other institutions have a similar statement. It seems possible that in those countries or regions where organizations can include these statements, sociologists may have more opportunity to practice sociology, or use more sociological methods.

Other ways that sociologists engage in international intervention include working directly with government agencies, or with government affiliated associations such as the World Health Organization (WHO), the World Bank, the International Monetary Fund, the World Trade Organization, or the United Nations (UN), or with any of the thousands of non-governmental organizations (NGOs). For example, one of the authors developed a training program for Chinese officials to deal with unemployment and reemployment problems in China (Wang and Statham, 2004). A web search on "sociologist at the UN" returned a chair of a panel of Civil Society (UN, 2008a), several members of a High-Level Panel about Gender Dimensions of International Migration (UN, 2006), and a moderator of a Human Rights Workshop (UN, 2008b). A brief search of WHO returned a sociologist working as a research director, and another as a program commissioner (WHO, 2008).

Table 2.6. Sociological Associations

Name	Missions	Key Research/Practice Activity
The International Sociological Association http://www.isa-sociology.org/	Represent sociologists everywhere	Facilitate and promote international research and training
The Asia Pacific Sociological Association http://www.asiapacificsociology.org/	Link sociological associations, . . . and . . . sociologists	Promote and assist the publication of social research. Encourage co-operation between sociologists, planners, and policy makers
The Latin American Studies Association (LASA) http://lasa.international.pitt.edu/	Foster intellectual discussion, research, and teaching	Recognize scholarly achievement and represent Latin American interests and views before the U.S. government and at times to governments elsewhere
The Australian Sociological Association http://www.tasa.org.au/	Further applied sociology . . . provide a network for sociologists	Hold annual conference . . . publish the *Journal of Sociology*

The Association for Applied and Clinical Sociology
http://www.aacsnet.org/wp/

Further applied sociology

Advance theory, research, methods, and training that promotes the use of sociological knowledge, and promote the use of applied and clinical sociology in local, regional, state, national, and international settings

The Association for Humanist Sociology
http://www.altrue.net/site/humanist/

Share a commitment to using sociology to promote peace, equality, and social justice

Holding an annual meeting to build the community and to share ideas and experiences

The European Sociological Association
http://www.europeansociology.org/

Facilitate sociological research, teaching, and communication . . . give sociology a voice in European affairs

Facilitate sociological research . . . and communication between . . . sociologists and other scientists . . . contribute to understanding and solving social problems improving the quality of life in Europe

African Sociological Association
http://www.afsanet.org/

Provide professional home for sociologists working on or interested in African issues

Devoted to the advancement of the study of "sociational life" rooted in, and concerned with the African condition. It is devoted to valorising distinct African voices and insights into the global sociological enterprise

Doing sociology at the institutional level includes direct intervention, including, as mentioned in the beginning of this chapter, things like improving access to clean water in one village or training people on how to advocate for their rights. In this section, we describe some of the direct interventions sociologists are doing, using examples primarily from the sociologists who volunteered descriptions of their work. The activities they describe include work in a variety of settings including using evaluations to train and build capacity, creating workshops on gender sensitivity, sexual harassment, sexual education, and abuse issues, empowering community development, and training in human rights education. These sociologists work in a variety of countries including Brazil, Cyprus, Ghana, Iran, India, Nigeria, Russia, and South America. These sociologists were contacted through various sociology related organizations and e-mail lists. These sociologists volunteered information about their activities in practicing sociology. We changed their names to maintain confidentiality.

DOING SOCIOLOGY IN EUROPE

Three sociologists from Cyprus described their work and situations. Cyprus lies in the Mediterranean Sea, just south of Turkey and just west of Syria. The population of Cyprus is almost 800,000. About 81% are Greek Cypriots, 11% are Turkish Cypriots and 8% are foreigners residing in Cyprus (Cyprus Government Portal, 2008). The quality of life in Cyprus is not too different from that of the rest of the European Union (EU) countries. For example, Cyprus's IMR of 7 per 1,000 is nearly the same as the average IMR of all MDC (U.S. Census Bureau, 2008), the GDP per Capita was $15,000 compared to the EU's $20,000 (USDA, 2008). People in Cyprus also enjoy freedom of religion, as do most people in the developed world (U.S. Department of State, 2008a). Also, the most recent government was elected in free and fair elections, and generally respects the human rights of its citizens (U.S. Department of State, 2008b).

The sociologists from Cyprus reported their experiences as sociologists in Cyprus. For the most part, their story is about difficulties in finding sociological work in Cyprus. The main point here is that there are limited opportunities for practicing sociology in Cyprus.

Kyrenia wrote "in Cyprus the percentage of young people who are tertiary educated is very high, it is one of the highest in Europe, and the result is that many young scientists cannot find a job that is compatible to their degrees. For instance we have members in the Cyprus Sociological Association that are cashiers, café owners, secretaries etc." She also wrote that sociologists cannot work in social services because that is the role of social workers, and sociologists also cannot teach sociology in the schools. Kyrenia continued, "Therefore, many sociologists try to find other solutions. For instance they establish counseling companies; they go to the Police Academy and after their graduation they work as policemen/women." One study came to a similar conclusion, that, in Cyprus, students with degrees in social and political sciences were among the least likely to be hired (Economics Research Centre, University of Cyprus, 2008).

The situation in Cyprus is improving, though. Loukia wrote "Only recently, the last 5–10 years television and radio producers had realized the contribution of sociologists presenting and explaining publicly some social problems. They tend to invite sociologists to their programs for some explanations when presenting a social problem."

Chloe wrote, "The most important change that has happened in Cyprus in the past few years is the accession of the island to the EU. This means that 3% of the GDP has to be allocated to research by 2010. This has given a boost to research and gave more possibility to sociology as an active component. . . . Cyprus is also involved in European projects. This has helped towards the direction of improving quantity and quality in research, especially academically."

Two other sociologists told us about working in other European countries: one in Russia and one in Kosovo. Andrei helps to empower community development in Russia: "we helped to create self-help groups among the poor populations" with the goal of eradicating poverty. There is little information about sociology in Russia. On the one hand, there is a Sociological Institute as part of the Russian Academy of Science (Russian Academy of Science, 2008) and there are thousands of sociology academics (Novikova, 2008). On the other hand, not many Russian faculty are published in peer reviewed journals outside of Russia, and a large number of sociologists leave the profession (Novikova, 2008).

Naim, in Kosovo, has worked for a number of international NGOs. His current position is to "coordinate an inter-ministerial and stakeholder Working Group for compiling a strategy for" agricultural development. His current position is to coordinate a governmental inter-departmental working group for compiling a strategy for agricultural development.

DOING SOCIOLOGY IN AFRICA

Two of the other participating sociologists work in Nigeria, which is on the coast of West Africa. Nigeria has the largest population of any African country and is the 14th largest geographically (Embassy of the Republic of Nigeria, 2008). Nigeria has 250 ethnic groups but the "dominant ethnic group in the northern two-thirds of the country is the Hausa-Fulani, most of whom are Muslim. . . .

The Yoruba people are predominant in the southwest. About half of the Yorubas are Christian and half Muslim" (U.S. Department of State, 2008c). Despite the fact that the country is one of the world's top crude oil producers (and a leading supplier to the United States), the quality of life in Nigeria is much lower than that of other LDCs, for the most part. The IMR of Nigeria is 96 per 1,000, much higher than the average IMR of LDCs (typically 52 per 1,000), but on par with the IMR of sub-sub Saharan Africa, 89 per 1,000 (U.S. Census Bureau, 2008). The GDP per capita of Nigeria is $466, rather lower than the average of $1,900 for developing countries (USDA, 2008). Human rights conditions in Nigeria are poor, including absence of a freely and fairly elected government and, overall, a poor human rights record (U.S. Department of State, 2008b). On the other hand, people enjoy relative freedom of religion (U.S. Department of State, 2008a).

Abeke works for a NGO with the goal of empowering women and communities to improve economic, social, and political rights of women. Abeke is the project director, which involves designing organizational programs—identifying community needs and sourcing funds (writing proposals) to implement such programs; overseeing program/project implementation. She also oversees the daily operations of the organization.

Ehioze works at the research unit of a financial institution. "I assist in designing tools for appraisal of service providers, obtaining feedback on client services, designing training that is tailored to address skills gaps. The basic approach is that I work within a system and understanding its dynamics is important in designing risk management framework. In designing intervention strategies to address vulnerabilities, we try to understand underlying human behavioral patterns and address potentially predictable expectations, while at the same time building scenarios for proactive actions."

Two other sociologists provided information about working in Africa, one in South Africa and the other in Ghana. Alan in South Africa works on local government planning and community development. He is part of a group that "physically goes into a community with questionnaires, focus group meetings, fieldwork, photography, planning sessions to research and study every social aspect of that community. Our reports are then presented before mayoral committees, decision makers and give direction to their decision making processes." Jacob, in Ghana works with an NGO as a monitoring and evaluation specialist, "tracking what smallholder farmers think of the success or otherwise of the program and how best we can improve on our assistance to these farmers."

There appears to be some opportunity for the practice of sociology in Africa, working either in institutions or independently. Opportunities for sociologists might be a relatively new phenomenon, for example, it was only recently that the International Sociological Association held a world conference in Africa (International Sociological Association, 2006). Similarly, until recently sociologists in South Africa had little interaction with sociologists outside of South Africa (Jubber, 2007). Thus, while sociology is practiced in Africa, there may be limited but emerging opportunities and roles for either academics or practitioners.

DOING SOCIOLOGY IN ASIA

Two of the sociologists reported working in India. India is the dominant nation of South Asia. The world's second-largest country in population, with 1.12 billion people, India is 80% Hindu, and 13% Muslim, with an and estimated 2,000 ethnic groups (U.S. Department of State, 2008d). The quality of life in India is somewhat mixed. India's IMR of 35 per 1,000 (U.S. Department of State, 2008d) is much better than the average for developing countries, of 63 per 1,000 (see Table 2). India's social structure is characterized by dramatic class and regional disparities, as seen in the recent hit movie, *Slumdog Millionaire.* While, the GDP per capita of India is $909 (U.S. Department of State, 2008d), somewhat lower than the average for developing countries (see Table 3), the country has a huge and growing middle class. Politically, the government of India had some degree of respect for citizen rights but there is also a good deal of corruption and abuse, including torture. Overall, there is inadequate enforcement of human rights laws, although there have been some investigations into individual abuse cases and punishment of perpetrators (U.S. Department of State, 2008b). Presenting a consistent mixed picture, the national government displays general respect for religious freedom, but some state and local governments were rather more restrictive (U.S. Department of State, 2008a).

On the one hand, academic sociology in India seems to be progressing, with a continuingly growing association, journals, and popular conferences (Indian Sociological Society, 2008). On the other hand, academic growth does not seem to translate to sociological involvement with applied issues. For example, there seems to be only a limited number of sociologists working with or in the government of India. A search from the government of India's website (http://india. gov.in/) found no sociologists as such (although as in the United States, sociologists may be working under other job titles). A Google search for sociologists with URL's ending in "gov.in" found only two sociologists, in advisory capacities (Ministry of Culture, 2005; National Water Development Agency, 2004). In one recent book review (Vasavi, 2003), the author criticizes Indian sociologists for not becoming involved with major societal issues. It is difficult to find any further information about the position of sociology in India.

One of the Indian practitioners we contacted, Dalaja, works on education and advocacy for a NGO. Recently Dalaja has been focusing on creating workshops on gender sensitivity, sexual harassment, sexual education, as well as abuse issues among teenage students and teachers in low income communities. These workshops are being developed for one specific organization. The administrators of the organization requested the workshops but based on conversations so far with people she will be working with, Dalaja feels that the workshops may not be well received by people working in that organization. The other sociologist, Aadesh is the lead researcher for a project on the coping strategies among the poorest in rural India. Aadesh, was involved in problem formulation, methodology development, conduct of actual research, analysis, and publication.

Dalaja writes that her sociological training was useful. "My sociological training actually is employed in critically analyzing the way in which I conduct research among already victimized groups. I find that while there are a lot of NGOs that work in the field, there is a surprising lack of ethical conduct or conversations about confidentiality in the field. I discovered this when I was collecting data for my dissertation. So, my future interest primarily lies in making sure that the participants of research study are treated ethically."

Conclusion

What are sociologists doing globally, and are they contributing? It is clear from this review that sociologists are active in a very wide variety of fields internationally. The position of sociologists in society seems somewhat mixed, at times fairly well accepted and involved in government or community projects as agents of change, and at other times, somewhat restricted to supporting the status quo. As indicated in the introduction, our participation seems largely in academics, but there are also many sociologists who take a direct role in applying sociology in the global community. In sum of where we are, there is still a good deal of room for growth among sociologists worldwide.

One of the issues that may be limiting sociologists in terms of direct intervention is lack of recognition. Pilar, from Argentina and now attending graduate school in Europe, wrote of this, "Usually when I am in other countries people don't know what sociology is or they mix it with psychology, so I am always obliged to say that I study society and that this is useful for teaching at University or for Public Policy (this is my short version for ordinary citizens of what sociology is)." Thus, one step that sociologists could take is to develop better information resources, easily available to the public, about sociology, describing what sociology is, and what sociologists do. The American Sociological Association began a project on public sociology (American Sociological Association, 2008), but this has had little impact. As sociologists and sociological practitioners have long noted, there remains need to publicize what our discipline is all about and what we can do—both here in the United States and globally.

Another related step to furthering the ability of sociologists to work in direct intervention (whether clinical or applied sociology, or what is coming to be considered "public sociology") is expanding recognition of our abilities to use sociology beyond "pure research." At least in the United States, the sociology community is increasingly coming to recognize intervention in the tenure and promotion process (Jaschick, 2007). As can be seen in the chapters of this book, sociologists are expanding the use and understanding of sociology outside the academic community, at least in the United States. Hopefully this trend will continue, and will further develop throughout the rest of the world as well.

Works Cited

American Sociological Association. 2008. Public Sociology Web Site. http://pubsoc.wisc. edu/news.php. Retrieved December 1, 2008.

Association of Applied and Clinical Sociology. 2008. www.aacsnet.org/wp/. Retrieved November 29, 2008. Mission statements.

Cyprus Government Portal. 2008. www.cyprus.gov.cy. Click on "About Cyprus" and then "Towns and Population."

Economics Research Centre, University of Cyprus. 2008. www.eurofound.europa.eu/ ewco/2008/05/CY0805019I.htm. Retrieved February 3, 2009.

Embassy of the Federal Republic of Nigeria. 2008. www.nigeriaembassyusa.org/. Retrieved November 5, 2008. Pages about history, people, business, and economy.

Indian Sociological Society. 2008. "About Us." www.insoso.org/aboutus.htm. Retrieved November 15, 2008.

International Sociological Association. 2006. World Congress of Sociology, Durban, South Africa. www.ucm.es/info/isa/congress2006/index.htm. Retrieved December 18, 2008.

———. 2008. www.isa-sociology.org/. Retrieved November 29, 2008. See main page statement and statutes page.

Jaschick, S. 2007. "Tenure and the Public Sociologist." www.insidehighered.com/ news/2007/08/15/tenure. Retrieved December 1, 2008.

Jubber, K. 2007. "Sociology in South Africa. A Brief Historical Review of Research and Publishing." *International Sociology* 22, No. 5: 527–546. Abstract available at http:// iss.sagepub.com/cgi/content/abstract/22/5/527. Retrieved December 18, 2008.

Ministry of Culture. 2005. "Anthropological Survey of India." www.ansi.gov.in/policy_ interventions.htm. Retrieved November 21, 2008. The National Advisory Committee for establishing a National Repository on Human Genetic Resource and Data includes Prof. E. Haribabu, a sociologist.

National Science Foundation, Division of Science Resources Statistics. 2006. "Table 13, Employed Doctoral Scientists and Engineers, by Field of Doctorate and Sector of Employment, 2003. Characteristics of Doctoral Scientists and Engineers in the United States, 2003." Arlington, VA (NSF06-320) (June 2006). Available at www.nsf .gov/statistics/nsf06320/tables.htm.

National Water Development Agency. 2004. http://nwda.gov.in/indexmainasp?linkid= 88&langid=1. Retrieved November 21, 2008. A committee of environmentalists, social scientists and other experts on interlinking of rivers. Set up by the the Government of India. The Ministry of Water Resources had constituted a Task Force on Interlinking of Rivers, which includes "Shri Rajinder Singh, Noted Sociologist."

Novikova, Helen. 2008. "Uneasy Questions for Russian Sociology." State University, Higher School of Economics. www.hse.ru/lingua/en/news/4508743.html. Retrieved November 26, 2008.

Russian Academy of Science. 2008. "Branch of Philosophy, Psychology, Sociology and Law." www.ras.ru/win/db/show_org.asp?P=.oi-852.vi-.fi-.id-852.ln-en.oi-855. Retrieved December 18, 2008.

Shackman, Gene, Xun Wang, and Ya-Lin Liu. 2002. "Brief Review of World Demographic Trends. http://gsociology.icaap.org/report/demsum.html. Retrieved November 12, 2008.

Shackman, Gene, Ya-Lin Liu, and Xun Wang, 2004. "Brief Review of World Political Trends." http://gsociology.icaap.org/report/polsum.html. Retrieved November 12, 2008.

———. 2005. "Brief Review of World Economic Trends." http://gsociology.icaap.org/ report/econ/econsum.html. Retrieved November 12, 2008.

Shackman, Gene, Y Liu, and X Wang. 2008. "Understanding the World Today." The Global Social Change Research Project. http://gsociology.icaap.org. Retrieved December 7, 2008.

United Nations. 2006. "Commission on the Status of Women. 50th Session. High-Level Panel." www.un.org/womenwatch/daw/csw/csw50/HighLevelPanel.html. Retrieved September 24, 2008.

———. 2008a. "Reform at the United Nations. Panel on Civil Society, Biographies." www.un.org/reform/civilsociety/bios.shtml. Retrieved September 24, 2008.

———. 2008b. "Reaffirming Human Rights for All 2008 Conference, the Importance of Education and Learning Human Rights as a Way of Peace and Communication among Peoples." www.un.org/dpi/ngosection/conference/workshthu11.shtml. Retrieved September 24, 2008.

U.S. Census Bureau. 2008. International Database, Population Division. www.census. gov/ipc/www/idb/. Retrieved September 19, 2008.

USDA. 2008. Real Historical Gross Domestic Product (GDP) Per Capita and Growth Rates of GDP Per Capita for Baseline Countries/Regions (in billions of $2,000), 1969–2007. www.ers.usda.gov/Data/Macroeconomics/. Retrieved September 19, 2008.

U.S. Department of State, 2008a. International Religious Freedom Report 2008, Released by the Bureau of Democracy, Human Rights, and Labor. 2008 report on International Religious Freedom. www.state.gov/g/drl/rls/. Retrieved September 19, 2008.

———. 2008b. Human Rights 2007. Released by the Bureau of Democracy, Human Rights, and Labor. March 11, 2008. www.state.gov/g/drl/rls/. Retrieved September 19, 2008.

———. 2008c. Background Note: Nigeria. July 2008. www.state.gov/r/pa/ei/bgn/2836. htm. Retrieved November 8, 2008.

———. 2008d. Background Note: India. June 2008. www.state.gov/r/pa/ei/bgn/3454. htm. Retrieved November 17, 2008.

Vasavi. V. A. 2003. Sociology in India. "Review of *Contemporary India*—A Sociological View, by Satish Deshpande." Review published in *The Hindu*, June 2003. www.hinduonnet.com/thehindu/br/2003/06/03/stories/2003060300100300.htm. Retrieved November 22, 2008.

Wang, Xun and Anne Statham. 2004. "Teaching About Social Welfare in United States: An International Education Education Program." *Education Global* 8:147–158.

World Health Organization. 2008. "Community-Based Care Can Improve Access." TB Community Involvement Publication. www.who.int/tb/people_and_communities/involvement/community_who_story_sep08.pdf. Retrieved December 1, 2008.

CHAPTER 3

The Role of Theory in Sociological Practice

Jay Weinstein, Eastern Michigan University

Theory plays a *central* role in sociological practice. In fact, in many cases it is the use of theory that sets applied, clinical, and public sociologists apart from other types of practitioners such as social workers, market researchers, and management consultants. You may have heard at one time or another that sociological theory and sociological practice are somehow opposite approaches. This is a misunderstanding. For nothing can be further from the truth. Theory and practice depend on each other, and together they provide sociological practitioners with an effective set of tools for improving human relationships.[1]

This chapter explores this connection between sociological theory and sociological practice. We begin with a brief examination of the way in which practicing sociologists *use* theories. Next, two contrasting theories of knowledge (or *epistemologies*) are presented: the nomological and the pragmatic. Here we argue that the latter provides the more realistic depiction of how scientific knowledge is created, especially in social science. The chapter ends with a call for practicing sociologists to apply theory, build practical knowledge, and improve society.

How Sociological Practitioners Use Theories

Practicing sociologists specialize in contributing to the solution of social problems, great and small. This might involve preparing a report on how relations among employees and managers in a small business can be improved, designing a survey that will yield useful information for a neighborhood recreation program, or devising policies to correct a major social injustice such as school segregation. In these and many other contexts in which they work, these practitioners enter the field armed with theories (i.e., explanations). Realizing that their theories do not contain absolute truths, they nevertheless employ them and the hypotheses (i.e., expectations) they generate as a framework for focusing on the important features of an otherwise incomprehensibly complex situation. They use theories as a builder uses scaffolding, to help reach places that would otherwise be inaccessible.

As practicing sociologists reflect on the results of their observations, they continually refine their theories to the point at which they believe that the solutions they propose are sound. Then they apply those solutions in a preliminary way, such as in a *pilot study*. Further testing of hypotheses and further refinement of the theory are then pursued. Eventually, the practitioner is satisfied that the proposed solution is the best possible one within the limitations of the time and resources available. As they complete their work, they "take down the scaffolding." The theories that were employed in the project have been changed, we hope improved, by the experience. Thus, the next project can be approached with a more powerful theoretical framework that has been informed by real-life experience. This process shows how (1) theory guides practice and (2) practice improves theory. And this is the sense in which theory is *central* to applied and clinical sociology (Kenig, 1987).

Two Models of Knowledge Creation

In this section, we momentarily set aside the relationship between theory and practice to discuss another claim that is often made but which, in fact, is seriously mistaken. This is the view that, because sociological theories cannot achieve certainty, the field is not truly "scientific." In this context, we consider two contrasting approaches to the quest for knowledge from the work of sociologist Nico Stehr (1992) and others: the *nomological* (also referred to as "nomothetic") model and the *pragmatic* model.

THE NOMOLOGICAL MODEL: THE LIMITS
OF KNOWLEDGE FOR KNOWLEDGE'S SAKE

The assumption behind the argument that sociology cannot be scientific is that other sciences (e.g., physics) can attain certainty. This is premised on the assumption that there are basic, universal laws, in this case of the mind—which is what the term "nomological" refers to. Those who understand how the non-social sciences actually operate are, however, well aware that the search for certain knowledge was abandoned decades, if not centuries, ago. Scientists do not overtly and directly seek to establish irrefutable inductive truths. They know, as sociologists should also know, that "irrefutable inductive" is a contradiction in terms. Rather, scientists seek *exceptions* to widely accepted beliefs; contradictions to what ought to be observed; and unfulfilled expectations in experimental outcomes. In this respect, all scientific knowledge is provisional; otherwise, there could be no such thing as scientific progress.

To be clear, I am not saying that scientific theory routinely contains obvious falsehoods. For, as mentioned above, a theoretic formulation that includes one or more sentences known to be false is, strictly speaking, not a theory. Each statement must find support from empirical evidence on some occasion and not yet be refuted. But if such statements are truly empirical, then it remains possible for them to be refuted at some future date—and, in the long run, it is likely that they will be refuted. To expect more, as some sociologists seem to do, is tantamount to guaranteeing that theirs will forever be an "impossible science" (Turner and Turner, 1990).

THE PRAGMATIC MODEL: "GOOD ENOUGH" FOR NEWTON

If we abandon the search for absolute theoretical truth, are we not then left without a criterion for judging the viability of a theory? How, after all, can one determine if theory A is superior to theory B, if both are equally likely to produce false hypotheses at one point or another? These appear to be the very kinds of questions that keep the debate alive about whether or not sociology is/can be a scientific discipline. They are also based on the prevalent misunderstanding of science outlined in the last section. For in posing them, one conjures up an image of a battle between, say, two physicists, each having developed a theory of the behavior of a newly discovered sub-atomic particle. The first physicist generates and tests a series of ten hypotheses, all of which are upheld by observation. The second physicist is successful in testing nine hypotheses, but falters on the tenth. At that point, an impartial judge declares that the first theory is the one that shall prevail, because it is "truer" or "more valid."

This neat and somewhat suggestive depiction of how "real" science works supports the pessimistic appraisal of sociology's prospects as a science. And perhaps for that reason it is held to be more or less accurate—at least implicitly so. However, we have known for some time that this image does not portray the mechanisms whereby some scientific theories survive and others are discarded. Rather than judgments being made on the basis of veridicality—the capacity to generate truth—they are far more typically made on the basis of practicality—the capacity to be effective in application to practical problems.

In the title of his recent book on William James, Harvey Cromier (2000) put it succinctly: "The truth is what works." As Stehr (1992) noted somewhat earlier, knowledge that has practical consequences, consequences that can be observed and which are in some way valued, is knowledge that survives and becomes certified. Knowledge that cannot be shown to make a difference in the world is likely to be forgotten. Moreover, these outcomes are largely unrelated to the ultimate truth-value of the theories behind the knowledge. As long as it "works," a scientific theory is *good enough*.

Before illustrating and elaborating on this point, let me immediately indicate what this means for sociological theory. Following Stehr, I am suggesting that the true test of theory is the extent to which it makes a difference in practice. If this is so, then the value of specific theories and even the question of whether or nor there can be such a thing as sociological theory can never be resolved solely within academic contexts. For in such contexts judgments must be made only in relation to the (inappropriate) nomological model. We must, in brief, take our theories into the *real* world if we have any hope of achieving our cherished goal of becoming *real* scientists.

This account of practical knowledge has its immediate roots in the pragmatist epistemology of the late nineteenth and early twentieth centuries, first outlined by Josiah Royce (1969), developed by C. S. Peirce (1998; Hookway, 2000), and applied by William James (Cromier, 2000), John Dewey (Hudman, 1990) and George Herbert Mead (1934, founder of the symbolic interactionist approach described in Chapter 4 of this volume)—all of them American philosophers. Thus, I have termed it the pragmatic model. As students of the pragmatist (or as James preferred "pragmaticist") movement are aware, this theory of knowledge was developed in conscious opposition to the idealist foundations of the nomological model.

Peirce (1898, 1985) provided one of the most succinct statements in his essay "How to Make Our Ideas Clear," first published in *Popular Science*. Here he characterizes the mind as an inverted hierarchy of beliefs. At the top of the hierarchy, nearest the surface, are our fleeting opinions that are supported only weakly by actual experiences. For instance, we may come to believe that our new neighbors are friendly based upon an initial meeting and short conversation. On such a basis, we would be cautious about what we might expect from them and not terribly surprised if we eventually learn that they are not as nice as we first believed. At the deepest level are the beliefs that we refer to as "knowledge." These have been verified time and again as we put them to the test in everyday situations: e.g., the belief that when we return from work our house will be where we left it in the morning. We are inclined to put considerable stock in such beliefs and to act on them with confidence (in this example, we would routinely proceed home in the usual direction).

The important thing to note, Peirce argues, is that the highest and lowest levels, and all levels in-between, differ from one another only in degree not in kind. The beliefs that we designate as knowledge are those that "work." And every act we perform is, in one way or another, a test of these beliefs. Thus, we cannot say that even our best verified beliefs represent eternal truths. During the earthquakes in Turkey some years ago, thousands of people returned from work in good faith, "knowing" the location of their homes, only to be dismayed that this knowledge no longer worked. In such cases, one is compelled to have a "change of mind" through a reconsideration of what one really knows.

So it is with scientific theories. Every time we act upon them, we are putting them to the test. But the entire range of argumentation and formal hypothesis testing one can marshal will never prove that our law-like generalizations constitute knowledge. If we can act effectively on the basis of such beliefs, then they are tantamount to knowledge—until they fail to work. At that point, our theories need to be corrected. Otherwise, like the startled, homeless earthquake victim, we will not be able to negotiate effectively through this world.

THE CASE OF NEWTON

For more than two centuries, scientists and laypersons alike held Newtonian physics to be the ideal case of eternal scientific truth. They were convinced that his law-like generalizations were in fact laws. Moreover, it was commonly assumed that the reason for Newton's success lay in the unerring ability of his system to produce verifiable hypotheses. Of course we now understand that Newton's laws were partial truths. Recent developments in physics such as relativity theory, quantum mechanics, and the widespread acceptance of the principle of indeterminacy have helped us to understand the limitations of the classical theories. For, considering what is now known about physical properties at the sub-molecular and super planetary levels, it is clear that Newtonian mechanics apply only to a limited range of observable phenomena (the middle range). And, even for the kinds of phenomena for which the classical principles still appear to be valid, they are only approximately so under normal conditions.

These differences between the physics of the early eighteenth century and the physics of today have caused scientists to rethink the nature of the physical world. In addition, they have prompted philosophers and sociologists of science to examine critically the nature of empirical truth.[2]

For example, it has often been remarked that newer discoveries such as quantum mechanics have "proved" that Newton's laws were "false." But this kind of observation is, at best, a metaphor. It would be more accurate to note that Newton's laws were never "true" in the first place; they were only not (yet) falsified. More important, perhaps, we now understand that the enduring character of the Newtonian system is *not* the result of its unerring and unexceptionable generalizations. Instead, his system worked; it proved to be good enough. Good enough for what, we might ask? As Stehr (1992) has argued, it was good enough to form the basis of the Industrial Revolution. Although it was by no means *absolute* knowledge, it was extremely effective as practical knowledge.

Knowledge for What?

The contrast between the nomological and the pragmatic models suggest a question posed some six decades ago by Robert Lynd (1939): "Knowledge for What?" That is, what is our purpose in developing and applying scientific theory? As noted above, from the nomological perspective, which is essentially the position to which most contemporary academic sociologists subscribe, the answer is "for knowledge." Yet, sociology aside, some pragmatist philosophers would also accept a version of this position. While granting that the ultimate test of our beliefs is in their application to real-world situations, one might still hold that the purpose of such testing is to establish which beliefs deserve to be maintained and which need to be revised. That is, the end of the pragmatic knowledge-creation process need not be to change the world but rather simply to create better knowledge—where "better" is defined here in relation to effectiveness.

THE SPECIAL CASE OF SOCIAL SCIENCE

It is at this juncture that Lynd and others have argued on behalf of social scientific exceptionalism. For the aspects of the world that would be altered by a pragmatist *sociologist* in the search for knowledge differ from those of interest to a pragmatist non-social scientist. In particular, whereas a physicist might wish to establish how a physical theory applies to the operation of a machine, a sociologist would need to effect change in an organization, social relationship, or another part of the *moral order*. So, the argument goes, the social scientist has a special responsibility to operate in good faith by testing knowledge not for manipulative ends but rather to bring about an authentic improvement in the setting(s) employed for such knowledge tests. Although it is obvious that, on an abstract plane, "improvement" is a highly value laden concept, Lynd, and the preponderance of sociologists who have preceded and succeeded him, have in mind the movement toward more inclusive forms of policy formulation and decision making. That is, the brief but well-grounded answer to the question of "Knowledge for what?" is "for democracy."[3]

Today it is perhaps easier to understand that non-social scientists, too, might have moral responsibilities. Following the events of World War II and the important educational work of the *Bulletin of Atomic Scientists*, most physicists are now overtly dedicated to promoting peaceful uses of atomic energy. Similarly, based on the discoveries of Rachel Carson, Barry Commoner, and other environmentalists, most contemporary biologists are openly concerned with the preservation of species and their environments. Thus, sociologists no longer are (if they ever were) the only scientists who routinely face ethically-charged theoretical problems.

Nevertheless, it seems to me that Lynd's observations still apply to social science in a special sense. Looking back on the century that has just passed— and its clear lessons about what happens when social scientists allow others to monopolize social "engineering," it appears at best pointless and at worst destructive to plead the case for "pure" sociology. I believe that those who hold that their only interest in developing sociological theories is to generate more research to improve theories, etc., are either enormously self-involved, oblivious to the world around them, or intellectually dishonest. Even more important, the argument against a (democratically) committed sociology, and in support of the development of apolitical theory, is seriously discontinuous with the foundations as well as the authentic intellectual breakthroughs of the discipline.   *So we should be political...?*

MORAL BANKRUPTCY, ABSTRACTED EMPIRICISM, AND GRAND THEORY

Thus, when C. Wright Mills posed his now oft-cited opposition between abstracted empiricism and grand theory, on one hand, and intellectual craftsmanship, on the other, he was simultaneously addressing epistemological and ethical concerns.[4] Strongly influenced by the work of Thorstein Veblen and the Chicago School tradition (the subtitle of Mills' Ph.D. dissertation: "The Higher Learning in America" is the title of one of Veblen's books), Mills explicitly connected sociological approaches to theory with the sociologist's moral commitments (Mills, 1969). In his view, the discipline was experiencing a period of moral bankruptcy in which practitioners routinely avoided engagement with such critical issues as the erosion of democracy in America. This stance was achieved and supported by a characteristic distortion of scientific activity, whereby empirical research and theory were pursued in isolation from each other. Empiricists did not theorize, but rather chose to let the facts "speak for themselves." Theorists did not ground

look up

their generalizations in empirical research, preferring instead to develop the all-encompassing—but empty—schema of theoretical sociology.

Mills' alternative, intellectual craftsmanship, combines theory and research in such a way that effective law-like generalizations can be created, tested, sustained, and revised. This approach, Mills believed, is productive of knowledge in an authentic scientific manner, without inflated claims of absolute truth or nihilistic assumptions to the effect that knowledge is impossible to attain. Moreover, he felt that developing sociological theory in this manner would help put sociologists in touch with the important social issues of our times.

It is at this juncture that another of Mills' well-known formulations emerges: the idea that it is the special task of sociologists to seek to connect biography and history. By placing the lives of individuals in historical context in a manner that only sound theorizing can do we are, Mills believed, better equipped to build a meaningful social science. Moreover, in the process we are also open to understanding and to contributing to the solution of the problems that stand in the way of achieving more fulfilling biographies and greater historical progress. On the other hand, as long as the development of real sociological theory is avoided, eschewed, or held to be a futile undertaking, it will be very difficult for sociology to realize its potential as a source of enlightenment and a means of improving the human condition.

What Should Be Done?

It should be obvious that there is a subtext to this presentation. That is, like Robert Lynd, C. Wright Mills, and other—less famous—sociologists, I believe that our current set of priorities that gives greater importance and a higher status to academic, nomological theorizing in comparison to the pragmatic model should be reversed. In my view, we are currently involved in a classic case of the tail wagging the dog. In part because of the prevalent misunderstanding of non-social science among sociologists and their lack of sympathy for the founding conception of sociology as a kind of technology, a disdain of intellectual craftsmanship characterizes the dominant (but not necessarily larger) segment of our profession.

For those who agree with this assessment and who would like to realign our theoretical priorities, several strategies are available—some of which are, to an extent, already being pursued. One such strategy is, of course, to practice what we preach—and to preach what we practice. The more successful we are in demonstrating that knowledge that works "works," the more likely we are to win support for applied approaches. Another fairly common strategy is to criticize our academic colleagues, pointing out the historical, ethical, and epistemological weaknesses in their search for absolute truth and/or their consequent abandon-ment of the search for *any* kind of truth. I for one believe that this approach is of limited effectiveness, and that it has a strong potential for alienating those who should be our allies. Such backlash effects are especially likely at this point in the history of the field. For many voices can now be heard from many ideological and methodological quarters claiming that sociology is in a state of crisis (with little agreement about what is meant by "sociology" and "crisis"; see Weinstein, 1997b).

Yes!.

Another strategy, which I think has considerable promise, is to seek converts. If my reading of the situation is in any way accurate, then many academics are "closet" applied sociologists. They work within the nomological framework—if they address theoretical concerns at all—because they believe they need to do so for the sake of academic success. This is the case despite the fact that most of them became sociologists in order to improve society (not merely to improve their resumes). Of course, early in the process of professionalization, one learns to suppress such "do-gooder" thoughts. But my suspicion is that the urge to develop and apply practical knowledge, to be a kind of Gunnar Myrdal—the Nobel Prize winner who conducted the possibly best-known "doing sociology" project ever undertaken in the United States and perhaps the world[5]—in one's own back yard, never really dies.

Moreover, I do not think that making a commitment to applied approaches, today, is professionally risky. To state my reasons for believing this would take us far beyond the discussion at hand. But I do think that there is a key to "com-ing out," to becoming the kind of sociologists we set out to be when we first declared our major. And this key lies with our students, undergraduates, and graduates alike. For in their naïveté concerning what constitutes an acceptable professional attitude, they entirely understand and sympathize with the search for applied theory and practical knowledge. Those students who are aware, or can be made aware, of the power they have (where would academic sociologists be without them?) have the capacity to exert pressure on their professors to admit to their own original motivations. For, in their naïveté, they know that, in Myrdal's words (1944), "the rationalism and moralism which is the driving force behind social study, whether we admit it or not, is the faith that institu-tions can be improved and strengthened and that people are good enough to live a happier life."

Works Cited

Cromier, Harvey. 2000. *The Truth Is What Works: William James, Pragmatism, and the Seed of Death*. Lanham, MD: Rowman & Littlefield Publishers.

DeMartini, Joseph R. 1984. "Applied Sociology as Knowledge Utilization: A Meeting Ground for Theory and Practice." Paper presented at the Annual Meeting of the American Sociological Association (San Antonio, TX, August 27–31).

Hartmann, D. J. and Sonnad, S. 2006. "The Applied Sociologist as Craftsman." Paper presented at the Annual Meeting of the American Sociological Association, Montreal Convention Center, Montreal, Quebec, Canada Online at www.allacademic.com/meta/p104065_index.html.

Hookway, Christopher. 2000. *Truth, Rationality, and Pragmatism: Themes from Peirce.* New York: Oxford University Press.

Hudman, Larry A. 1990. *John Dewey's Pragmatic Technology.* Bloomington: Indiana University Press.

Kenig, Sylvia. 1987. "The Use of Theory in Applied Sociology: The Case of Community Mental Health." *The American Sociologist* 18 (September): 3

Kuhn, Thomas S. 1970. *The Structure of Scientific Revolution.* Chicago: University of Chicago Press.

Lakatos, Imre and A. L. Musgrave, eds. 1970. *Criticism and the Growth of Knowledge.* Cambridge: Cambridge University Press.

Lazarsfeld, Paul F. and Jeffrey G. Reitz. 1970. *Toward a Theory of Applied Sociology.* New York: Columbia University Bureau of Applied Research.

Lynd, Robert. 1939. *Knowledge for What?* Princeton, NJ: Princeton University Press.

Mead, George Herbert (C. W. Morris, ed.). 1934. *Mind, Self and Society: From the Standpoint of a Behaviorist.* Chicago: University of Chicago Press.

Mills, C. Wright. 1959. *The Sociological Imagination.* New York: Oxford University Press.

———. 1969. *Sociology and Pragmatism: The Higher Learning in America.* London: Oxford.

Myrdal, Gunnar (with the assistance of Richard Sterner and Arnold Rose). 1944. *An American Dilemma.* New York: Harper and Brothers, 2 volumes.

Nisbet, Robert. 1969. *Social Change and History.* New York: Oxford University Press.

Peirce, Charles Sanders. 1985. *How to Make Our Ideas Clear/ Über die Klarheit unserer edanken.* Frankfurt am Main: V. Klostermann.

———. 1998. *The Essential Writings,* ed. by Edward C. Moore. Amherst, NY: Prometheus Books.

Royce, Josiah. 1969. *The Basic Writings,* ed. by John J. McDermott. Chicago: University of Chicago.

Stehr, Nico. 1992. *Practical Knowledge: Applying the Social Sciences.* Newbury Park, CA: Sage.

Straus, Roger, ed. 2002. *Using Sociology: An Introduction from the Applied and Clinical Perspectives.* Lanham, MD: Rowman & Littlefield.

Suppe, Frederick, ed. 1974. *The Structure of Scientific Theories.* Urbana: University of Illinois Press.

Turner, Stephen P. and Jonathan H. Turner. 1990. *The Impossible Science: An Institutional Analysis of American Sociology.* Newbury Park, CA: Sage

Weinstein, Jay. 1996. "The Place of Democracy in Applied Sociology." *Journal of Applied Sociology* 13:1.

———. 1997a. *Social and Cultural Change: Social Science for a Dynamic World*. Boston: Allyn and Bacon.

———. 1997b. Applied Sociology Is the Answer, But What Was the Question?" *Michigan Sociological Review* 11 (Fall).

Notes

1. DeMartini (1984) has a detailed discussion of this connection. Straus (2002) provides a comprehensive discussion of the relationship between theory and sociological practice as well as substantive examples in clinical and applied sociology. Lazarsfeld and Reitz (1970) provide a pioneering statement of the theory of applied sociology.

2. An obvious and singularly acclaimed landmark in this recent inquiry into the character of scientific truth is Thomas Kuhn's argument concerning paradigm shifts. See Kuhn (1970) and his earlier critics Lakatos and Musgrave (1970), and Suppe (1974).

3. Some time ago I published an article in the *Journal of Applied Sociology* (Weinstein, 1996) that argues in favor of a close connection between sociology and democracy. Peter Rossi e-mailed me a comment, "I basically agree with you, but the devil is in the details." That observation has served as an important reminder as I have continued to explore the sociology/democracy interface over the subsequent few years. For a more extended discussion of this claim, see Weinstein (1996, 1997a: Preface).

4. In their discussion of the foundations of applied sociology, Hartmann and Sonnad (2006) focus specifically on the craftsmanship theme.

5. *An American Dilemma: The Negro Problem and Modern Democracy* (1944).

CHAPTER 4

Clinical Sociology
CHANGING MEANINGS, CHANGES LIVES

John Glass, Collin County Community College, Texas

Like other behavioral sciences, sociology has a number of theoretical perspectives that are used to explain social behavior. Some focus on large-scale, collective behavior, and others focus on small-scale, face-to-face interaction. One of the more popular perspectives in the latter category, developed almost one hundred years ago, is symbolic interactionism; the following will demonstrate its utility for practicing sociology.

Symbolic interactionism has two basic tenets; first, that the objects we encounter in daily life have no inherent meaning and second, that they acquire meaning through our interaction with them. This may sound mysterious, but actually it's not; let's take the example of some sticks to make these two points clearer.

The first point is that sticks, in and of themselves aren't meaningful to us. This means that most of us pass by sticks lying on the ground each day and don't pay much attention to them. We ignore them because they are not relevant to us. We would however, pay attention to them (assign meaning to them), if we found ourselves in a situation where we needed them for some reason. For instance, when we go camping and we need to get a fire going, we start looking for sticks. Once found, they take on the meaning of "kindling" as we use them to start a fire. They can take on other meanings, however. After we eat dinner and are sitting around the dwindling campfire, we notice that we have an itch far down in the middle of our back. Not wanting to bother anyone, we look around for one of those sticks that we used as kindling to scratch the itch; the stick's meaning has now become, "backscratcher." The next morning, we are throwing a football around and it gets lodged in a tree. One more time, we turn to the sticks, looking for a long straight one that we can use as a "pole" to dislodge the ball. Notice that in these three cases, the objects (the sticks), have not changed, they have retained the same properties; what has changed *is the meaning that was assigned to them*, based on the way we interacted with them. This demonstrates both tenets of symbolic interactionism. First, the sticks have no inherent meaning; if the meaning was in the sticks, then the meaning wouldn't have changed, it would have remained the same no matter what we did with them. The fact that it did change based on our interaction with them, however, demonstrates the second tenet.

Now we can begin to consider how these two powerful insights into human behavior might be useful to social interaction. Prior to providing a specific example, however, an additional point is needed; an answer to a basic question . . . what constitutes an object? We have discussed how meaning arises with objects, but what exactly is an object? Very simply, an object is anything of which we become aware. This includes objects with material properties (such as sticks, tables, cars, pens, trees, etc.) and objects that do not have any material properties (such as ideas, thoughts, feelings, etc.). Just as sticks take on different meanings when we interact with them, so can feelings, thoughts, ideas, etc. For instance, we may find ourselves in a situation in which other people are making negative comments about us (we aren't smart enough; we should do better, etc.). Usually, people in this situation feel painful emotions in response to these comments or objects. Employing a symbolic interactionist perspective, we can see how someone could assuage those feelings by realizing that the meaning being assigned is temporary, situational, and in fact, fleeting. Why? Because the meaning of whom one is, to him or herself and to others, *changes over time and in response to different situations*. In other words, *there is no **one** meaning that defines anyone*. We can also note that the emotions that we are experiencing in response to the comments are physical sensations that are indicative of being exposed to a painful situation; they are not verification of the comments or objects. A demonstration of an actual application of this method will clarify these points even more.

For several years I worked as a substance abuse counselor in a court-mandated, residential treatment program for felony probationers. I was the only sociologist on staff. As such, my clinical approach was more inclusive than most. I not only understood my clients' behavior in terms of the lives that they had lived, but also in reference to the situation that they found themselves in—here, a judicial treatment center. Specifically, I understood the power that institutions have to shape thinking and behavior and in this particular case to shape thinking and behavior related to the use of illicit substances. Institutions have the ability to do this through the manipulation of meanings attached to objects.

My clients were men who had committed a crime either due to, or related to, substance use. They were sent to our treatment program as an alternative to time in jail or the penitentiary. The purpose of the program was two-fold: to reduce and or eliminate their substance use and to reduce or eliminate their criminal behavior.

At the time, the prevailing approach to substance abuse treatment was strongly influenced by 12 Step programs such as Alcoholics Anonymous. This being the case, there were some features of substance abuse and dependence that were thought to be common to those with either diagnosis. These included denial of a problem with the substance, denial of a chronic addictive condition (a disease), resistance to change, unwillingness to comply with treatment recommendations, and others. As such, treatment counselors were expected to "break through" clients' denial, educate them about their "disease" and "convince" them that the only hope for a life free from substance abuse (and its consequences) was through the practice of abstinence.

This approach had worked well for many people and was considered to be an effective means of treatment (and it continues to remain an effective means of treatment for many people). Many of my clients, however, had been through treatment before, had heard all about addiction, denial, and abstinence and were not convinced that all of those ideas applied to them. The fact that they did not readily agree with a counselor's assessment of their situation, however, was considered to be evidence of "resistance." This, like denial, was expected to be confronted at all times by counselors as addicts were, almost by definition, considered to be unwilling to change their behavior.

Needless to say, this often became a very tiring affair for both counselor and client. Being a sociologist, it also became an ethical matter as there were times when I felt that my task as an institutional agent was to "brainwash" my clients into believing things about themselves that they did not agree with. Something had to change.

One day, I was meeting with Tommy (not the client's real name), an intravenous heroin user. I decided to take another tack as the denial-resistance-confrontation approach was not working. I simply started asking him very simple questions; was he happy with his life? If not, did he think his unhappiness was related to his use of heroin? If so, did he think *stopping* the use of heroin would result in an *increase* in his happiness with life? If he thought that, could he and I work together toward achieving that? With those simple questions, the entire counselor-client dynamic changed. I no longer had to work to try and convince him (or anyone else) of anything. I now only had to assist someone in taking action that would result in improvement in his life. In other words, instead of working *against* each other, we were now working *together*.

How is this an example of the application of symbolic interactionism? He and I, through our interaction with each other, managed to change the meaning of a significant object in his life, his use of heroin.

Within the treatment setting I described above, the meaning of the use of heroin was "addiction"—a chronic, progressive "disease" with no cure that one had to accept, had to relinquish "denial" about, or had to be less "resistant" to the treatment process. That meaning wasn't working for Tommy, though. That meaning of his heroin use was not resulting in him changing his thinking and his behavior; it was not leading him toward refraining from the use of heroin. By simply changing the meaning of the object, i.e., the meaning of his heroin use, an opportunity arose for him to consider stopping the use of heroin. No longer did he need to be convinced of having an addiction, of needing to be less resistant, of needing to not be in denial. Note that the object, his heroin use, was still the main issue and getting him to stop the use of heroin was still the main goal. The reasons for doing so, however, were different (even though pragmatically they were the same; abstinence from heroin—regardless of why—will result in improved ability to obtain happiness from life) since the meaning of the object of interest was different. From that time on, our counseling sessions were more amenable, more productive, and more supportive.

This is one example of how symbolic interactionism was used as a sociological intervention. There are, of course, many other opportunities to use this approach. In fact, the best use of this approach is probably in one's daily life. By consistently paying attention to how meaning is created, how it is applied to objects, what the consequences are of some meanings as opposed to others, and above all, how meaning can be changed, individuals can discover myriad opportunities for an increased sense of freedom, spontaneity, and creativity in their own lives.

CHAPTER 5

If Crime Is the Problem, Is Community or Problem Solving Policing the Solution?

Chet Ballard, Valdosta State University, Georgia
Rudy Prine, Valdosta State University, Georgia

Efforts by the authors to apply sociology and criminology to assist communities in solving social problems take the form of a series of collaborative research projects, spanning years 1998–2008. The project work includes a variety of community institutions and individuals who are interested in community organization, crime, law enforcement, and the interactions among them. The project collaborators are the authors, three police departments, key local law enforcement administrators who contributed specialized skills, knowledge, or community organizational contacts, and their respective city managers. The focus on broader community organization allowed a more thorough examination of social patterns related to crime, victimization, and citizen perceptions of local law enforcement efforts known in the literature as "community policing" and also as "problem-solving policing" (Prine, Ballard, and Robinson, 2001; Ballard and Prine, 2002).

Context: Crime as a Social Problem Requires an Interdisciplinary Approach

Crime is one of the problems that Americans are most concerned about. People tend to associate the issue of crime with concerns about the breakdown of society. Crime is any violation of criminal law, yet what is considered to be a crime varies over time and across cultures (Siegel, 2009). Quite apart from the financial costs of crime, or even the pain and trauma individual victims suffer, when law enforcement is unable to guarantee that law-abiding citizens can go about their daily business, and if people are too afraid to leave their homes to visit public places like shops or parks, the entire community experiences a reduction in quality of life (www.civitas.org.uk/blog/crime/). In sum, crime matters to us all.

While headlines, TV news, and other media make it seem otherwise, the situation is getting better, not worse. The trend in crime in America has been downward over the past thirty-five years as measured by the National Victimization Report data which chronicles violent and property crimes from 1973 to the present time (Criminal Victimization, 2007, Bureau of Justice Statistics (www.ojp.usdoj.gov/bjs/cvictgen.htm). Earlier in the present decade crime rates spiked upward, but in *Crime in the United States 2007*, the FBI reports that the nationwide violent crime rate dropped for the first time since 2004, down 1.4 percent from 2006. Property crimes saw a 2.1 percent decline from 2006. It seems that the bump upward in crime earlier in this decade was not the start of a long-term trend of more, and more violent crime (www.fbi.gov/ucr/cius2007/index.html).

Sociologists, criminologists, politicians, and the public disagree over whether public policy responses to crime such as "targeting all street offenses," three strikes laws, mandatory sentences for drug offenders, and a rapid expansion of the prison population in America are causes for observed lower crime rates. The age structure of the American people, economic and employment factors, and changes in policing practices are regarded as equally important in making sense of the longer term pattern of lower rates. Regarding age, criminologists use the term "population at risk" to identify specific groups that commit crime at higher rates and generally speaking this refers to ages fourteen to twenty-one. As the percentage of this age group's population increases within a community, so too does the risk of increased criminality (Schmalleger, 2009).

Sociologists and criminologists have developed theories to explain the relationship between economic factors and risk of crime such as relative deprivation, general strain theory, and modified rational choice theory. Advances in crime and society research have led to integration of theories linking individual criminality to broader structural factors. Changes in a community's economy affect neighborhood stability and patterns of social interaction. If community residents have lower levels of interaction with their neighbors they are less likely to serve as guardians for the common good, less likely to be concerned about suspicious behavior, and less likely to report crimes to the police (Curran and Renzetti, 2000).

Criminologists have long believed that variations in crime rates are at least partially explained by police patrol patterns. If a specific neighborhood is targeted by law enforcement then it is more likely that arrests will result. Similarly if drug and other vice-related activities occur in areas of the community which are exposed, i.e., within a public landscape, then arrests are simply easier to make (Doerner, 2007).

In theory, research, and practice, there is a good intellectual fit between sociology and criminology in explaining deviance and societal disruption. Many view criminology as a sub-field of sociology with jurisdiction over the examination of three general factors: the making of law, the breaking of law, and the reaction to the breaking of law. For example, there is linkage between corporations' unethical accounting practices and fraud. The criminologist would analyze arguments on whether such accounting practices should be placed into the criminal code. The infamous Enron criminal case eventually led to the Sarbanes-Oxley law on corporate accountability. Currently there are twenty-six separate FBI investigations into possible wrongdoing associated with accounting frauds in the sub-prime mortgage market financial disaster as reported on National Public Radio (www.npr.org/templates/story/story.php?storyId=96019338).

Sociologically, the criminal justice system response should include behavioral as well as legal considerations. While the criminologist is more likely to focus on law and procedure, as well as psychological or individual-level explanations of fraudulent behavior, the practicing sociologist would explore social interaction patterns involving power between positions in the corporation and structural-level interests such as institutional networks with other corporations and government regulators.

Applying Sociology and Criminology to Neighborhood Social Control Efforts

The 1960s will be remembered for cities set ablaze as race riots, counter-culture demonstrations, and political protests challenged institutional legitimacy and authority resulting in violent citizen-police confrontations aired in living color on TV. Violence in the streets left Americans with a dreadful image of the nation's metro areas, and fear of street crime reached far outside cities into suburbs and the countryside. Using violence to restore order in neighborhoods rocked by discord heightened an "us" versus "them" policing mentality resulting in the popularity of paramilitary-style strike forces and swat teams, all the while distancing the police further and further from routine street-level interactions with residents. As a reaction to this assault mentality and isolation, community policing emerged as an alternative to the combative and militaristic style of policing popular in this time period.

Community policing makes policing services different from traditional law enforcement. The community policing strategy would prefer to solve the problem that leads to an arrest rather than make an arrest of a resident. Police who work from a community policing strategy still respond rapidly to emergency calls and still arrest offenders, but community policing *is* problem-solving policing. Most calls to the police are calls for service and in the vast majority of such cases, those services can better be provided by agencies other than the police (www .joburg.org.za/content/view/88/75/). Officers who know both a community's problems and its residents can link people with other public and private agencies that can help solve community concerns before individual troubles turn into community problems. Building structures of trust and sharing information across community agencies in order to resolve resident problems is the core of community and problem-solving policing. As policing focus shifts to solving problems, officers spend more time working with citizens to prevent crime and resolve disputes. Better police-citizen communication means officers are more likely to proactively use and share crime information with the public and view the public as partners not as adversaries. No single agency can solve complex social problems alone. A combined community-police effort is a practical way to restore safety to neighborhoods and business districts according to the Santa Clara Police Department (www.scpd.org/community/community policing .html).

The police partner with the community in a combined effort to understand the causes of crime and to resolve underlying social problems which often lead to criminality. Community policing places responsibility for public safety on the whole community rather than the police alone. If residents are to enjoy a safe community and reap the benefits of an enhanced quality of life, they must have meaningful opportunities to share responsibility for the security of neighborhoods. Police officers are encouraged to become deeply familiar with residents and their neighborhoods, stopping to listen to resident's comments and complaints, with much higher street-level visibility. This has produced community policing programs that feature cops walking the beat, bicycle patrols, and establishment of officers inside schools to build trust with young people (school resource officers). Analogous to the four-part model of program evaluation taught in applied sociology classes, police are being trained to problem-solve using a four step process. First, the officer identifies what problem is to be addressed. Next, questions are asked to learn as much as possible about the problem. Then a customized problem solving response which directly responds to the identified problem is tried. Last, the officer evaluates the response to determine if the problem was resolved and what follow-up efforts must be planned. This technique is described in detail on the San Antonio Police Department's web pages (www .sanantonio.gov/saPD/COPPS.asp?res=1280&ver=true).

Efforts to reduce or prevent crime take a number of forms, but increasingly, police agencies are seeking greater citizen input and support for their efforts, moving from top-down to more democratic models of policing practice. As Rebach and Bruhn (1990) note, intervention at the community level involves four steps: assess, plan, implement, and evaluate. Each of the steps presents substantive challenges for police departments.

- Should police hire an outside expert to conduct an assessment of citizen perception of policing effectiveness?
- Should the police conduct an in-house assessment?
- Should community residents be provided with an opportunity to comment and assess the police?
- Should the police partner with university faculty to bring an independent and overtly scientific perspective to the task?
- Will the data collected be used to plan and implement changes?
- Who determines whether to implement data-supported changes?
- Who will determine whether the changes implemented have worked?

Problem-solving policing has developed a strategy which incorporates needs assessment/assets mapping and program evaluation into a strategy for addressing crime and the equally important issue of fear of crime in communities. Community policing does not diminish law enforcement. Instead, it provides officers with more tools to use with residents to improve public safety and personal feelings of security.

Community policing improves community-police interactions immediately, but its real value is in a long-term decline in crime rates and precipitous decline in fear of police and fear of criminal victimization by residents. Now in its third decade of deployment in cities and communities across the nation, community policing has a track record on which to understand its successes and failures. Crime rates over the past thirty years have been declining across all Crime Index categories (murder, assault, etc.) as noted in the Federal Bureau of Investigation, Uniform Crime Reports (www.fbi.gov/ucr/ucr.htm).

Though not the sole cause, community policing can take some of the credit for the improving crime picture in America. Delivery of policing services has expanded beyond arrest and removal of offenders from the community. Today it is increasingly common for victim's services to be integrated into the problem solving approach applied by departments embracing a community policing strategy (Sutton et al., 2005). The isolation and separation of police from the community lessens as more democratic policing strategies are put into practice. Input from community residents is more frequently sought and valued as part of the problem-solving approach used by larger and smaller law enforcement agencies.

The police are the community's front line agents with training and authority to identify problems and provide first responder assistance to residents with immediate concerns. Calls and referrals for assistance to other community agencies are not viewed as failure of the police officer to handle the situation on the spot. Instead, this more inclusive and collaborative approach is making law enforcement more effective. Community policing has begun to fulfill its promise as the community organization best able to empower citizens to fight crime by taking a greater role in the management of their residential and business affairs within a problem-solving policing environment. Moving from a reactive response to crime, community policing has put in motion proactive responses to community problems which hold the potential to further reduce crime and improve public safety. Opening the door to greater citizen involvement in public safety work while incorporating more social service delivery into policing has resulted in a net gain in accountability of the police to the community. There is more visibility, more transparency, and more trust.

To paraphrase Sir Robert Peale's observations of policing in London, the community is the police and the police are the community (www.met.police.uk/history/index.htm). The ongoing quest is to find ways to solidify that connection into a seamless web. One beginning step is for police departments to seek citizen input regarding both community police relations and citizens' perception of problems within the community. Bringing the community into the police department is indicative of acceptance of an assets-based approach to community organization. An "us" versus "them" mentality is replaced with a view that keeping communities safe is the shared responsibility of the police and the residents. The assets-based approach to community organizing and community building recognizes the significant role that residents play in assisting or thwarting policing practices.

University Partnerships with Police: Applied Research as a Policing Resource

Application of the strategy of program evaluation from applied sociology is increasingly evident in studies of community policing and evaluations of how well policing services are delivered to community residents. Police departments that operate from a community policing perspective recognize the value of bringing community residents into the assessment and planning process. They also recognize how local university faculty and students can serve as an important resource in their efforts to understand deviance and criminality in their communities. Within this brand of policing strategy, democratizing input into decisions about local community social control not only includes inviting residents to partner with police, but also includes educators who have an important role to play in understanding social disorganization and criminal behavior. Applying sociological knowledge to the study of which assessment strategies are most effective is one example of how collaborative efforts between academics and practitioners can produce positive community change (Straus, 2002).

Police agencies seeking to understand how crime and policing are perceived by community residents enter into collaborative efforts with college faculty (and students) to study and make sense of the situation in its specific community and cultural context. Collaborating with academic faculty, police chiefs, police department leadership, and city managers hammer out strategies to best understand and evaluate delivery of policing services to community residents. Community policing is based on trust and one common sense strategy is simply to ask respondents to indicate their level of trust in the police. Rather than an either-or answer to the question of trust, we designed a rating scale for measurement of citizen trust of the police with answer codes which ranged from complete trust to complete distrust.

The First Step:
Determining the Purpose of the Study

Collaborative community policing research starts with two essential questions: what information is to be sought and how should it be obtained? We have conducted community policing studies in three communities and in each the research was initiated by either police department administrators or city managers (one was a former student of one of the authors). In sponsored research as opposed to researcher-initiated studies, it is the sponsor who has final say on what the purpose of the study will be. It is the collaborating researcher's task to assist the client in clearly defining what the purpose of the study is and which of its objectives will be measured (Kretzman and McKnight, 1993). It was determined that the police needed citizen input to determine the answer to several questions: "How is the police department doing?" "Are citizens' satisfied with police services?" "Are citizens reporting crimes when they are victimized?" "Does race of the officer or citizen matter?" "Which crimes would residents like the police to prioritize for greater enforcement?"

As we will discuss later in this chapter, unlike traditional sociological research, applied and clinical research tends to be conducted for a set of clients, funded by them and to have a pragmatic focus (that is, designed for use by or on behalf of those clients). In this specific case, client-driven research, even though collaborative, involves satisfying the needs of city officials, police chiefs, police command staff, and community residents, each with potentially different needs and interests. Once the purpose and objectives of the study are defined, identifying what data to collect and how it is to be collected was determined through meetings with a city manager and police chief. With most of the key stakeholders sitting at the same table, differences in opinion are quickly resolved. Determining what community residents want to get out of the survey and what issues they want to share with the police is more difficult, especially when you consider that the public is the ultimate consumer of policing services and much more diverse (social class) than the city and police officials in the communities studied. In the three communities we studied, the majority of community residents were white and, interestingly, the police chiefs were African American. To hear from residents, we conducted a focus group of community residents in one community. From that meeting, important questions emerged for inclusion in our research, such as "Do residents have interaction with police officers?"; "Do residents feel safe in their neighborhoods?" and "How does race affect police decisions?"

Armed with focus group input, we constructed a survey to measure several dimensions of the perception of crime, personal victimization and delivery of policing services. The key variables were: level of personal safety, crime levels in the neighborhood, trust, visibility of the police, levels of interaction between citizens and police, reporting of victimization, satisfaction with police response to victimization, and overall performance grade earned by police. Additional survey questions addressed resident/police race relations. We asked whether residents felt race of the resident or officer affected police decisions. We asked if citizens had personally witnessed police abuse due to race. The last question on the survey was open-ended and allowed citizens to write any suggestions that they had for the police. As one might expect the open question produced a wide range of comments from a simple "thank you" or "job well done" to complaints about specific officers or traffic hot spots in the community (Ballard and Prine, 2004).

Although all three communities studied are small in population size (less than 25,000), there was variation by racial/ethnicity, education, and income levels to account for during data analysis. We included demographic variables including, age, gender, race, household income, education, and length of residency. The sociological value of collecting demographic data from a study population is self-evident in academic research circles, but when viewed from community and police department angles of vision, sensitivities about collecting information about race, class, and gender must be addressed and justified. Residents and police administrators ask, "Why is this important?"; "This is none of your business"; or "Why does the police department want to know this about me?" Applied researchers need to be prepared to defend their protocols to audiences outside academia and recognize that community residents will not be as convinced of the value of asking about race, income, or education level as we were.

A Second Step:
Who Will Be Studied and How?

Now that we understand which variables to measure to find out what community residents believe about their police department, another more thorny problem must be resolved, namely how to get the data and which community residents to include. If this were solely a researcher-initiated piece of academic-audience research, the answer would be clear. Identify the population of interest, determine whether to study the entire population or sample, define a sampling design which will produce the number of cases and representativeness desired, and proceed to implement the study design (Maxfield and Babbie, 2008). But in a client-driven collaborative research project, questions must be answered about how the research is to be funded and how much funding is available. This has a direct and profound impact on how the study will be conducted and which methods will "fit the budget." For example sampling design is highly dependent on time, money, and practical concerns.

Regarding which community residents should be included in the study population, the police departments and city governments felt very strongly that every household should have the opportunity to participate. They wanted there to be no doubt that every household had been reached and every household had an opportunity to share their perceptions of the police department. From their point of vision, this trumped the argument that a simple random sample of households would be more representative of the community and more efficient than a mass mailing. They asserted, "We do not want complaints from the public on why they didn't have the opportunity to participate." From the researcher's point of view it is hard to visualize an angry crowd of citizens storming the police headquarters demanding their right to participate—if only resident interest in community policing research were so strong! The decision made was to use the city utility department's list of households with electrical hook-ups, which insured that each household on the city's mailing list would receive a copy of the community policing survey in a mailing from the city.

The less than 30 percent response rate observed in research projects conducted in the three communities underscores the differences between a client-driven piece of research and response rates observed in researcher-initiated projects. Of course funding affects both research-initiated and client-initiated projects, and in reference to the sampling design described above, all three communities decided to survey all households but none had budgeted for follow-up mailings. Hence, the weak response rate. To increase the response rate, a business-reply envelope, for return of the survey at no cost to the resident, was supplied in the mailing to each household.

With the cooperation of one city manager we were able to place the community policing survey online, accessible from the city's web pages (Ballard and Prine, 2002). Although Internet survey delivery seems commonplace today, just a few years ago it was a new resource especially well-suited for wired smaller communities and one of our study communities was just that. We were able to take a platform used mainly for dissemination of local government announcements and turn it into a survey response tool. While slight discrepancies were observed on demographic characteristics of those who responded online compared to mailed surveys, the survey results from the electronic sample were very similar to those from the mailed survey sample.

The Time Dimension and the Importance of Longitudinal Data

In one of the three communities, the authors have collaborated with the city manager and police chief on four separate occasions over a ten year period. Replication is an important aspect of social research and a rarity in the community policing research literature. We were able to establish baseline and trend data on crime and victimization and to place locally collected data in state, regional, and even national context.

Despite the fact that Americans are objectively safer today than they were in 1973, fear of crime is consistently ranked high on the list of what citizens consider to be significant social problems. Fear of victimization is a rational response to a subjectively defined threat of victimization:

> To be afraid of crime is to show moral outrage and disapproval for the way society seems to have loosened its moral standards and deterioration in the norm of conformity to a set of traditionally-understood rules. For people who live in high crime areas, the fear of crime tends to be an everyday experience that reduces their quality of life. Yet for those people who live more protected lives, the fear of crime tends to be a more diffuse feeling that reflects a broader expression of concerns about social change. (Jackson in Murray and Farrall, (Eds.), 2008; p. 148)

Sociologically speaking, perception is reality, that is, the public's fear of crime presents a challenge to law enforcement agencies which must grapple with the disconnect between objectively declining crime rates and citizens' subjective feelings of fear. For instance, this disconnect is evident by age. The actual risk of victimization and the perceived risk among age groups are different. The elderly are actually at lower risk of being victims of crime but exhibit higher levels of fear of crime (Hancock and Sharp, 2000).

Criminological and sociological research confirms that perceptions are significant in shaping criminal behavior as well. Paternoster and Mazerolle (1994) argue that perceived sanctions are just as important as real punishments in deterring non-conforming behavior. His work also shows that perceptions of informal sanctions from peers and family are just as important, if not more so, as formal responses from the criminal justice system. Most people feel safe in their own neighborhood but women, blacks, and Hispanics say they are more fearful of crime than whites, according to recent study by the National Crime Prevention Council (NCPC), a private, nonprofit, educational organization.

It is not surprising that the public's perception of crime differs from reality. Every day the media follows the marketing mantra of "if it bleeds it leads," with story after story of murders, assaults, and robberies. Studies show there is no empirical relationship between the amount of crime reported in newspapers and TV and local crime rates (Davis, 1951 in Pope, Lovell, and Brandl, *Readings in Criminal Justice Research*; Kappeler, Blumberg, and Potter, 1993, see same source). In our study communities, police and city officials lament the media coverage of all things negative about crime and the police. "Rant and Rave" columns in their local newspapers have a way, in the words of one police officer, "of shaping the discussion on crime." While the bulk of crimes in our three study communities are property crimes, media coverage will be visible and loud on any violent crime, further explaining the perception gap between what is and what is perceived to be.

Media's need to sensationalize crime and subsequent misrepresentation of crime for political gain by elected officials may pressure police to redirect resources or acquiesce to public pressure about needed policing strategy regardless of what the real local crime situation may be. We found support for this proposition in a police department personnel study we were asked to perform in one of our study communities. There was a perception, among officers, that it was more important for administrators to avoid citizen complaints than to engage in pro-active policing. This makes for an interesting three way dynamic; officers desire to aggressively enforce the law; citizens don't want to be profiled or harassed; and police administrators want a supportive and non-complaining public.

An additional note about citizen fear: national surveys indicate that most women and a substantial number of men are afraid to walk outdoors at night, even in their own neighborhoods. The home security business has grown into a billion-dollar industry with one in four American households touched by crime (mostly property crime) each year. We turn to the police as the legitimate authority to enforce laws, arrest offenders, and maintain order. In our community policing research, we found that 80 percent of residents felt relatively safe in their neighborhoods (Ballard and Prine, 2004). As the front line of defense between the public and the criminal, the police are symbols of the entire justice system. So much more visible and reachable than other criminal justice system personnel, they are the "human face" of the criminal justice system. Most community residents will rarely, if ever, interact with judges, prosecutors, or correctional officers during the course of their everyday affairs.

The police "cannot possibly arrest all suspected lawbreakers. There aren't enough police, and even if there were, there wouldn't be enough courts to try the accused or enough jails to hold them" (Coleman and Kerbo, 2002:442). It is not in the interest of justice for the police to arrest every offender, irrespective of the circumstance. Therefore, police must use discretion and judgment in deciding how and how many lawbreakers to remove from the community. Demonstrated beautifully in *The Andy Griffith Show*, Sheriff Taylor applied common sense, humor, and a thorough knowledge of the community to make determinations of whether an offender should be arrested or not. Compare this use of discretion to Deputy Fife's bureaucratic and zealous adherence to rules and regulations frequently to the detriment of justice. Policing today is more complex than the vagaries encountered by Andy and Barney in Mayberry. More than ever, American society is socially diverse with even the most minor conflicts between residents and police having the potential to become a serious or even deadly incident.

In our community policing research, we found evidence of how differences in race and social class affect perceptions of the police. Our studies show the dyads of African American resident and white officer encounters draw more attention than within race encounters. Minority residents see the police officer as representing more than simply law enforcement. Rather, white and black officers may be seen as representative of all institutions and authorities operating in the community. Again, perception is reality concerning race, especially when one of the actors is of a different race, social class, gender, and the other represents a position of authority. For a statistically small but substantively significant number of community residents, the race, social class, and gender of the police officer matters. It is precisely this perception which studies of community policing document and use to improve policing service delivery to residents across these social lines.[1]

Police agencies are facing increasing challenges to traditional policing with newer approaches and more democratic enforcement strategies gaining popularity. Police in hundreds of communities are returning to foot patrols. "They are surveying citizens to learn what they believe to be their most serious neighborhood problems" (Kelling in Hancock and Sharp, 2000). Indicators that police and community leaders are serious about including residents in discussions about how to keep communities safe include the revival of interest in "Neighborhood Watch" programs and community policing structures created within departments.

Maxfield and Babbie (2008) agree that community level victimization surveys fill an important gap left by a reliance on national indicators of victimization. While a police administrator might want to know how his/her community compares to regional or national findings, policies are carried out at the local level. It follows that local information is most relevant to help shape policy and the evaluation of policy and practice. Sherman (1992) supports the use of research in developing law enforcement policy with the stipulation that the relationship is ongoing. His work on arrest policy for misdemeanor level domestic violence shows that there are significant differences across communities and while arrest seems to be a deterrent in some jurisdictions it seems to exacerbate problems in others. Local data collection is a practical way to supplement regional, state, and national data sources.

While there is an understanding that community based research may not reach the level of methodological sophistication found in the National Community Victimization Survey (NCVS), there are certain factors that should be included in a victimization survey. In our community policing research, we captured the basic factors of interest in the national surveys but customized the surveys to include significant local differences as well. As a result of the collaborative process with city and police officials, a set of questions about awareness and use of crime victims' services was added to the core community policing survey to gather data relevant for partner agencies who work with the police to improve police performance and improve resident safety.

Completing the Loop:
Research as a Cyclical Process

The real reward in "doing" sociology and criminology is when the researcher is able to see the results of his/her work being implemented in the community for positive social change. In one of our community policing studies conducted in 1998, citizens' responses indicated a need for improved communication between officers and the public. The police department used this data to install a training module on communication, a "refresher" course for all officers. Was it successful? Follow-up surveys in fact showed a decrease in the number of residents who made communication a priority item.

Another issue that drew a great deal of attention from residents was traffic concerns (everyone has an opinion on traffic problems). There were both general comments like, "crack down on speeding," and specific ones, "Police need to watch the 1600 block of Oak Street between 3:00–5:00 pm because it's like a race track." Our research led to police sergeants identifying specific locations for patrol and/or radar monitoring, and the department used our data to apply for an equipment grant. The successful grant resulted in the purchase of an automatic speed indicator digital display ("Your speed is . . ."), which has become a common sight on roadways.

When a city and police department commit to community policing or problem-solving policing, there is an effort to use scientific data to understand community problems and community residents. Participating in on-going research and evaluation also helps the department to apply for and maintain Commission on Accreditation of Law Enforcement Agencies (CALEA) standards. It is rewarding to enter a police department and see the CALEA certificate framed and proudly displayed in the lobby and to know that you played a small part in the department's achievement of this recognition and honor.

Client-Driven Versus Researcher Initiated Research Issues

There is quite a difference between a researcher-initiated and a client-initiated study of citizen perceptions of community policing. In the academic setting, researchers would begin a study of how citizens perceive the police department by doing a review of the literature, considering existing conceptual models and relevant theories, developing hypotheses, then defining the study population or sample. But when the police department is your client paying for the research, the process starts with a meeting to hear which questions the client wants answered in the research, what resources are available, and perhaps most importantly the timeline for conducting the research and deadline for delivery of research results. In researcher-initiated research projects, the researcher may take quite a long time to search the relevant literature, explore theoretical conceptualization, and prepare a research design. The audience for researcher-initiated studies is frequently professional academics and the researcher crafts each aspect of the research with an eye on publication of the study in an appropriate professional peer-reviewed journal.

Contrast this with police department-initiated research wherein all major parameters of the study are defined by the client, especially time, money, and how results will be disseminated. In our community policing research, we have used the collaborative research process between the university and our clients to produce data-based findings to inform police and city decision makers and we have also prepared manuscripts using the same dataset for publication in academic journals. However, these two types of research products, the applied research report and the academic manuscript take very different formats and have decidedly different purposes and publics.

Everything from the study population size to data collection methods to the dissemination of findings is impacted by time and money. Researcher-initiated work inside academia may have an open-ended timeline . . . "as long as it takes," with the guiding goal of publication for promotion and tenure framing the timetable. Police department sponsored research works on the time schedule of the police chief and his supervisor in city government. In some cases, the research product gets disseminated no further than the client who pays to have it produced. Researcher-initiated studies have literature reviews which take more time than some entire client-sponsored piece of research takes to produce. For example, a client who needs a piece of research completed yesterday may insist upon an impossibly fast study timeline and create all manner of chaos with traditional research design processes requiring researchers to be creative and flexible in ways uncommon in traditional academic research projects. For example, in our community policing research, we have mediated between the client's interests and the interest of science on many occasions. When a police department is cutting back due to budget shortfalls, the client cannot expect that academic partners will be able to do more with less and in less time. We have been fortunate that our city and police department partners recognize that a contract with a for-profit research firm will be many times the price that practicing sociologists who are full-time academics will charge, but the tradeoff will be lower cost for more time required to do the project. A for-profit research company could do the project quickly and render a hefty bill for those services. Smaller cities and police departments partner with universities to keep from breaking their budgets.

Practicing sociologists and criminologists who work primarily in academic settings have, generally speaking, access to institutional resources such as student labor (student assistant, work-study, internship, service-learning), which keeps costs lower for clients. Faculty members reap dual benefits from delivery of university-based services which result in positive changes in the community and they use their applied work to enhance student education while building their own promotion and tenure and post-tenure portfolios. For students, the textbook and class room lessons come alive as they work collaboratively with clients. This is participatory learning considered optimal for training students in research methods and statistics. In our project, we included students in every decision-making aspect of the community policing research work. Students were at the table when meetings between the city managers, police chiefs, and faculty members took place and participated in conversations which shaped research design decisions. Clearly students play a critical role in data entry, file management, and data analysis. Working closely with faculty, students get an insider's feel for the context of social research and are involved in interpretation and discussion of what the data means.

For example, when one police chief made a decision to change the data collection protocol, the student working with us on the project heard discussions about the pros and cons of changing the protocol, why the change was necessary, and how it could best be implemented with the least harm to the overall data collection effort. The survey research design used in the project relied on a utilities hook-ups list maintained by city government which served as the sampling frame for the project. The police chief and city manager felt it would be very important to target a small but growing Latino population and made a case for a drastic change in the survey protocol to insure a greater return rate by Latino residents. We also believed it was important to reach the Latino members of the study population and approved the proposed change in the data collection design. Rather than rely solely on mailed surveys, Spanish-speaking members of the local county extension service office hand delivered surveys to Latino households and assisted with any language barriers while encouraging and facilitating completion of the survey.

Conclusion

Taken as a whole our research projects certainly have not been perfect. We believe, however, that we have effectively negotiated real world problems and engaged police departments, city officials, and the service population in efforts to improve policing. Project results indicate that it is possible to accomplish a lot with limited financial resources. By combining the resources of a regional university with a motivated police department and a supportive city hall, momentum for positive change grows. The police administrators and city officials bring access to communities and a desire to understand residents better to the table. We bring expertise in research design, data analysis, and report writing to the table. For the practicing sociologist and criminologist, the sharing of knowledge and resources is a creative and energizing partnership. Each collaborator has something to contribute and each has to compromise in order for the research project to succeed. The real world is different from the laboratory and practical results matter more than perfection.

The product of the research is information, which police administrators and city officials use to make improvements to policing services in their communities, and by extension, enhance the quality of life of residents. We have extended the classroom for the students who are directly involved in the collaborative research and indirectly to students in our classes. "This topic reminds me of our community policing research" is a refrain heard often by students in our classes as we bring the lessons from the field into the classroom. In closing, there are real benefits for all concerned: police departments develop community policing policy informed by community input, the city demonstrates its commitment to include all segments of the population, and the community gets a more responsive police department.

Works Cited

Ballard, Chet and Rudy Prine. 2002. "Citizen Perceptions of Community Policing: Comparing Internet and Mail Survey Responses." *Social Science Computer Review*. 20 (4) Winter.

———. 2004. "Thomasville Residents' Perceptions of Community Policing and Police Department Performance Survey Results," a sponsored research report presented to the Thomasville Police Department and Thomasville City Manager, Thomasville, GA, July.

City of Johannesburg, Community Policing Forum. 2009. "Aiming at Cyberspace in Randburg." www.joburg.org.za/content/view/88/75/. Retrieved May 1, 2009.

Civitas Blog. 2004. "Anti-Social Behavior Order Is No Substitute for Effective Policing." www.civitas.org.uk/blog/crime/. Retrieved on October 25, 2008.

Coleman, James William and Harold R. Kerbo. 2002. *Social Problems*. 8th Edition. Upper Saddle Hills, NJ: Prentice Hall.

Commission on Accreditation of Law Enforcement Agencies, CALEA. www.calea.org/Online/CALEAPrograms/LawEnforcement/lawenfprogram.htm. Retrieved on December 19, 2008.

Curran, Daniel and Claire Renzetti. 2000. *Theories of Crime*. 2nd Edition. Boston, MA: Allyn and Bacon.

Doerner, William G. 2007. *Introduction to Law Enforcement: An Insider's View*. 3rd Edition. Dubuque, IO: Kendall/Hunt.

Federal Bureau of Investigation, Uniform Crime Reports. www.fbi.gov/ucr/ucr.htm. Retrieved November 18, 2008.

Hancock, Barry W. and Paul M. Sharp (Eds.). 2000. *Criminal Justice in America: Theory Practice and Policy*. 2nd Edition. Upper Saddle River, NJ: Prentice Hall.

Jackson, Jonathan. 2008. "Bridging the Social and the Psychological in Fear of Crime Research." In Lee, Murray and Stephen Farrall (Eds.), *Fear of Crime: Critical Voices in an Age of Anxiety*, Oxford: Routledge-Cavendish, pp. 143–167.

Kappeler, Victor, Mark Blumberg, and Gary Potter (Eds.). 2000. *The Mythology of Crime and Criminal Justice*. Long Grove, IL: Waveland Press.

Kelling, George. 2000. "Police and Communities: The Quiet Revolution." In Hancock, Barry W. and Paul M. Sharp (Eds.), *Criminal Justice in America: Theory Practice and Policy*. 2nd Edition. Upper Saddle River, NJ: Prentice Hall.

Kretzman, John and John McKnight. 1993. *Building Communities from the Inside Out: Centre for Urban Affairs and Policy Research*. Chicago: ACTA Publications.

Maxfield, Michael G. and Earl Babbie. 2008. *Research Methods for Criminal Justice and Criminology*. 5th Edition. Belmont, CA: Wadsworth.

Metropolitan Police of London, United Kingdom. www.met.police.uk/history/index.htm. Retrieved December 19, 2008.

National Public Radio. 2008. "FBI to Get to the Root of the Financial Crisis" by Dina Temple-Raston and Renee Montagne. www.npr.org/templates/story/story.php?storyId=96019338. Retrieved October 23, 2008.

Paternoster, Raymond and Paul Mazerolle. 1994. "General Strain Theory and Delinquency: A Replication and Extension." *Journal of Research in Crime and Delinquency*. 31 (3).

Pope, Carl, Rick Lovell, and Steven Brandl (Eds.). 2001. *Voices from the Field: Readings in Criminal Justice Research*. Belmont, CA: Wadsworth.

Prine, Rudy K., Chet Ballard, and Deborah M. Robinson. 2001. "Perceptions of Community Policing in a Small Town." *American Journal of Criminal Justice*. 25 (2) Spring.

Rebach Howard M. and John G. Bruhn (Eds.). 1990. *Handbook of Clinical Sociology: Research and Practice*. New York: Plenum Publishers.

San Antonio Police Department, Community Policing. www.sanantonio.gov/saPD/COPPS.asp?res=1280&ver=true. Retrieved October 4, 2008.

Santa Clara Police Department, Community Policing. www.scpd.org/community/community policing.html. Retrieved October 3, 2008.

Schmalleger, Frank. 2009. *Criminal Justice Today*. 10th Edition. Upper Saddle River, NJ: Prentice Hall.

Sherman, Lawrence W. 1992. *Policing Domestic Violence: Experiments and Dilemmas*. New York: Free Press.

Siegel, Larry J. 2009. *Criminology: Theories, Patterns, and Typologies*. Belmont, CA: Wadsworth.

Straus, Roger A. 2002. *Using Sociology: An Introduction from the Applied and Clinical Perspectives*. New York: Rowman and Littlefield Publishers.

Sutton, Nicola, Graham A. Draper, and John Jones. 2005. *Community Policing: Exploring Issues in Contemporary Policing*. Toronto, CN: Emond Montgomery Publishing.

Thomas, William Isaac and Dorothy Swaine Thomas. 1928. *The Child in America: Behavior Problems and Programs*. New York: Knopf

U.S. Department of Justice. 2007. *Crime Victimization*. Office of Justice Program, Bureau of Justice Statistics. www.ojp.usdoj.gov/bjs/cvictgen.htm. Retrieved December 19, 2008.

Note

1. The idea that "perception is reality," it merits note, is a key principle of the symbolic interactionist perspective discussed in Chapter 4. This is often referred to as the "Thomas Theorem," originated by an early 20th Century American sociologist, W. I. Thomas who first stated it in a study of child delinquency (Thomas and Thomas, 1928).

CHAPTER 6

Issues in Criminal Justice Evaluation
EVALUATING MICHIGAN'S DRUG COURTS[1]

David J. Hartmann, Western Michigan University
Gayle M. Rhineberger-Dunn, University of Northern Iowa

Applied work in crime, law, and deviance can take many forms. Our own work, for example, has generally fallen into four areas: evaluations of interventions, analysis of existing social policies, efforts to design new policies to pursue social objectives (at both the municipal and state level), and basic data collection efforts (including targeted surveys and data reviews and, more broadly, needs assessments). While such distinctions are useful, actual projects like the one described here often span categories. Furthermore, those students interested in the emerging discipline of evaluation will notice that this project also exemplifies an important but still underutilized evaluation genre, that of evaluability assessment.

Satisficing in (Applied) Research

Long ago, the pragmatist philosopher, John Dewey identified inquiry with problem oriented thinking (1938). The pragmatists had much to say that is still relevant to applied sociologists but this insight is more fundamental than most.[2] As we collectively attempt to identify a problem, we largely determine both the research design and the potential use of the findings. Problem definition is emergent and constructed and it is therefore important that a statement of the problem respect and report that context. There is wide agreement among both policy makers and practitioners, for example, that drug courts should address the interdependent problems of crime, substance abuse, and an overburdened corrections system. In responding to a Request for Proposals (RFP) explicitly articulated around these issues, we agreed to accept these problem statements and at least the potential utility of the drug court approach. It is important to remember that even in evaluation work and almost always in more basic kinds of research, a well informed researcher might choose to dispute or modify these taken for granted definitions. As Weber famously put it, "The specific function of science, it seems to me, is . . . to ask questions about those things which convention makes self-evident" (1949, p. 13).

In any event, even accepting the importance of interdependent crime and substance abuse as worthy of investigation in Michigan's drug courts, the ability to shed light on such problems is limited by time and budget and expertise. The first part of our evaluation tries to balance the need for informed advice on far-reaching and inter-dependent problems with a severely circumscribed timeline. In many ways, the compromises arrived at during this stage determined the type of work we did and the use that was made of it subsequently. The lesson is general and in stark contrast to the Enlightenment ideal—we do not discover the truth for all time, we make progress on local problems. At every turn, researchers are required to define and limit their inquiry. The pragmatist's guide is also the standard for applied researchers in sociology—focus the work so as to maximize its use for the problems that are most pressing. Those problems are necessarily to at least some extent local and emergent and value laden (a more pejorative term is political) and so our attention to them must be as well.

Drug Court Characteristics

Drug courts—increasingly called drug treatment courts—are an emerging favorite in the range of approaches to deal with the individual and societal problems of substance abuse. They take a long-term court supervised treatment approach for offenders or accused offenders with drug problems (Belenko, 2001). As of August, 2008, American University (2008a,b) cites 1,938 drug courts—1,206 adult, 474 juvenile, 235 family, and 23 combination—in the United States with another 107 in some stage of planning. They report that over a quarter of a million clients have been enrolled and close to 80,000 have graduated.

This is a rapid and impressive growth for a model that is just under twenty years old. The Dade County (Miami) program in 1989 is usually considered the progenitor of this line. As the U.S. General Accounting Office (GAO) first noted in 1997 and Belenko confirmed in 1998 and 2001, we notice a relative lack of empirical, much less rigorous outcome evaluation studies. Terry (1999, p. 15) has argued that "little is available that reveals much about the impact of treatment drug courts on the outcomes for which they were created." The GAO

(USGAO 1997, p. 13), similarly, has reviewed 20 evaluation studies and has few "definitive conclusions concerning the overall impact of drug courts."

The Request for Proposals—Getting a Handle on Drug Courts in Michigan

Recognizing the need for a rigorous outcome assessment of its drug courts, in 2001 the Michigan State Court Administrative Office (SCAO) awarded Western Michigan University's Kercher Center for Social Research the task of evaluating the Michigan Drug Court Grant Program to answer two critical policy questions: 1) Are drug courts cost effective?" and "2) How can significant outcomes benefiting communities with established drug court programs be measured?" Additionally, the SCAO requested that we develop an evaluation protocol enabling the SCAO "to perform future continuous evaluation of program participants." To accomplish this task, three test sites were chosen: Kalamazoo Men's Drug Court, Macomb County Juvenile Drug Court, and City of Detroit Drug Court. The Kalamazoo Men's Program was chosen because of the evaluators' familiarity with the program and key actors and because it was a part of a nationally known jurisdiction with well-developed record keeping mechanisms. The other two programs were chosen, after consultation with the SCAO office, because they met the criteria of having mature record keeping and providing particularly helpful comparisons (e.g., a juvenile court, one from the east side of the state, or a rural setting). One court was the juvenile program in Macomb County and the other was the adult court in Detroit. We did not intend for or assume that these sites would represent all Michigan drug courts, but would simply give a sense of the range of situations in Michigan.

For these three sites, our specific objectives were to collect and report available outcome assessment information and determine the capacity of each site to support a rigorous model of outcome evaluation for drug treatment courts. To accomplish these objectives, project collaborators first produced a "model outcomes protocol" based on basic principles of evaluation design as well as a review of the drug treatment court literature. The protocol included a recommended set of outcome and context measures, recommendations as to the timing of measurement, recommended design features (e.g., a control group), and recommendations for management information systems (MIS) and staff support.

The protocol was applied to each of the three test sites through an analysis of existing data and site visits. Since the required timeline for this study called for development of a set of outcome measures within four months of the contract award, and then completion of a draft of the site analyses six weeks later, we realized we would be dependent on existing outcomes analysis at each site. Our site visits included a review of capabilities and levels of support for dimensions of the model protocol. A compromise "core outcomes protocol" was reached wherein the payoffs of the model protocol were balanced against the resource demands it would impose.

SCAO Outcome Site Protocol[3]

The three parts of the model protocol correspond to three basic questions: who to measure, when to measure, and what to measure. The first part, "Selection and Comparison Group Issues," addresses two basic points: who gets in to the program and to whom will they be compared. It is important that eligibility criteria and selection process be explicit and consistently followed so that one knows what kind of selection bias, relative to program intent, may occur. Basic evaluation design requires isolation of potential program effects through comparison of change in outcome measures for the treatment or experimental group to changes for a comparison (ideally a randomly assigned control) group. Otherwise, changes might not be due to the drug court but be a natural result of maturation, changing economic conditions, or a variety of other factors. It is important that, as much as possible, the same data elements are collected and retained for both the experimental and the control group members.

The second part, "Frequency of Measurement Issues for both Experimental and Comparison/Control Group," addresses issues of when and how often to measure. The timing and frequency of measurement should be comparable for the experimental and control groups. It is important that in-program and follow-up data be systemically collected and retained for both graduates and unsuccessful discharges from the program, as well as for comparison group members. Since follow-up data are not used by the drug court for client processing, the schedule of follow-up can be determined by the evaluation needs and budget. Quarterly or at least twice per year contacts are preferable both because self-report information tends to be more reliable when it is taken at more frequent intervals and because long delays in contacting former clients are associated with more difficulty in locating the potential respondent (Hartmann, Wolk, and Sullivan, 1995). Follow-ups should be continued for at least two years after discharge for all three groups (successful and unsuccessful discharges from drug court and the comparison group).

The third part, "Outcome Measures: In-Program and Follow-Up," outlines the primary outcomes or core measures that are significant for all drug courts. Since the essence of outcomes assessment is to measure change in key indicators, whenever possible, measurements should be made for a pre-program period through official records (as for criminal behavior) and self-reports (e.g., of substance use) as well as during and after the program. Based on our experience and review of the current drug court literature, we suggest including measures of the following variables: criminal activity, substance use, employment, discharge status, and family and health outcomes for juvenile and family courts.

Applying the Model

The first step in conducting evaluations is, in fact, to determine the feasibility of the evaluation work for the particular programs and sites one has in mind. This is called evaluability assessment and was a primary use of the three outcome sites. This sort of analysis should routinely be done before evaluation of complex systems like drug courts, particularly when they have an inconsistent record of evaluation work.

Basically, evaluability assessment assesses the feasibility and likely usefulness of an evaluation. It explores the feasibility of evaluation by looking at four potential barriers to effective work at each site (Wholey, 1994, 1). 1) Are there clear goals and objectives and an understanding of potential costs? Without that clarity, it may not be possible to agree on goals to be evaluated. 2) Are those goals plausible as well as well defined? If not, they may need to be revised before evaluation begins. 3) Are relevant performance data obtainable? This is crucial and must be checked thoroughly. Sample data reports or even a pilot project may be advisable. 4) Can evaluators and clients agree on the intended uses of evaluation information? Is evaluation intended to guide goal modification, to help publicize the value of the program, or to plan for changes in the program structure or operation? Basically, how will the information be used?

Evaluability assessment can take a long time and substantial money but will save considerable resources in the long run. To be effective, it must involve intended users at both the operations and policy levels since both are needed to make sure there is clarity of goals and access to data. The intent of the program can be discerned from program documents but also from interviews and group discussions. That intent, particularly in a clear program design (a model of how the program is supposed to operate to accomplish its goals), is not always widely shared. The program design is the basis for evaluation, however, so all who will be involved must understand it. If staff do not understand why certain information matters, they will be less likely to maintain it or to collect it for evaluation.

Next, the evaluability assessment explores the actual operation of the program and documents how it differs from what was intended. This is a process evaluation and involves site visits, data reports, and conversations with staff. If actual operation differs from what the agreed on design is, changes in program design or operation should ensue before the full evaluation begins. The nature of that full evaluation, possible designs and probable uses of results, should be understood by actors at each site and the evaluability process provides the opportunity for that discussion.

Certainly, there can be substantial difficulties in carrying out such an assessment. Establishing and keeping trust, learning specialized vocabularies, uncovering long unquestioned assumptions about program operation and orientation, and maintaining the spirit of a common interest in program improvement are crucial.

Site Analyses

We used three test sites for two purposes: first to present the outcome data that was currently collected and available and second to see how much of the ideal model appeared sensible and doable in those sites. Based on that analysis we presented a suggested "core protocol for SCAO sites" that we believed would provide solid outcome measurement within reasonable budgetary and time constraints. Part of that core protocol was an estimate of the sort of resources that should be provided or facilitated for sites to make their tasks feasible.

Our approach to the three sites was clearly an example of evaluability assessment. Before asking all sites to carry out a complex and expensive evaluation, an assessment of the ability of particular programs and sites to support evaluation work was required. In question, "Was the evaluation of interest feasible for the program and site?" For the three sites, we 1) collected and reported available outcome assessment information and 2) determined the capacity of each site to support a rigorous model of outcome evaluation for drug treatment courts.

We found basically that sites were committed to data collection and analysis to assess program effect but lacked capacity in key areas. They were collecting many of the indicators of program operation and performance that would be needed in a full outcome model: e.g., number of enrollees, source of referral, reason for selection/rejection, acceptance/refusal by referral, Addiction Severity Index (ASI) score, Behavioral Severity Assessment Program (BSAP) score (for mental health assessment), dates of participation, demographics, status hearing attendance, dates of treatment. These indicators were generally maintained only for enrollees.

Further, they were collecting such information in hardcopy client files or, at best, in multiple databases. This may have allowed aggregation of descriptive statistics for one variable at a time (e.g., number of participants by race) but would not routinely support comparison of variables, groupings of cases by other variables, or linking of variables across databases. One site felt they could learn to do at least bivariate reports (that is, cross-tabulations, tables with multiple columns for different groupings) within their new client-processing database since it was adopted in part to have more flexible reporting capabilities. Another site was still in the process of converting files to the computer but had some hand written reports.

These three sites routinely collected employment data, drug test data, and recidivism data on clients while they were in the program. These were the major available outcome measures. These measures were not analyzed for subgroups of clients or in comparison to unsuccessful discharges or a comparison/control group. They did not routinely collect outcome measures related to health and family functioning, although treatment providers often had these data. Treatment providers also had data on treatment modality and the dosage and intensity of treatment for clients but generally that information was not in the drug court databases.

Most significantly, like most operating programs, these three drug court sites did not routinely designate a comparison/control group and so did not collect data on comparison/control group members. Nor did they generally collect post-program outcome measures with the important exception that they were beginning to query standard databases for recidivism (e.g., Law Enforcement Information Network (LEIN), Internet Criminal History Access Tool (ICHAT)). Again, Kalamazoo was doing this themselves while the other two were contracting out the service. Only Kalamazoo had completed such an analysis.

Suggested Core Outcomes Protocol

As previously noted, one purpose of this evaluation was to develop an evaluation protocol which the SCAO would use to uniformly evaluate all Michigan drug courts. Based on our analysis of the three test sites, several requirements were identified for a core outcomes protocol to work properly, beginning with an electronic database. Many jurisdictions do not have such a database and many others do not have the staff resources to collect client data, especially from control groups or at follow-up, or to enter and process the data once collected. Asking courts to take on meaningful evaluation work without these resources is unfair and unrealistic.

This database should be distinct from the database(s) used for client processing. It should contain all variables that will be analyzed for outcomes evaluation purposes, and be maintained by evaluation staff with continuous data collection and coordination from other data sources. It should support statistical analysis and graphical displays of outcomes (e.g., Statistical Package for Social Science [SPSS] or Statistical Analysis System [SAS]).

Each person referred to the drug court should have a record, which would include source of referral, precipitating offense, and reasons for selection/rejection from the program. Demographic indicators should also be included. Although it is not likely that any full needs or risk assessment will be done on referrals, whatever is done and used should be recorded.

A comparison or control group should be defined and comparable information recorded for those persons as is kept for drug court clients. The location and type of program and supervision in place for each comparison/control group member should be specified. Access to those persons for data collection must be set up in advance and monitored for completeness. The comparison/control group can be drawn from referrals who refuse or from a matched group of other persons. We do not recommend a comparison group of referrals not selected for the drug court since there should be systematic differences in need/risk. A record in the evaluation database must be built for each comparison/control group member.

Location information to be used for follow-up should be collected at intake and exit as should contact information for a collateral informant. Any required releases for data collection should be signed. The dates of transition points should be recorded (e.g., referral, enrollment, phase movements, discharge, termination of probation, detentions). These are required so that time in program by component and time at risk variables can be constructed.

Treatment (drug court) and comparison/control group members should have a multi-dimensional biopsychosocial needs assessment at intake and exit from programs. The ASI is a good example that includes substance dependency and history but also other domains of functioning. Treatment data, including type, dosage, and intensity should be recorded.

In-program outcomes including recidivism, drug use, employment, days in detention, and education (particularly for juveniles) should be routinely recorded, as should any changes in program or incarceration status associated with negative outcomes (including dates). Additionally, discharge status and dates must be recorded. Reasons for discharge, successful/unsuccessful status, and resultant placement (e.g., released from supervision, nature of supervision, incarceration) should also be recorded. Retention rates should be monitored and routinely reported. Both successful and unsuccessful discharges from the drug court remain in the database for continued data collection and analysis. The same is true for comparison/control group members.

Follow-up data collection should begin when persons are discharged and are not incarcerated. If a person is unsuccessfully discharged and goes to a term of incarceration, that should be recorded but follow-up would wait until release from detention. Follow-up contacts should occur at least every six months and should ask respondents about substance use, employment, family and social functioning, and any other outcomes deemed important. Official records of criminal activity should be accessed (e.g., a statewide computerized information system) as should records of time spent in detention. Since official records can be incomplete for extended periods of time, they should be re-checked over time. Juvenile and adult criminal records must be checked for juveniles, particularly at follow-up where most will age out of the juvenile system.

Both in-program and follow-up outcomes should be frequently and routinely monitored so that a culture of outcomes review is built. Outcomes should be related to demographic indicators, risk/needs scores, treatment received, and discharge status as well as membership in drug court or comparison/control group. Analysis of outcomes should include bivariate and multivariate explanations.

To accomplish this ambitious and time-consuming protocol, evaluation expertise in the form of local partners should be contractually retained. Local evaluation plans should be submitted for review to SCAO to ensure the core elements are present and a feasible system will be created. An evaluability analysis should be conducted at each site as part of the preparation for outcomes evaluation.

Results of the Report

While this evaluation story is clearly one of compromise based in compressed timelines, limited data availability, and diverse site operations, each limitation was explicitly acknowledged and turned into a part of the evaluation design. The focus became one of developing a model protocol in two steps—a draft ideal and then a more realistic one based on an evaluability assessment. This strategy was approved by the funder and resulted in information well-suited to assist policy in this area. In addition to informing the SCAO as to the current functioning of drug courts (a process evaluation of multiple sites was carried out concurrently with the outcome work described here), our model protocol and data elements became central to the development of Public Act 224 passed in Michigan which controlled state funding for drug courts. The senior author served as an advisor to the senate committee that drafted the legislation. That act specified a modified version of our evaluation protocol as a required component.

This codification of evaluation elements and expectations subsequently encouraged a stability of evaluation work in this area and facilitated centralized training and MIS development. These may all turn out to be largely positive results. At the same time, it may be largely negative that a core data set and standard protocols become taken-for-granted in the same way as the original problem definition has now been codified. The model in place lends itself far better to tinkering than radical critique. That critique, should it come, may have to arise in more basic research than that following our evaluation model.

Conclusion

This applied research project both met some initial needs for data and set the stage for more systematic evaluation to follow. It first followed an evaluability model to see what sort of sustained evaluation might be possible, pushed that envelope a bit, and had, and continues to have, a role in on-going policy debates. It was sensitive to various stakeholders—primarily legislators, government professionals, and practitioners, and to a lesser extent clients and treatment professionals. But it clearly suffered from the weaknesses of much applied work—it largely accepted a problem definition and a proposed model for addressing the problem. At worst, such research can show the proposed solution is unimpressive. It is not designed to identify superior options and so tends to be conservative on both problem definition and solution. It is, to borrow two of Kuhn's phrases, a paradigm of normal science—circumscribed and modest—but nevertheless contributory to a cumulative advance.

Works Cited

American University. (2008a). *Summary of Drug Court Activity by State and County.* Bureau of Justice Assistance Drug Court Clearinghouse Project. Accessed September 23, 2008. http://spa.american.edu/justice/documents/2150.pdf.

———. (2008b). *Summary of Drug Court Activity by State and County: Juvenile/Family Drug Courts.* Bureau of Justice Assistance Drug Court Clearinghouse Project. Accessed September 23, 2008. www.spa.american.edu/justice/documents/2418.pdf

Belenko, S. (1998). "Research on Drug Courts: A Critical Review." *National Drug Court Institute Review*, 1(1).

———. (1999). "Diverting Drug Offenders to Treatment Care: The Portland Experience." Pp. 108–138 in Terry, W. C. (ed.), *The Early Drug Courts: Case Studies in Judicial Innovation.* Thousand Oaks, CA: SAGE.

———. (2001). "Research on Drug Courts: A Critical Review." *National Drug Court Institute Review* 1:1–42.

Dewey, John. (1938). *Logic—The Theory of Inquiry.* New York: Henry Holt and Company.

Hartmann, D. J., Wolk, J. L., and Sullivan, W. P. (1995). "State-Wide Self-Report of Treatment Effectiveness: Promise, Pitfalls, and Potential." *Alcoholism Treatment Quarterly* 13:45–57.

Terry, C. W. (1999). "Judicial Change and Dedicated Treatment Courts: Case Studies in Innovation." Pp. 1–18 in Terry, W. C. (ed.), *The Early Drug Courts: Case Studies in Judicial Innovation.* Thousand Oaks, CA: SAGE.

U.S. General Accounting Office. (1997). *Drug Courts: Overview of Growth, Characteristics, and Results.* Washington, DC.

Weber, M. (1949). *The Methodology of the Social Sciences*. New York: The Free Press.

Wholey, J. S. (1994). "Assessing the Feasibility and Likely Usefulness of Evaluation." Pp. 15–39 in Wholey, J. S., Hatry, H. P., and Newcomer, K. E. (eds.), *Handbook of Practical Program Evaluation*. San Francisco, CA: Jossey-Bass.

Notes

1. This paper is adapted from a research report undertaken at the request of the Michigan Supreme Court, State Court Administrative Office (SCAO). Like many large scale empirical projects, it was produced by an interdisciplinary team of faculty and graduate students. These collaborators are gratefully acknowledged: Ron Kramer, Subhash Sonnad, Matt Rushlau, Mary Anderson, Jon Neil, Paul Gregory, and Kristen DeVall.

2. Chapter 3, as the reader may recall, provides a more detailed discussion of pragmatism.

3. A detailed description of the Outcome Site Protocol is available from the first author upon request.

CHAPTER 7

Evaluation in Education

FROM GOALS TO CAPACITY DEVELOPMENT[1]

James G. Hougland Jr., University of Kentucky

In a period of increased public accountability, educational organizations and initiatives are subject to pressure to demonstrate that they are achieving worthwhile results. American public schools, for example, have been required under the terms of "No Child Left Behind" federal legislation as well as mandates in several states to administer exams that are intended to provide information on the schools' success in achieving predetermined standards. New educational programs at any level that receive funding from most federal agencies and many private foundations are required to undergo formal evaluations to examine their success.

Evaluations can take many forms, but goal-oriented approaches—those that are focused on the goals and objectives of a program and that attempt to measure how well or poorly the program has done in achieving them (Worthen, Sanders and Fitzpatrick, 2004)—are among the most frequently attempted. Outcomes-based evaluations—focusing on "the state of the target population or the social conditions that a program is expected to have changed" (Rossi, Lipsey and Freeman, 2004: 204)—often are guided by the goals underlying a program. Thus, a program that is intended to reduce drop-out rates among high school students may reasonably be evaluated on the basis of the extent to which drop-out rates actually have decreased.

Focusing on program goals offers several advantages to an evaluator, but such an approach also can lead to unanticipated complications and dilemmas. To begin with several *advantages*, a goal approach, first, encourages early and frequent communication between program staff and the evaluator. This communication is necessary for the evaluator to develop a thorough understanding of what the long-term goals and the shorter-term objectives actually are. Some information may be included in official documents, but probing program staff members about their understanding of the actual purposes of the program and the indicators that would signal success will lead to a much more thorough understanding of the purposes underlying a program. Second, identifying goals and placing them in meaningful categories provides an organizing framework for evaluation activities and reports. Third, a goal approach sets the stage for valid conclusions about success by setting standards against which progress can be measured.

Despite these advantages, some *disadvantages* also exist. A focus on indicators of successful goal achievement alone can be misleading because indicators may be examined without looking carefully at the context in which the program is operating. Programs that are being evaluated are dynamic entities that often face changing and challenging circumstances, and a careful evaluation should take this into consideration. Rossi and colleagues have noted:

> The interpretation of outcome measures and changes in such measures is difficult. Responsible interpretation requires consideration of a program's environment, events taking place during a program, and the natural changes undergone by targets over time. (Rossi, Lipsey and Freeman, 2004: 231–232)

In this chapter, I describe my efforts to evaluate an educational program focused on information technology. While goals played an important role in the evaluation, I soon discovered that other considerations are equally important.

The Research Setting and Selected Findings

Initiated in 2001 with major funding from the National Science Foundation (NSF), the Kentucky Information Technology Center (KITCenter) represents a major initiative on the part of the faculty and administration of the Kentucky Community and Technical College System (KCTCS) to enhance instruction and capabilities regarding information technology (IT) throughout Kentucky.[2] While KITCenter is multifaceted, its major emphasis has involved professional development (based on an extensive set of face-to-face and remote workshops) on the part of community and technical college faculty to enhance their ability to develop a new IT curriculum and to teach courses within it.

As KITCenter's external evaluator, I have worked with KCTCS faculty and administrators to develop a set of goals against which performance should be evaluated. Shorter-term goals have involved faculty credentials, curriculum development, course offerings, and student enrollment. I also have worked with the faculty to take a longer-term perspective to ask whether the students who enroll in the updated and enhanced IT courses are able to obtain degrees or certificates, and, if so, whether their educational experience sets the stage for more advanced education or job placements within their field. For those who have found employment, I also have asked how their employers perceive the quality of the training they have received. For such questions, I worked with the faculty to establish quantitative indicators of success. For example, the faculty and I agreed on the following two goals regarding employment and employer satisfaction:

1. Employment: *Of the students who have completed the IT program and who have not transferred to a senior institution, 80 percent will have entered a job related to their degree by the end of the final year of NSF funding.*
2. Employer Satisfaction: *Ninety percent of employers who have hired IT program graduates will express satisfaction with their preparation and performance when they are surveyed.*

As I have reported elsewhere (Hougland, 2008), deciding whether these two goals have been realized proved more difficult than anticipated. Regarding employment, 84 percent of program completers[3] reported that they were employed, but only 46 percent said that they were employed in IT, so the 80 percent threshold specified in the goal was not met.[4] However, the goal fails to recognize the complementary roles of employment and ongoing education in the lives of many people who complete education programs in two-year institutions. Almost one-third of the completers contacted on my behalf were continuing their education while also holding a job. While the goal was not satisfied as stated, it seems that earning an IT credential has set the stage for continuing professional development on the part of many of the program participants. At a minimum, a more complex and nuanced goal appears to be needed.

What about the second goal? Are 90 percent of employers satisfied? It turns out to depend on the standard that is set. In interviews with employers of program completers working in IT, employers were asked whether they considered the completers' performance to be "excellent," "very good," "somewhat good," "somewhat poor," or "very poor" in several aspects of their work.[5] Overall results were:

Excellent:	34 percent
Very Good:	40 percent
Somewhat Good:	22 percent
Somewhat Poor:	3 percent
Very Poor:	1 percent

If we consider "somewhat good" or better to reflect satisfaction, the goal was easily achieved. Ninety-six percent of the employers considered overall performance to be "somewhat good" or better. However, taking only "excellent" or "very good" as indicators of employer satisfaction leads to a different conclusion. Only 74 percent of the employers were satisfied when "somewhat good" was excluded from the definition. Although employers clearly leaned toward being satisfied, the project's success in meeting its goal regarding employer satisfaction turns out to depend on a rather arbitrary decision about whether or not to accept a particular response category. When this is considered in combination with the arbitrary selection of 90 percent as the level necessary for saying the goal has been achieved, a goal-oriented approach begins to appear problematic. Decisions to label a program a success or a failure can be based as much on arbitrary definitions as on the program's substantive success in improving lives. This being the case, it seems appropriate to subject goal-oriented approaches to evaluation to very careful scrutiny. The insights of researchers working in the area of organizational sociology have proven helpful in thinking through the implications of goal-oriented approaches.

A Critical Appraisal of Goals in Organizations and Program Evaluation

At one time, the role of goals in organizations was viewed in straightforward terms. Child (2005: 48) summarizes traditional conceptions of goals as follows:

> In a textbook bureaucracy, each level of organization is responsible for setting goals and making decisions at that level and below. Goals, characteristically, are set by the senior team and acted upon by line managers. Decisions that require coordinated action across units are referred to higher levels in the organization for resolution. The senior team acts as policy maker for the rest of the company.

In reality, goals are likely to play a more complex and less predictable role in most organizations. This occurs for many reasons, including the following six.

First, any one organization is likely to have multiple goals, which vary according to specificity and time frame (Hannan and Freeman, 1977). Some may represent achievements that are expected within the next few weeks, while others may focus on future decades.

Second, many organizations have made strategic decisions to move to decentralized models for goal setting and decision making. In decentralized organizations, the authority to make major decisions is no longer confined to top executives. People throughout the organization are expected to make decisions regarding their area of responsibility. As Child notes, decentralized units are more likely than centrally located executives to perceive and to adjust rapidly to changing circumstances. Moreover, allowing goals to be set in decentralized units will increase an overall sense of commitment to achieving them. However, the decentralization of goal setting is likely to lead to a set of competing and potentially contradictory goals within the various units of an organization.

Third, even if decision making remains centralized, goals may be separated from the means that are established to achieve them because members of organizations will be rewarded by their ability to stick to procedure rather than their contributions to achieving more abstract goals. In a classic statement of this concern, Merton (1957) noted that, with their emphasis on adherence to rules, organizations are vulnerable to *goal displacement*, a process in which goals are forgotten as members of an organization come to see following the rules as an end in itself. In an educational organization, goal displacement may occur when, for example, officials meticulously inspect all instructors' course syllabi to be sure that they contain required language but pay no attention to what students actually are learning in courses.

Fourth, regardless of an organization's degree of centralization, competing and potentially contradictory perspectives will exist within the organization. Some observers of organizations contend that they are most appropriately viewed as *coalitions* of participants who "exhibit divergent views and interests regarding what the organization is and what it should be doing" (Scott, 2003: 353). Members of such a coalition are likely to be pursuing their own interests even as they pay lip service to the formal goals of the organization (Cyert and March, 1963; Pfeffer and Salancik, 1978). To the extent that organizations are political entities characterized by shifting coalitions, the stability of any given view of an organization's goals is open to question.

Fifth, members of the coalition affecting an organization's goals may not be located entirely inside the organization's boundaries. Stakeholders who are interested in influencing an organization's goals and activities often include external actors (Pennings and Goodman, 1977). Given that organizations often are trying simultaneously to please investors, creditors, suppliers, customers, government regulators, community leaders, and other external actors, they often find it difficult to perform well on all criteria of interest to these disparate stakeholders. In one study of small businesses, Friedlander and Pickle (1968) found a pattern of low and sometimes negative correlations between various criteria of success. Devoting a major effort to trying to please one stakeholder might actually rob resources from other initiatives favored by other stakeholders.

Sixth, because they operate within a larger environmental context, organizations are confronted with changes (in, among other things, competitive pressures, available technology, the legal and regulatory climate, and cultural understandings) that may render some traditional goals obsolete. However, it often is the case that societal changes affect various actors in an organization in different ways. A traditional goal may continue to be viewed positively by some even as it is being abandoned by others. Regarding one such instance, James Wood, Samuel Mueller, and I noted:

> One way of meeting this problem is through [the] mechanism [of] "goal submergence," a process by which organizational leaders de-emphasize a traditional goal to those members (and potential members) who find it disturbing while continue to stress the goal to those who value it. (Hougland, Wood and Mueller, 1974: 409)

We developed the "goal submergence" concept to explain the actions of a major religious denomination with respect to the changing attitudes about alcohol. The Methodist Church officially supported temperance goals for many years after the 1933 passage of the Twenty-First Amendment to the U.S. Constitution. The Twenty-First Amendment repealed prohibition by authorizing states to allow the sale of alcoholic beverages that had been illegal during the prohibition period. Despite the denomination's official support of temperance goals, changes in the structure of boards, financial appropriations, formal behavioral standards, etc. indicate that the denomination was quietly decreasing its support for temperance goals even as they continued to receive verbal support (Hougland, Wood and Mueller, 1974: 410–412). If an organization responds to social change through goal submergence processes, it is likely that many official statements of goals will become obsolete long before they are officially abandoned.

For reasons such as the six just discussed, goals play a rather complex role in organizations. Goals often provide a useful initial look at an organization's or project's reason for existence, but they also introduce pressures to reduce statements of desired achievements and even of broad missions to specific quantitative targets. All too often, these specific targets may reflect what is easy to measure rather than what is truly important. If, for whatever reason, an organization falls short of its specific targets, this may be interpreted as a failure despite a difficult economic environment, unavailability of needed technology, and other mitigating contextual factors or evidence of constructive steps to deal with the problem. Observations of such problems during her tenure as an American Sociological Association Congressional Fellow prompted Dr. Joyce Miller to offer the following note of caution:

> I have cautioned program developers not to establish goals that are impossible to achieve (since success will be measured with respect to these goals). Further, I have cautioned funding agencies about trying

> to hold agencies accountable for aspects of programmatic efforts over
> which the agencies have no control. ([Miller] Iutcovich, 2002:1)

Such considerations have led me to the position that "applied sociologists attempting to evaluate an initiative on the basis of goal achievement . . . must be sensitive to the difficulties involved in defining goals appropriately and in interpreting the organization's experience with respect to those goals" (Hougland, 2008: 3).

These reservations about goals do not mean that goals should play no role in program evaluation. I noted at the beginning that goals can be helpful in conceptualizing and organizing an evaluation. Moreover, the funding agencies that often require evaluations are unlikely to be satisfied with an evaluation that pays no attention at all to goals. However, my efforts to evaluate KITCenter and other educational programs have led me to supplement attention to goals with other considerations.

Capacity Development: Another Consideration in Evaluation Research

While the achievement of goals and objectives will retain a central place in evaluation research, additional questions should also be addressed. Most such questions should be examined in the context of a set of coherent goals. One such approach is *capacity development*, a term borrowed from work on international development. In this context, *capacity* can be thought of as:

> an organization's ability to achieve its mission effectively and to
> sustain itself over the long term. Capacity also refers to the skills and
> capabilities of individuals. (Alliance for Nonprofit Management,
> 2004)

In the context of international development, *capacity development* entails taking stock of an entity's existing resources and its stated goals and taking steps—drawing on local and external resources—to promote the *sustainability* of efforts that have been initiated to achieve the entity's goals. One international body has conceptualized capacity development as occurring at three levels:

- Individual: "enabling individuals to embark on a continuous process of learning—building on existing knowledge and skills and extending these in new directions as opportunities appear."
- Organizational: "building on existing capacities" but also developing new capacities and structures as needed.
- Systemic: developing or improving policies and legal systems at the national level or higher (Todd and Risby, 2007: 2).

When these ideas are taken to the level of an organization introducing new programs, the levels conceptualized by Todd and Risby change only a little when one considers whether the new programs can be sustained over time:

- The *individual* level is exactly as they describe it. Individuals must not only obtain knowledge and skills. They must be able to build upon them and to apply them to new challenges and opportunities.
- At the *organizational* level, it is important that the organization develop a capacity to sustain what has already been established while also being prepared to modify structures and policies in the face of change.
- The *systemic* level in this case does not involve entire nations, but it does involve the highest levels of organizational governance. Particularly, if the organization consists of several units spread across a large area and having some decision-making authority at the local level, it is important to ask what is happening in the overall system's headquarters to allow accomplishments to be sustained.

In sum, then, applying a *capacity development* perspective to a new program in a set of educational organizations leads one to ask not only whether goals are being achieved but also, in the context of those goals, whether the effort can be *sustained* over time. This becomes a particularly important question when external funds (such as a grant from a foundation or a federal agency) were used to initiate the program. Sustaining a program after the external funds are no longer available will occur only if individuals, the organization, and the overall governing body have developed the capacity to support the long-term strength of the program.

Evaluating KITCenter in Terms of Capacity Development

Aside from the official goals that have been established to evaluate KITCenter, it is possible and useful to examine KITCenter in terms of its capacity development and, therefore, its sustainability even in the absence of external funding. Because KITCenter's eligibility for renewed funding from the NSF ends in 2009, attention to its sustainability was very timely.

On the *individual* level, KITCenter's heavy emphasis on workshops suggests that a key question is whether former workshop participants are making tangible use of the skills they gained in the workshops. In addition, it is useful to ask whether students who have completed KITCenter degrees or certificates are better equipped for ongoing professional development and occupational success than they otherwise would have been. The utilization of skills by former workshop participants is directly related to capacity development because most are employed either by KCTCS or by the secondary schools that will prepare students for future enrollment in KCTCS or other higher education programs. Their professional qualifications, therefore, are essential for the sustainability of IT instruction in KCTCS. The qualifications of completers are more indirectly tied to sustainability of IT programs within KCTCS because most of them leave KCTCS after achieving their educational objectives. However, they are the representatives of KCTCS training in the eyes of employers and instructors of more advanced programs. As a result, their success will have an impact on the willingness of key actors to recommend enrollment in KCTCS IT programs to prospective future students.

In late 2007 and early 2008, former workshop participants responding to a survey[6] reported various tangible uses of knowledge gained in KITCenter workshops:

- Twelve percent of former workshop participants had earned certification because of knowledge gained form a KITCenter workshop;
- Of those with teaching responsibilities, 29 percent have started teaching new courses because of knowledge gained from a KITCenter workshop;
- Of those with teaching responsibilities, 93 percent report that they are better prepared to meet the needs of IT students;
- Most (77 percent) report that workshops have increased their ability to help co-workers with IT problems.

When respondents reflected on workshops' impacts on co-workers who had attended, they also saw tangible long-term impacts:

- 16 percent noted that some of their co-workers had obtained certification because of the workshops;
- 25 percent said that their co-workers were now prepared to teach a course they had not taught before;
- 40 percent pointed to improved instruction in courses that their co-workers had previously taught;
- 47 percent said that their co-workers were better able to support the efforts of classroom instructors;
- 61 percent said that their co-workers could provide better support for IT needs in the organization.

Former workshop participants' subjective reactions are consistent with this pattern of utilization. As Table 1 shows, almost all participants believe that the workshops have had at least some impact on both their personal IT abilities and

Table 7.1.   Perceived Impacts of KITCenter Workshops (N = 371)

IMPACT	Little or no impact	Some impact	Significant impact	Truly substantial impact
Your personal IT abilities	6%	44%	40%	11%
IT in your organization	7%	41%	37%	15%

the state of IT in their organization. Slightly more than half rate the workshops' impacts as "significant" or better. Substantial numbers of workshop participants are utilizing the knowledge they have gained both for their personal work and for the enhanced quality of IT in their organization.

As reported earlier, most completers are employed or pursuing additional education, and several are doing both. Most of the completers told interviewers that they give their IT training in KCTCS considerable credit for their later success. Of those who are employed, more than half (56 percent) believe their KCTCS training helped them to get the job, and 28 percent believe they are earning more than they would have without the KCTCS training. They also point to several positive outcomes of their IT training. When asked to rate the quality of their training with respect to several aspects of their work ability, most chose "good" or "excellent" (rather than the alternative choices of "fair" or "poor") for their view of the program's success. For example, percentages choosing "good" or "excellent" for the following outcomes were:

- Teaching them to work as part of a team: 69 percent
- Preparing them for a rewarding career: 68 percent
- Preparing them for future responsibilities: 78 percent
- Helping them to make a lasting impact in the workplace: 74 percent
- Enhancing their overall IT abilities: 89 percent

As also was reported earlier, 74 percent of the employers of completers rated the quality of their work as "excellent" or "very good." Specific areas receiving particularly high ratings included reading skills, willingness to accept new assignments, ability to work with equipment, willingness to strive for improvement, and ability to cooperate with co-workers. This finding may be important in two respects. First, a substantial majority of employers appear to be sufficiently impressed with KCTCS IT training that they would most likely be willing to refer prospective new students to KCTCS programs, thereby contributing to their sustainability. Second, as also was the case with students' ratings of their own abilities, the high ratings are not confined to technical skills. In particular, the completers' ability to work as part of a team and to accept new assignments may bode well for their future success in team-oriented and rapidly changing workplaces. Because of their personal success, many completers may become effective advocates when interacting with prospective new enrollees in KCTCS IT programs.

Several developments at the *organizational* level appear to be consistent with sustainability. Within KCTCS:

- All KCTCS institutions (sixteen community and technical colleges covering all regions of the state) have developed an IT curriculum. Several that offered no IT certificates when KITCenter was established now offer one or more certificates.
- The number of individual instructors teaching IT courses decreased for several years beginning in 2002, but the number of IT instructors in KCTCS institutions increased (from 231 to 244) between Fall 2006 and Fall 2007 (the most recent fall semester for which official data are available).[7]
- The percentage of KCTCS IT faculty employed on a full-time basis has increased (from 50 percent in Fall 2001 to 76 percent in Fall 2007) since KITCenter's inception. A critical mass of full-time faculty members is important for ongoing program development because it is full-time faculty members who will be involved in curriculum development, negotiations for resources, and other critical tasks outside the classroom.
- System-wide use of remote labs for IT instruction has increased. This has increased the system's capacity to serve students in smaller and more isolated institutions.

Kentucky's secondary schools (including high schools and advanced technology centers) also play an important role in KITCenter's sustainability because they will provide many of the students seeking IT instruction in community and technical colleges. It is noteworthy that secondary school faculty and staff members account for 43 percent of KITCenter workshop attendees. Of fifty-five advanced technology centers in Kentucky, about ten IT programs existed in 2001. The number increased to thirty in 2007. Of about three hundred public high schools in Kentucky, twelve IT programs served fewer than three hundred students in 2001. By 2007, more than one hundred IT programs served more than 4,000 students.[8]

Secondary students, of course, may choose any number of institutions for the pursuit of higher education, but KCTCS has encouraged their enrollment by establishing dual enrollment programs that allow them to begin taking courses at a community and technical college while completing secondary school requirements. The program appears to have attracted students. Of 612 students who completed a formally recognized IT career cluster in 2005–2006, 23 percent entered a KCTCS institution.

Less can be said about capacity development at the *systemic* level, but a few points stand out as important:

- Several faculty members, representing about one-fourth of the colleges within KCTCS, have taken the lead in coordinating KITCenter activities, and many more have been involved in teaching workshops. This involvement (through KITCenter and earlier grants) has led to the development of a statewide informal network of faculty members who share an interest in the ongoing development of IT instruction. While face-to-face meetings of this geographically scattered set of faculty members may occur less often without funding to pay for transportation costs, contact is likely to continue through the Internet and other means.

- A high-ranking official in the system's headquarters has been given responsibility for maintaining KITCenter after external funding has ended. He has announced a decision to continue using the KITCenter name and logo, and his office will have access to some internal funding.

- The KCTCS System Office has established a system-wide curriculum committee for IT. While individual colleges make their own decisions about which specializations to offer, they do so within a unified curricular framework established by the system-wide committee. The curriculum committee has at least two effects with positive implications for sustainability. First, it provides a unified set of courses and certificates for all colleges and faculty members. Second, its periodic meetings provide an opportunity for face-to-face contact between faculty members who ordinarily work in different locations throughout the state.

Despite these developments, sustaining KITCenter as an organizing framework will have its challenges. Workshops have been the central defining feature of KITCenter, and the necessary funding for them will become much more scarce in the absence of support from the NSF. While KITCenter's core faculty are expected to maintain ties, several have become involved in new projects that will take their time and energy. Such developments, combined with normal staff turnover and ongoing uncertainty in the job market for IT professionals, introduce uncertainty regarding KITCenter's future. Nevertheless, a focus on its capacity development leads to a degree of optimism about its long-term viability that might not be generated by a more narrow focus on its achievement (or lack of achievement) of formal goals.

General Implications for the Evaluation of Educational Programs

In this chapter, I have reported on portions of the evaluation of a single initiative within a community and technical college system. Without denying the importance and value of examining a program's success in achieving formal goals, I have attempted to show that a broad, long-term analysis of capacity development is valuable for understanding the likelihood that innovative efforts can be sustained over time.

Education in general is subject to a variety of attempts to subject it to formal evaluation. Any innovative program that is supported by federal funds is likely to face a requirement for formal evaluation. Legislative mandates, including "No Child Left Behind" at the federal level and many education reform initiatives passed by individual state legislatures, also involve evaluation—often focusing primarily on students' performance on mandated examinations. Most educational institutions are subject to formal accreditation reviews by regional bodies that look thoroughly at the institution's formulation of goals and the thoroughness of its efforts to assess the extent to which goals are being realized.

Specific mandates, including "No Child Left Behind" and legislative requirements in some states, may be modified or even partially abandoned over time. Even so, it is reasonable to predict that such formal evaluations, often comparing performance to predetermined standards, will remain an important part of the educational landscape. Particularly when funding requirements, legislative mandates, and accreditation standards are involved, formal, goal-oriented evaluation takes on considerable importance. Without minimizing the importance of evaluations tied to ongoing standards, I would suggest that it also is advisable to ask whether those programs or educational institutions that are found to be performing well with respect to formal standards are developing the capacity to maintain that performance. At the same time, it may be important to ask whether those programs or educational institutions that currently are falling short of satisfying formally established standards are developing the capacity to allow one to predict more satisfactory performance in the future.

Exact questions to be asked will vary according to the nature of the institution and the goals it is attempting to achieve, but questions that may be pertinent for many purposes would include:

- Aside from fulfilling formal requirements, to what extent are faculty members participating in opportunities for professional development? To what extent are they proactively cultivating professional contacts beyond the boundaries of their own organization?
- If shared governance (including faculty involvement and, in many institutions, parental or student involvement) receives lip service, to what extent does it actually occur? If, for example, a school has established a site-based decision making body consisting of faculty members and parents, to what extent is its authority respected by the principal and superintendent?
- To what extent do faculty members who are developing new programs receive financial support from the administration?

These are merely examples of the kinds of questions to be asked, but, for any evaluation of an educational program or initiative, going beyond formal requirements to meet official standards can generate important insights. In particular, attention to capacity development can help us understand whether new initiatives and programs will have long-term impacts.

Works Cited

Alliance for Nonprofit Management. 2004. "Capacity Building and Organizational Effectiveness." www.allianceonline.org/about/capacity_building_and_1.page. Accessed July 17, 2008.

Child, John. 2005. *Organization: Contemporary Principles and Practice.* Malden, MA: Blackwell Publishing.

Cyert, Richard M., and James G. March. 1963. *A Behavioral Theory of the Firm.* Upper Saddle River NJ: Prentice Hall.

Friedlander, Frank, and Hal Pickle. 1968. "Components of Effectiveness in Small Organizations." *Administrative Science Quarterly* 13: 289–304.

Hannan, Michael T., and John Freeman. 1977. "Obstacles to Comparative Studies." Pp. 106–131 in Paul S. Goodman and Johannes M. Pennings, eds. *New Perspectives on Organizational Effectiveness.* San Francisco: Jossey-Bass.

Hougland, James G., Jr. 2008. "Employer Satisfaction with Program Completers: Challenges of Contact and Interpretation." *Journal of Applied Social Science* 2: 1–12.

Hougland, James G., Jr., James R. Wood, and Samuel A. Mueller. 1974. "Organizational 'Goal Submergence': The Methodist Church and the Failure of the Temperance Movement." *Sociology and Social Research* 58: 408–416.

Merton, Robert K. 1957. *Social Theory and Social Structure.* 2nd ed. Glencoe, IL: Free Press.

[Miller] Iutcovich, Joyce. 2002. "Congressional Fellow Report: The Politics of Unrealistic Expectations and the Rhetoric of Accountability." *Footnotes* (American Sociological Association). www.asanet.org/footnotes/julyaugust02/fn7.html. Accessed December 26, 2008.

Pennings, Johannes M., and Paul S. Goodman. 1977. "Toward a Workable Framework." Pp. 146–184 in Paul S. Goodman and Johannes M. Pennings, eds. *New Perspectives on Organizational Effectiveness.* San Francisco: Jossey-Bass.

Pfeffer, Jeffrey, and Gerald R. Salancik. 1978. *The External Control of Organizations.* New York: Harper & Row.

Rossi, Peter H., Mark W. Lipsey, and Howard E. Freeman. 2004. *Evaluation: A Systematic Approach.* 7th ed. Thousand Oaks, CA: Sage Publications.

Scott, W. Richard. 2003. *Organizations: Rational, Natural, and Open Systems.* 5th ed. Upper Saddle River, NJ: Prentice Hall.

Todd, David, and Lee Risby. 2007. "Evaluation of GEF Capacity Development Activities: Approach Paper." Washington, D.C.: Global Environmental Facility Secretariat. www

.gefweb.org/uploadedFiles/Evaluation_Office/Ongoing_Evaluations/Cap%20Dev%20Info%20Doc%20No1.pdf. Accessed December 24, 2008.

Worthen, Blaine R., James R. Sanders, and Jody L. Fitzpatrick. 2004. *Program Evaluation: Alternative Approaches and Practical Guidelines*. 3rd ed. Boston: Allyn and Bacon.

Notes

1. This is a revised version of a paper presented at the 2008 Annual Meeting of the Association for Applied and Clinical Sociology, Jacksonville, Florida. It is based on research supported in part by evaluation subcontracts between the Kentucky Community and Technical College System and the University of Kentucky, with funding from the NSF grants DUE-0101573, DUE-0101445, and DUE-0532651.

2. KCTCS is a statewide system of community and technical colleges. KCTCS colleges are located in all regions of Kentucky.

3. In this chapter, I refer to "completers" rather than "graduates" because community and technical college programs have a variety of completion points. Graduation with a formal degree is a goal for some students, but others are more focused on obtaining certification in their area of training.

4. Statistics are based on interviews with completers conducted via telephone by trained and supervised interviewers employed by the University of Kentucky Survey Research Center (UK-SRC). Interviews were conducted about two years following completion so that employment and education patterns would have time to stabilize. Interviews were completed with 256 of 294 individuals contacted, for a cooperation rate of 87.1 percent.

5. Using contact information provided on a voluntary basis by completers employed in IT, UK-SRC interviewers conducted telephone interviews with supervisory personnel in a variety of organizations employing KCTCS completers. Interviews were completed with 79 of 94 eligible individuals contacted, for a cooperation rate of 81.9 percent.

6. E-mail messages were sent to the last known address of former workshop participants. Messages included an invitation to participate in a web-based survey as well as a link to the survey. Those who did not respond to the initial request received up to three reminders via e-mail. Responses were received from 371 respondents, for a cooperation rate of 43.4 percent. In some cases, error messages were generated by obsolete e-mail addresses, but it is unlikely that this happened in all cases. Thus, some who are classified as not cooperating may never have received a request to participate in the survey.

7. Comparisons are based on fall semesters only for the sake of consistency. Fall semesters and spring semesters tend to differ in terms of student enrollment.

8. Data from KCTCS reflect official statistics reported by KCTCS to the Kentucky Council on Postsecondary Education. However, data regarding secondary schools are based on estimates by knowledgeable staff members of the Kentucky Department of Education.

Jets Pizza IL 017

1907 W Springfield Ave Suite A
Champaign, IL 61820
Phone:217-352-9992
www.jetspizza.com

Ord #56

WALK-IN

1/17/2018   3:16 PM

| 2 Slices Bottle   5.50
  Cheese Slice
  Cheese Slice
  Pepsi

| Subtotal   5.50
                              Tax   0.52
                            Total   6.02

Paid Cash   6.02

Amount Due   0.00
Dana D.

Paid in Full

CHAPTER 8

Community Research Tactics and Social Change

ASSESSING NEEDS AND ASSETS IN AN
INNER CITY NEIGHBORHOOD

Jeffry A. Will, University of North Florida
Tracy A. Milligan, University of North Florida
Tim Cheney, University of North Florida

In the following pages, we will outline an extensive needs and assets assessment of a targeted area of East Jacksonville, Florida. Our chapter, serves as both a case study of how the sociological practitioner can contribute to community development efforts, and also represents the report we provided to our clients. This study was carried out by the Northeast Florida Center for Community Initiatives (CCI) as part of a collaborative effort with FreshMinistries, Inc., of Jacksonville, funded as part of the Compassionate Capital grant program of the federal government. FreshMinistries describes itself as "an interfaith nonprofit organization working to improve people's lives and bring hope to those living in distressed conditions" (www.freshministries.org). This project included extensive data collection efforts, meetings with community residents, service providers, and FreshMinistries staff, as well as qualitative field work by CCI staff. While there were a number of obstacles and hurdles to overcome (discussed later in more detail), we believe that the information presented here can serve as a foundation from which on-going efforts focusing on the East Jacksonville Core neighborhood can be developed.

As a "snap-shot" of the community, the report we developed provides a wealth of data and information that may already be known to the Jacksonville community, but that has not been synthesized to be used in a coherent plan of action. It is our hope that the information we provided and which is related in this chapter will be used to spur action—an issue raised by a large number of informants in the study—and not merely relegated to a bookshelf to accumulate dust. Indeed, CCI is dedicated to working with the community members and

FreshMinistries to use this information to bring about positive change for East Jacksonville.

Research Design and Methods

Between January 2007 and July 2007, research team members from CCI built an extensive and diverse data set on which our report was, incorporating quantitative, qualitative, and archival data collection strategies. These strategies included:

- Conducting a "windshield" survey to develop a community physical profile.
- Participating in community resident dialogue/town hall meetings.
- Conducting community resident surveys and focus groups.
- Conducting interviews and focus groups with service providers, educators, religious leaders and other officials.
- Developing an economic and social indicators database, including data from the U.S. Census Bureau, Duval County Health Department, Police Department, educational sources, quality of life indicators, and others sources.

A Demographic Picture of East Jacksonville Core

WINDSHIELD SURVEY

A windshield survey, as the name implies, allows for data to be gathered about the physical neighborhood through observation, usually through a car windshield. It can also be conducted when walking through a neighborhood. The results of this survey were then combined with other geographic data collected primarily from the 2006 property appraiser database of the City of Jacksonville and secondarily from the 2000 U.S. Census, 2000–2006 Supervisor of Elections data and 2007 crime data from the Jacksonville Sheriff's Office (JSO). These data sources help to put the windshield survey into context through a comprehensive examination of the neighborhood. First, however, a general look at the neighborhood will help acquaint the reader with the geographic area being discussed.

As of 2002, there were 206 neighborhoods defined by the city of Jacksonville, which cover virtually all of the developable land in Duval County. While most of these neighborhoods have names derived from the main road or waterway that runs through them or by the key subdivision that dominates them, a few have names based on their geographic location in relation to downtown Jacksonville. For instance, as their names imply, mid-Westside is located west and slightly north of downtown, Midtown is located directly east of downtown, and the Southside neighborhood is located directly south and across the St. Johns River from downtown. Included in this group is the neighborhood of East Jacksonville, which is located east and slightly north of downtown. The East Jacksonville neighborhood, commonly referred to as "East Jax," has boundaries that extend from 8th Street on the North, the St. Johns River on the East, the Arlington Expressway to the South, and a somewhat ambiguous West boundary that falls on an old line of railroad train tracks (see MAP 1; this map is available in color at www.unf.edu/coas/cci/publications.htm). The tracks—or at least what is left of them—are located in the Ionia St./Spearing St. corridor.

As detailed by the 2000 U.S. Census, the five tracts that make up the East Jacksonville Core neighborhood[1] have a population that is almost 75 percent African American. Independently, these tracts range from 94.5 percent (Tract 4) to 65.5 percent (Tract 10). This predominately African American neighborhood is statistically quite different from Duval County where 65.8 percent of residents

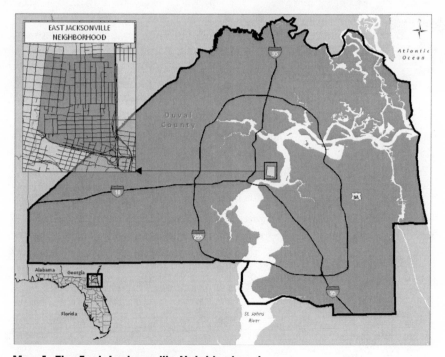

Map 1. The East Jacksonville Neighborhood
Source: City of Jacksonville, FreshMinistries

are white. While these numbers essentially show the majority race to be African American in the East Jacksonville Core and white for Duval County, the numbers of non-African American minorities are, for all intents and purposes, equal. Duval County has a 6.4 percent rate; while the core neighborhood also has a 6.4 percent rate overall. Within tracts, the percents range from 1.2 to 14 percent.

In Duval County as a whole, a majority of households (71.1 percent) with children under age eighteen are headed by married couples. Only 22.5 percent of these households are headed by unmarried women, and 6.4 percent by unmarried men. In the East Jacksonville Core neighborhood, however, the percentage for married and female headed households with children under age eighteen is almost completely opposite. Overall, the core has a 56.4 percent unmarried women rate and a 35.8 percent married headed household rate. In Duval County, the median household income in 1999 was $40,703. In the East Jacksonville Core neighborhood, the median household income ranged from a low of $7,857 to $27,446. Duval County has a poverty rate of 11.9 percent, while the East Jacksonville Core neighborhood has rates that are three and four times that.

It was clear from the data gathered that the residential structures in East Jacksonville Core neighborhood are, on the whole, much older than we find in much of the rest of the city. Residences in the area are also much smaller and are located on undersized lots compared to those found in Duval Country overall. In addition, a review of property use codes and the windshield survey indicate a number of vacant buildings, closed businesses, and a significant number of residences that are in only fair or poor condition. Map 2 below (available in color at www.unf.edu/coas/cci/publications.htm) displays some of the results from the windshield survey, illustrating the conditions of both types of residential and the non-residential parcels. As one can see, the perimeter of the neighborhood contains mostly "good" parcels, while the "fair" and "bad" parcels are located on the interior of the core neighborhood. There are very few "new construction" sites in the core area. Given that most of the housing was built in the pre–World War II era, this is not a surprising picture. The lack of recent building represents an important area of focus for core neighborhood improvement efforts as the potential impact of such new construction on the overall neighborhood could improve resident quality of life through jobs, increased property values, and retail store attraction.

With the data that were available, we were able to locate where police responded to incidents and subsequently made arrests within the core neighborhood from 2001 through the first half of 2007. Several important points need to be made about the distribution of incidents and arrests in the core neighborhood. First, it is important to note that there appears to be little variation on the number and distribution of incidents across the years since 2001. Indeed, the

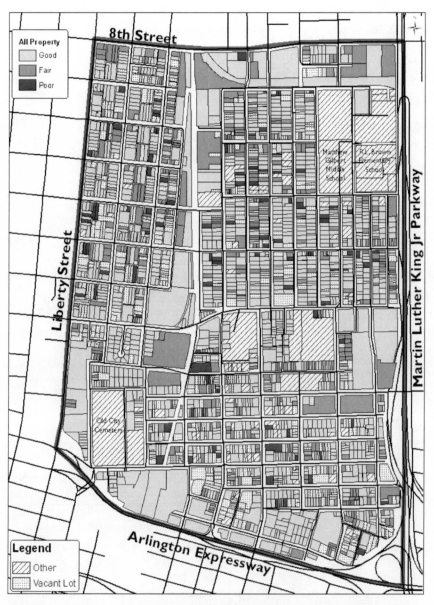

Map 2. All Property Classification Within the East Jacksonville Core Notes: for apartments or businesses with multiple buildings, the overall condition was given. See Methods for property grade classifications.
Source: Windshield Survey Database, Jacksonville Property Appraiser

police are quite busy in the neighborhood, and there appears to be little easing in the number of calls despite efforts by community leaders and authorities. Second, although spread throughout the core neighborhood, there are several areas where there appear to be significant concentrations of arrests and incidents. Most noticeable are the large number reported around the schools and areas in the far south where a number of abandoned buildings and vacant lots are located.

Perceptions and Experiences of East Jacksonville Core Residents

TELEPHONE SURVEY

As part of the needs and assets assessment, the University of North Florida (UNF) Polling Lab, in conjunction with CCI, conducted a telephone survey with adult residents of the East Jacksonville Core neighborhood in April 2007. The goal of the survey was to gather opinions of neighborhood residents regarding a few specific topics including the general quality of the neighborhood, public services, safety, education, and the family learning environment. The UNF Polling Lab was able to obtain 103 completed surveys, a 19 percent response rate.

The telephone survey provided the research team and other stakeholders a perspective of the East Jacksonville Core neighborhood on a number of topics and issues. The telephone sample of residents was demographically similar to the overall neighborhood, supporting the validity of the respondents' responses. For instance, while there was a higher percentage of female survey respondents compared to the overall neighborhood, the distribution of age, employment, and income were comparable between the two groups.

The ratings of the neighborhood and various neighborhood services such as public schools and neighborhood businesses were split with approximately half reporting them to be excellent and good and the other half rating them as fair or poor. The large majority of respondents tended to perceive these services as good or fair. There was strong consensus concerning the number and quality of jobs available in the neighborhood with many of the resident respondents rating each of these aspects of neighborhood jobs as poor.

While a majority of the resident respondents reported being afraid to walk alone at night in particular areas around their home, nearly all of the respondents felt safe and secure at night while in their home. Many of the surveyed residents rated public safety services such as rescue, fire, and the police as excellent or good, but were split in regards to the police working with people in their neighborhood to solve problems. Responses were also divided for rating public spaces such as streets and parks. Many of the residents surveyed believed that the removal of trash in the neighborhood is fair or poor.

A number of assets were discovered through the questions concerning health and the family environment. For example, many of the survey respondents claimed to always have access to health care services for themselves and their children. In addition to health care, children residing in the households surveyed also tend to receive parental homework assistance and frequently visit the library. Approximately half of the households represented in the telephone survey also had access to a working computer, access to the Internet, and owned more than fifty books. Furthermore, slightly more than half of the resident respondents had volunteered their time within the past six months to help at a local agency such as a school, church, or community organization.

Arguably, the most promising asset gleaned from the telephone survey is that a majority of those surveyed felt that people like themselves can have a big or moderate impact in making their community a better place to live. Such a response indicates a hope and promise within many of the residents that can be harnessed to improve the neighborhood. The challenge will be to get residents of all statuses and in all stages of life to take a stake in shaping the future of their neighborhood.

COMMUNITY MEETINGS OBSERVATIONS

One of the initiatives FreshMinistries has already begun in the East Jacksonville Core neighborhood includes organizing and coordinating monthly community meetings every fourth Thursday evening. According to FreshMinistries staff, the meetings have been organized for and are advertised to the residents in the East Jacksonville Core neighborhood that was defined for the needs and assets assessment. The community meetings are intended to be a forum for community residents to voice their concerns about issues in the neighborhood. In addition, these meetings provide opportunities for residents to discuss ideas and actions to be taken to solve issues thus identified and for FreshMinistries to distribute information on resources available that would assist in such actions. The meeting attendees are also involved in a number of neighborhood events sponsored by FreshMinistries. Given the purpose and nature of the community meetings, the CCI decided that these gatherings would provide valuable information for the needs and assets assessment.

Those attending the meetings during CCI's period of observation were current and past community residents, pastors, as well as representatives (or invited speakers) from the JSO, City Code Enforcement, and other local service agencies or businesses. The number of residents attending the meetings varied, ranging anywhere from only three to approximately thirty. Crime-related issues were often discussed at the community meetings. Meeting attendees complained about drug-related activities, loitering, prostitution, and the lack of police enforcement. The JSO officer listened to the complaints and concerns of residents, explained actions that should take place in regards to specific complaints, and shared what the police department is doing within the neighborhood. The JSO representative requested residents to call in criminal activity, explaining that calls can be anonymous. Despite the promise of anonymity, residents expressed frustration that their identities are not always kept confidential and consequently fear retaliation from the perpetrators they may report.

Another common topic of discussion at the meetings over the seven-month observation period concerned problems associated with abandoned houses and the lack of trash collection. Residents were not only concerned that the abandoned houses were eyesores in the neighborhood, but that they were being used for illegal activities. Unkempt shrubs and streetlights were also brought up as being unsightly and providing criminals with a means of concealing their activities. Another housing-related complaint made by residents entailed defective siding on some of the neighborhood low cost homes.

There was also a number of FreshMinistries-sponsored neighborhood events that community meeting attendees were encouraged to assist, coordinate, and/or attend. For example, a spelling bee was arranged for the students of a neighborhood school and volunteers were required to help make the event a success. FreshMinistries staff also attempted to recruit volunteers to arrange a community festival.

FOCUS GROUPS AND INTERVIEWS

Conducting interviews and focus groups with a variety of residents afforded the research team the opportunity to obtain a comprehensive perspective of residents in East Jacksonville Core neighborhood. It was almost unanimous that safety concerns (crime, drugs, etc.) are major issues confronting the community. Many of the discussions centered on drug-related crimes and fear of reporting criminal activity. Problems with neighborhood youth were also thought to be of concern for many. There was general consensus that proper parenting is at the root of a lot of these problems. The prevalence of teen pregnancy and young parenthood were some specific issues expressed by many respondents. Other top needs and issues of East Jacksonville Core neighborhood residents included education, employment, housing, and health.

In general, most of the interviewees were aware of some services and programs in their area. By far, respondents expressed a desire for services and activities aimed at neighborhood youth the most. This need is particularly evident at the local library where a relatively large number of children hang out after school. While library staff offer some structured activities for the children, these children need more space and assistance than the library can accommodate.

Fear of being pushed out of the neighborhood was another theme found in some of the interviews and focus groups. This fear emerged in discussions regarding both housing and education. While the general consensus was that the new construction and renovation occurring in the community were promising, some were afraid that these changes would displace many of the poorer residents. Respondents also expressed concerns that the neighborhood children are being pushed out of their neighborhood. They reported that instead of attending the neighborhood schools, they are bussed to schools outside of their neighborhood.

While respondents generally struggled in finding an asset within the neighborhood, a number of strengths emerged from the discussions. The residents themselves were identified as being an asset to the neighborhood. Their resiliency and compassion for one another were perceived as a positive foundation from which neighborhood improvements can grow. Other assets acknowledged by respondents included the numerous churches and specific programs within the neighborhood, and recent home restoration and construction.

One of the common themes resonating throughout almost every interview was the passion and commitment of the interviewees to improve the quality of life of the population they served. It was also routine that they used their own money and resources to help others. It is their dedication that provides hope that the neighborhood can grow and prosper in the near future.

Summary

In the previous pages, we have presented the results of an extensive Needs and Assets Assessment of the East Jacksonville Core Neighborhood. As discussed, there are a number of problems facing this neighborhood, which was not surprising. There are also, however, a significant number of assets in the neighborhood, including a core group of citizens, pastors, and service providers, who are intent on making things better. This finding was, in many ways, not so much expected. East Jacksonville is often described as "the worst" neighborhood in the city, and little attention has been paid to those assets in the past.

There are some serious issues facing the East Jacksonville Core neighborhood. The residential structures are quite old, and many are in fair or poor condition. Many are small houses and are appraised at significantly lower rates than much of the rest of Duval County. On the other hand, there are areas of the neighborhood that are in much better condition than many in Jacksonville would have suggested. These "promising pockets" represent an important asset for the neighborhood, and a resource to build improvements around in the future.

Similarly, the business infrastructure of the neighborhood is also in serious disrepair, with many vacant buildings and vacant lots, and little in the way of economic opportunity for those living in the community. Again, however, there is some optimism in that, while vacant, some of these business properties could provide the base for a renewal of the local economy in the neighborhood, without the dislocation of residents so often accompanying urban renewal and development. Combined with the few already established businesses, this represents a great opportunity for growth.

As is confirmed by media portrayals, and responses from focus groups and interviews, there is significant crime and police action within the core neighborhood area. And, this activity has been consistent for a number of years. While some efforts have been successful in dealing with the criminality, it is clear that significant work remains.

The community meetings were observed by CCI staff during a time of organization and development. Like many grassroots initiatives, it takes time and persistence for such efforts to take root and flourish. FreshMinistries staff used various incentives to entice residents to the table and brought a wide variety of agencies to showcase available resources and ways residents can get involved in their community.

It is clear from the community meetings that the residents of the East Jacksonville Core neighborhood face a myriad of challenges. However, the presence of City agencies, such as JSO and City Code Enforcement, illustrates a commitment from the City to assist the residents in the neighborhood. The motivation and energy elicited from the neighborhood residents can be seen as possible strengths in the area when developing approaches to address issues more central to the target neighborhood. Continued residential and City involvement will foster a working relationship in which significant progress in addressing the issues facing the neighborhood will become possible.

Recommendations

As we presented in our report, while there are a number of areas which it may not be realistic to recommend action—or which may be outside the abilities of FreshMinistries or CCI to act upon—the findings from this Needs and Assets Assessment do provide information that suggests a number of ways and areas in which action can be taken. Many of these recommendations are taken directly from the community residents interviewed for this study, while others are based on their reflections. These recommendations include:

- Create collaborative efforts to provide additional/focused organized youth sports.
- Work to re-deploy the Police Athletic League (PAL) facility in the core neighborhood.
- Extend library availability.
- Increase pressure on the city to address garbage and crime issues.
- Draw upon broader community service resources.
- Development of a Community Action Group (CAG).
- Facilitate the introduction of other community service efforts.
- Create economic opportunity through existing infrastructure and assets.

There are a number of other activities, for example, a "Clean Up the Neighborhood Day," campus visits and college application support, or parenting support classes, which can also be suggested. But the primary concern here is that the recommendations above be implemented to empower the neighborhood residents. Throughout the interviews and focus groups, it was clear that the residents, and community leaders, were not looking for "outsiders" to come in and take charge, but for the resources and opportunities to be available to, in the words of a former community leader in the area, "give a hand up not a hand out." To that end, perhaps the most important recommendation that we offer is that FreshMinistries (and CCI) *NOT* abandon the neighborhood—as so many of the residents interviewed were sure would happen. Action around the recommendations above will go a long way to both build up the neighborhood, as well as to bring together people from across the broader Jacksonville community.

Postscript

A year after our report was compiled, the CCI research team reconnected with FreshMinistries staff members to obtain an update on their progress within the East Jacksonville Core neighborhood, particularly with regard to the project recommendations. Of particular interest were the recommendations to: 1) Develop a Community Action Group (CAG); 2) Work to re-deploy the PAL facility in the neighborhood; 3) Draw upon broader community resources, services, and agencies to serve the neighborhood; and 4) Expand on economic development using existing infrastructure and assets. While the follow-up conversations found that not all of the recommendations had been acted upon, significant progress was, and continues to be, found in the neighborhood.

Although the neighborhood association in which meetings were observed for the research project has not formally created a CAG as was recommended in the report, the Eastside Neighborhood Alliance has become more organized in recent months according to FreshMinistries staff. For instance, officers have been elected by the local residents. Subsequently, these elected officers have taken on more responsibility for the group and some of them have attended a Weed and Seed training to assist them in carrying out their roles. In addition, the Alliance has been successful on a number of occasions in collectively voicing their needs and desires for their community to governmental officials and local agencies.

For example, the residents expressed their concerns over a proposed apartment complex slated for their community to their city council representative. The representative was originally in favor of the project, but changed his position based on the residents' fears that the complex was too large for the proposed parcel and that the anticipated rent was not affordable, leaving the apartments vulnerable to the market and becoming Section 8 housing. The development of the apartment complex has not proceeded at this point. Members of the Alliance have also been active in representing their community in regards to a nearby contaminated site that has been mandated by the Environmental Protection Agency (EPA) to be cleaned. They have attended meetings and collaborated with the Eastside Environmental Council to ensure that the cleanup is done to their satisfaction to protect the health and safety of the residents and that the community will benefit from any proceeds produced from the process.

The Eastside Neighborhood Alliance has further operated as a CAG by communicating their needs to neighborhood service agencies. Over the past summer, the neighborhood PAL renovated and added additional space, including room for a computer lab, to its facilities. PAL currently provides an after school program and is in the process of restoring the fields in order to offer organized sports for the neighborhood youth. While the renovations were already planned for the facilities, the Alliance was instrumental in getting the sports programs included in the plans. The Alliance invited PAL to a community meeting where residents were able to express their needs and desires, one of which was for sports programs to be available to the neighborhood youth, particularly older youth. It is interesting to note that when CCI was conducting the research, PAL personnel were not able to be reached to set up interviews even after several attempts. Recent attempts to contact PAL, however, have resulted in a quick response, indicating a greater presence in the neighborhood.

Significant effort has also been made to draw upon broader community service resources in the neighborhood, another recommendation presented in the original report. In addition to the work with PAL, a number of other efforts by the East Jacksonville Community Resource Center were also mentioned by FreshMinistries staff in the follow-up conversations. For instance, the staff indicated that the group was working on partnerships with Northeast Florida Community Action (NEFCA) to be able to refer clients to NEFCA services, and they were working with the Department of Children and Families (DCF) to be a Family Support Service Neighborhood Center. Additionally, several other groups have stepped up to provide some financial support for efforts in the neighborhood. The Jaguar Foundation (created by the owners of the Jacksonville Jaguars, the National Football League team in Jacksonville) provided funds to work with thirty-eight youth in job preparation and employment opportunities. In addition, Comcast Cable and local supermarket chain, Winn Dixie, have also provided funds for supplies and materials used by the community group. The Center is also working on developing a relationship with Florida Community College of Jacksonville (FCCJ).

The one area in which FreshMinistries has still not made significant movement is the creation economic opportunity through existing infrastructure and assets in the neighborhood. While they are still working on providing more needed services and resources, it is clear that more space is needed to provide these services. The existing infrastructure, particularly the storefront area in the southern most region of the neighborhood, has as not yet been tapped for that space. At this writing, however, expansion of the efforts is uncertain. With the economic decline of the current period, the resources such expansion requires are not expected anytime soon.

It is clear that while not all of the projects FreshMinistries has set out to accomplish have been implemented, and that not all of our recommendations have been realized, FreshMinistries has indeed remained quite active within the community. This is particularly important, given the fears expressed by a number of community residents during the interviews and focus groups that 1) the research would have little impact on what FreshMinistries would do, and 2) that regardless of what we found, FreshMinistries would abandon the neighborhood. It appears from our follow-up conversations with representatives of the agency, FreshMinistries has plans to serve the neighborhood for the foreseeable future.

Note

1. A *census tract* is a geographic region defined (in this case by the government) for the purpose of taking a *census*. Tract 4 and 5 cover the majority of the East Jacksonville Core neighborhood—with the outside boundaries falling on mainly industrial or city use. Tract 10 also covers the jail and part of the "revitalized" downtown core. The additional land covered by Tracts 11 and 12 is similar to the core neighborhood.

CHAPTER 9

Free-Range Humans

SOCIOLOGY'S ROLE IN SHAPING THE FUTURE OF THE BUILT ENVIRONMENT FOR AN AGING WORLD

Tina A. Quartaroli, University of Central Missouri
Michael L. Hirsch, Huston-Tillotson University

One in three Americans are now over age 50, as the country stands braced for the tidal wave of 78 million baby boomers just starting to crest age 65 (U.S. Department of Health and Human Services, 2008). By 2050, more than one-fifth of the population in the United States will be over age 65 (Cockerham, 1997)—81 million individuals age 65 or older versus 38 million in 2007 (U.S. Social Security Administration, 2007). Given this dramatic demographic shift, it is hardly surprising that sociologists have ramped up attention to aging-related issues. Discussion of issues in aging has become standard fare in social problems textbooks (Leon-Guerrero, 2008; Eitzen, Baca Zinn and Eitzen Smith, 2009); increasing numbers of social gerontology programs continue to emerge in higher education (Friedsam, 1995) and applied work in social gerontology has blossomed in the public and private sectors (Putney, Alley and Bengston, 2005).

While practicing sociologists can assist in the resolution of any number of challenges generated by this unprecedented demographic tilt, in this chapter we focus on the way in which built and furnished environments help or hinder an older population. The natural process of aging or "senescence" itself requires a major rethinking of the design and use of public and privates spaces. A world built for the young and able bodied imposes numerous environmental challenges on individuals as strength, stamina, and perceptual and cognitive abilities decline.

Taking into account such challenges, we created an instrument that can be used to assess the suitability of public physical environments for the needs of an aging population. In this chapter we will explore how practicing sociologists can contribute to the creation of a world of maximum mobility and sustainability for older persons, that is, a world dedicated to free-range humans.

Senescence, Environmental Press and the Prosthetic Environment

Senescence is the natural biological process of aging. Though theories abound as to the root cause(s) of this process, the outcome is one of lessened vitality, strength, perceptual acumen and cognitive ability. All aspects of this process have implications for one's ability to engage the environment. A recent survey of major U.S. cities finds the rate of disability among the 65 and older population range from a low of 31% in Las Vegas to a high of 58% in St. Louis (Disabled, 2006).

Lawton's theory of environmental press focuses on the interactions between person variables or competencies and environmental variables or *environmental press* as a framework for understanding older persons' abilities to adapt to their environment (Lawton, Brody and Turner-Massey, 1978; Lawton, 1983). In other words, environmental press refers to the degree to which one's ability to achieve one's ends in daily, mundane life tasks is challenged or thwarted by the nature of your surroundings (Lawton, 1983, 1985; Crandall, 1991). While one may wish to do laundry in the basement, climbing stairs with a laundry basket may become insurmountable. Here the "press" of the environment overcomes the ability to complete a desired task. Mounting incidents of environmental press may exacerbate or trigger physical and/or mental decline in well-being (Lawton, 1983; Wahl, 2001).

Lawton (1980) further suggested that design elements in the built environment which enhance perceptions of independence may improve both the physical and mental well-being of older persons. Some of these concepts eventually became incorporated into what is now commonly known as "universal design," a term coined by Ron Mace (1998), founder and original program director of the Center for Universal Design at North Carolina State University. Under Mace's vision and guidance, universal design grew from a focus on "accessibility" for the disabled into a holistic design concept that seeks to accommodate persons of all ages and abilities. It is often referred to in relation to home modifications allowing for "aging in place," the concept of an aging adult remaining in the family home perhaps until death. When activity is complicated by architecture designed for youthful mobility, structures may be retrofitted into a "prosthetic environment" (Crandall, 1991; Carstens, 1993; Marcus and Francis, 1997) using universal design and other design features to allow greater ease of use as physical and/or mental age-related challenges arise.

The prosthetic environment is structured in such a way as to make up for the loss of ability that accompanies the process of senescence. When vision fades, the prosthetic environment increases the intensity of lighting and the size of print. When bending over becomes difficult, electrical sockets and dishwashers are installed higher from the ground minimizing this difficult motion. When hearing is compromised, the prosthetic environment decreases echo and background noise and increases sound amplification and visual cues. The built environment can be constructed in anticipation of the outcomes of senescence (a principle of universal design) or it can be retrofitted to accommodate changing needs, the latter being an expensive proposition. While the large majority of applied research on the prosthetic environment and universal design for aging populations has focused on the home environment and the "aging in place" movement, this instrument addresses public and service-oriented physical environments, going beyond standard Americans with Disabilities Act (ADA) guidelines to encourage increased safety, mobility, and ease of use, and thus a more active, "free-ranging" engagement within the public sphere for aging persons of diverse abilities.

Assessing the Built Environment

Having demonstrated the need for free-range environments, we now need a tool or an instrument to assess or measure the adequacy of existing environments to meet the needs of aging populations. The construction of this instrument extrapolates lessons from the process of senescence, environmental press and the prosthetic environment. It can be used by researchers or others to assess building interiors, exteriors, public infrastructure and community services. It can be adjusted for community and project-specific realities and needs, and updated to incorporate new knowledge and technology.

Instrument construction begins with consideration of diminished capacities generated by senescence, moves to reflection upon the environmental press issues they pose, which in turn suggest prosthetic environment modifications that could be made to help maximize and sustain one's normal routine. Below are examples of concrete conditions that aging populations experience and the solutions offered by a free-range environment.

Process of Senescence (condition)	Prosthetic Environment (solution)
1) Low vision	A) Bright, non-glare lighting
	B) Consistent light intensity
	C) Large and crisp signage with contrasting colors
	D) Clear, well-defined paths with no unexpected barriers

E) Highlighted steps/stoops

F) Non-glare surfaces (floor, wall, countertops)

G) Large print

H) Solid, lighter-color floor covering

I) Strong color contrast between floor and walls

J) Glass window safety markings

K) Solid, level flooring

L) Tactile markings

M) No dark rugs or mats

2) Diminished hearing

A) Minimization of background noise

B) Minimization of echo/acoustic insulation

C) Visual and audible warning systems

D) Sound amplification

E) Communication training

3) Slowed reaction time

A) Elimination of surface faults

B) Installation of hand rails

C) Wider turning radius

D) Rumble strips as driver alerts

E) Windows in entry doors

4) Diminished strength, speed and stamina

A) Rest points in public spaces

B) Automatic doors or doors with less than 10 lbs of resistance

C) Slowly closing doors

D) Large medians for pedestrians

E) Longer "walk" times at crosswalks

F) Chairs with arms

G) In store assistance/delivery services

H) Elevators/chair lifts

I) Public transportation

J) Solid, level flooring

K) Minimal grade, ramped walkways/no doorway thresholds

L) Curb cuts

5) Chronic conditions, e.g. arthritis

A) Door levers instead of knobs

B) Automatic doors or doors with less than 10 lbs of resistance

C) In-store assistance/delivery services

D) Disability parking spaces

6) Use of walkers or wheel chairs

A) Wide doorways, aisles

6) Use of walkers or wheel chairs, continued	B) Minimal grade, ramped walkways/no doorway thresholds C) Bathroom handrails D) Raised commodes E) Curb cuts F) Disability parking spaces G) Wider turning radius
7) Diminished cognitive abilities	A) Memory cues, e.g., push/pull signs on doors B) Color-coded signage C) Communication and awareness training
8) Impaired thermoregulatory system	A) Indoor: heating and cooling set to optimal temperatures B) Outdoor: shaded/covered rest/waiting areas

We included the examples above in the construction of a multi-faceted survey instrument used to examine the built environment with a focus on the assessment of public spaces. Outdoor and indoor public spaces are addressed by the assessment tool. Title I of the ADA of 1990 prohibits private, government agencies, etc., from discriminating against individuals with disabilities. Tax codes also provides incentives for making businesses more accessible to people with disabilities. While some items fall under ADA guidelines and assist in ADA compliance, most are not readily associated with "disability" and are thus less likely to be considered during initial design and construction. The instrument begins with a coversheet for city block assessment as follows:

Public Infrastructure Critique—Block
Parking (hundred block/side of street recorded)

- Surface faults ___yes ___no
    If yes, location(s) _____
- Spaces clearly marked ___yes ___no
- Disability parking ___yes ___no
    If yes, location(s) _____

Crosswalks
- Clearly marked ___yes ___no
- All stop intersections ___yes ___no

- Traffic lights ___yes ___no
    If yes, timed duration for crossing_____
- Islands between lanes ___yes ___no: If yes, width _____
- Curb cuts/ramps ___yes ___no
    If yes, width/ramp degree of cuts_____
    IIf no, height of curbs_____

Sidewalks
- Ramps to disability parking ___yes ___no
    If yes, width/ramp degree of cuts_____
- Surface faults ___yes ___no: If yes, location(s) _____
- Clear walkways ____yes ____no
    If no, location(s) and type of impediment(s)_____
    _____
- Steps ___yes ___no If yes, location(s) _____
    _____
- Steps highlighted ___yes ___no If yes, describe _____
    _____
- Hand railings ___yes ___no If yes, location(s) _____
    _____
- Public benches ___yes ___no If yes, location(s) _____
- Shaded/covered rest/waiting areas ___yes ___no
    If yes, locations_____
- Municipal sign condition ___very good ___good ___poor
- Municipal lighting quality ___very good ___good ___poor
    If inadequate, describe_____
- Evening light consistency ___very good ___good ___poor

This part of the instrument is heavily concerned with issues of locomotion or the walk-ability of the public street and sidewalk. It takes into account environmental press issues related to speed, stamina, use of walkers and wheelchairs as well as issues of illumination related to diminished visual ability (low vision) and slowed eye adjustment to variations in lighting.

Walking is the most important form of exercise among older persons (Ruchlin and Lachs, 1999). Examination for surface faults, cracks, breaks, unevenness of pavement, etc., bring to bear issues of low vision (less ability to discern faults) as well as slowed reaction time (less ability to prevent a fall caused by tripping). Among the frailest elderly, with exaggerated loss of vision and especially slow reaction time, surface faults are particularly difficult to negotiate. The risks of falling are extremely important to note. In 1998, it was estimated that 10,000 premature deaths were caused by falling and it is projected that falling will cost the United States $32.4 billion annually by 2020 (Kovacs, 2005).

The second page of the instrument is blank save for a header. This page is used to pinpoint problems. Researchers make proportional drawings of the assessment area denoting trouble spots. Trouble spots include broken pavement, uneven sidewalks as well as inadequate and/or uneven evening illumination. Page three of the survey examines building exteriors and entry ways on the street under inspection. It is as follows:

Building Exterior—Building Address

Exterior Signage
- Business sign ___yes ___no
  If yes, sign condition is ___ very good ___good ___ poor
- Hours listed ___yes ___no
  If yes, sign condition is ___ very good ___good ___ poor
- Building address ___yes ___no
  If yes, sign condition is ___ very good ___good ___ poor
- Surface glare ___yes ___no
  If yes, glare is ___very intense ___intense ___not intense

Walkways
- Steps ___yes ___no: If yes, location(s)_____
- Ramped ___ yes ___ no: If yes, incline degree_____
- Clear walkways ____yes ____no: If no, location(s) and type of impediment(s)_____
  _____
- Shaded rest/waiting areas ___yes ___no If yes, locations_____
  _____

Doorway
- Wheelchair accessible ___yes ___no ___
- Width of doorway_____
- Threshold ___yes ___no: If yes, height_____
- Window in door ___yes ___no
- Door ___manual ___automatic
  If manual, door opening device ___knob ___lever ___push bar ___handle
  If automatic, with thumb push ___yes ___no, pressure activated ___yes ___no
- Entry/exit signs ___yes ___no
- Push/pull signs ___yes ___no
- Timing of door closure_____

Night Lighting/Illumination
- Steps ___ yes ___no
- Walkways ___ yes ___ no
- Signage ___ yes ___ no
- Hours ___ yes ___no
- Building address ___ yes ___ no
- Business sign ___ yes ___ no

Bold signage assists with diminished visual capacity as well as serving as memory cues. Sign condition factors, in relation to low vision, include size of signage, size and clarity of lettering, use of contrast colors, and lighting. Night illumination is especially important both in its consistency because of slowed eye adjustment, and for brightness as those in their mid-70's need up to three times the brightness as younger persons (Christenson, 1990).

The attention spent on doorways reflects the way in which senescence makes them increasingly more difficult to navigate successfully as individuals age. Doorways fitted with well marked automatic doors absent of thresholds and equipped with sensors to assure safe passage are especially desirable. Windows in non-automatic doors are particularly helpful in allowing safe passage through the doorway. Abruptly opened doors may hit and injure individuals on the out-swing side. Slowed reaction time increases the chance of experiencing a door strike.

Non-automatic doors pose several potential problems. Individuals suffering from arthritis may be unable to grasp and turn a knob or to grasp a handle and press down with their thumb to undo the door latch. Door weight may be too great to push or pull open. Doors that close too quickly may hit a person still moving over the threshold.

Readily available shaded rest/waiting areas are also noted. Older persons are more vulnerable to heat illness because the body's cooling mechanisms become impaired with age and age-related health conditions and medications (Worfolk, 2000). Temperatures as little as 10 degrees higher than the regional average can cause fatal heat stroke or dangerously exacerbate a number of health conditions common in older populations (Sykes, 2005).

The focus of the instrument's fourth page is building interiors. The interior assessment addresses issues of vision (e.g., floor faults, colors and patterns, surface glare, flickering lights), reaction time (e.g., floor faults, elevator door timing), stamina (e.g., chairs, stairs), strength (e.g., raised commodes, grab bars, chair arms, stairs), hearing (e.g., background noise, echo, visual fire alarms) and cognitive abilities (e.g., aisle signs, color coding). Presence or lack of curbside and/or in-store assistance addresses the entire range of capabilities. Accommodations for wheelchairs, walkers, and canes used for walking (physical disability) or navigation (vision disability) purposes are also important to note. Page four of the assessment tool is as follows:

Building Interior—Business Name and Address

- Aisle signs ___yes ___no
- Aisle width _____
- Aisles clear ____yes ____ no: If no, location(s) and type of impediment(s)_____
_____

- Floors
Floor pattern (describe)_____
Floor color(s) _____
Floor sloping ___yes ___no: If yes, location(s)/degree_____
Faults ___yes ___no: If yes, location(s)_____
Moisture ___yes ___no: If yes, location(s)_____
Rugs/mats ___yes ___no: If yes, location(s)_____
Steps ___ yes ___no: If yes, location(s) _____
Ramps ___yes ___no: If yes, location(s)/degree_____
- Lighting quality___ very good ___good ___ poor
    If inadequate, location(s)/descriptions_____
- Lighting consistency ___ very good ___good ___ poor
    If inadequate, location(s)/descriptions_____
- Surface glare ___yes ___ no
    If yes, glare is ___very intense ___intense ___not intense
    If yes, locations(s)_____
- Excessive and continuous background noise ___yes ___no
    If yes, describe_____
- Acoustic quality___ very good ___ good ___ poor ___ dBs
    If inadequate, describe_____
- Indoor temperature _____ high _____low _____ avg
    If inadequate, describe_____
- In-store seating ___yes ___no
    If yes: tilted backs ___yes ___no
    arms ___yes ___no ___some (percentage _____)
    well-padded seats ___ yes ___ no ___some (percentage_____)
- Public bathroom ___yes ___no
    If yes: disabled accessible ___yes ___no
    raised commode ___yes ___no
    support rails ___yes ___no
- In-store service ___yes ___no: If yes, describe_____
- Curbside service ___yes ___no: If yes, describe_____
- Fire alarms ___yes ___no: If yes: ___ audio only ___ visual only ___audio and visual
- Multiple stories ___yes ___no
    If yes: elevator ____yes ___no
    If yes: tactile buttons ___yes___ no
    audio announcements ___yes ___ no
    timing of door closure_____

If yes: stair access only ___yes ___no
If stair access only: location clearly marked ___yes ___ no
number of stairs_____
height of individual stair_____
depth of individual stair_____
non-slip treads ___yes ___ no
railing ___yes ___no: If yes, describe_____
_____

Interiors are examined for the same surface faults looked for during exterior examinations. In addition, other common interior items such as floor mats and throw rugs must also be recognized as trip hazards. In much the same way, sloping floors and slick surfaces, especially when wet, are also dangers to successful locomotion and are to be noted and eliminated.

Color schemes are noted, as strong contrasting colors make it easier for a person with low vision to distinguish between walls and floors (Altman, 2002). Along the same lines, lighter color flooring/floor covering is desirable as very dark areas on the floor such as carpets or mats can be perceived as holes by persons with low vision (ibid). Light glare is an extremely common source of difficulty for older persons as is uneven or flickering light (Sanford, 1999) and is also noted. Hearing loss affects one-third of persons 65 and older and half of persons over 80 (Keen, 2003) and is exacerbated by acoustic quality issues such as excessive background noise (Suss, 1993) and echo (Roberts, Besing and Koehnke, 2002). Acoustic analysis is, therefore, performed.

Older persons are especially susceptible to cold temperatures making indoor temperature measurement a critical component of interior assessment. Even mildly cool room temperatures of 60–65°F can interfere with the body's ability to regulate its temperature and cause serious health problems including hypothermia (Extreme Cold and the Elderly, N.D.). More than half of all deaths from hypothermia occur in people over 65 (Hypothermia-Related Deaths, 1998). Temperature analysis is performed with particular attention to waiting, eating, viewing and other areas where people are likely to remain seated for extended periods of time.

The fifth page of the instrument is similar to the second in that is it a blank sheet save for a header. This page is used to sketch the building interior denoting placement of aisles, chairs, etc., as well as highlighting the trouble spots discovered during the interior examination process.

Community Service Assessment

While assessment of the built environment has been the primary focus of our discussion thus far, another important component of maintaining the free-range status of our aging citizens is the presence or absence of public and private for profit and not-for-profit entities serving their needs such as point-to-point transportation services. Issues of need are related to the size and health of a community's aging population. While census data can provide part of the information needed to begin such an assessment, additional data collection may be required to determine service need. Once the level of service need has been determined, an assessment of whether or not the need is being met can begin.

Lastly, as new technologies and services emerge like those growing out of University of Florida's Gator-Tech Smart House program (see Helal, 2009), service needs will evolve. Here it is the responsibility of the applied researcher to meet the needs of clients as well as stay abreast of new developments in his or her area of specialization.

Using the Results

Communities and businesses that wish to maximize the engagement of their aging citizens or customers will often hire consultants to advise them on reaching, and meeting the needs of this growing segment of their population. Organizations such as Future Age Consulting Inc. (www.futureageconsulting.com) and IDEAS Consulting Inc. (www.ideasconsultinginc.com) specialize in assisting communities and businesses with communication and awareness trainings facilitating positive and productive intergenerational communication in business and other service settings, with community advancement programs to encourage older citizens toward more active civic engagement, with retrofitting old structures to meet the needs of an aging population, and with the design of new structures to ensure maximum range of personal and civic engagement.

Governing bodies, often slow to change their policies, have become increasing proactive in adjusting public infrastructure to meet the needs of these citizens more adequately. Whether it is modifying the structure of their roadways and street signage to meet the needs of its aging drivers (Conradi, 2002), constructing large and safe medians for elder pedestrians crossing the street (Dunn, 1994), accommodating the construction of so-called granny flats (White, 2003a), nurturing a walkable new urbanism (White, 2003b), or addressing the needs of older citizens stranded in suburbs designed for the young and middle-aged (Swope, 2005), policy makers recognize that they have a vested interest in creating an environment that can be successfully navigated by this fast-growing population.

Assessment results with the use of this instrument can help both public and private entities transform their properties into welcoming places rather than locations to be avoided. By doing this they benefit themselves by increasing commerce and civic participation at the very same time that they create a wider range of freedom of action for an increasingly-large population. Additionally, by drawing attention to the flaws of the existing environment vis-à-vis the needs of the current older population, pressure will build to ensure that new construction fully incorporates elder-friendly design.

Conclusion

Work for practicing sociologists comes in many forms and guises. In this chapter we have looked at the challenges a large aging population poses for society and how practicing sociologists can use their knowledge to help society create an environment within which its older citizens can lead independent and productive lives. Just as sociologists have a long tradition in highlighting the problems of our society, so too must they find ways to apply their craft in finding the solutions to these problems. By drawing attention to the structural impediments to safe and easy movement within the built environment for our aging citizens, sociologists can assist in the creation of an environment that is truly conducive to free-range humans.

Works Cited

Altman, Adelaide. 2002. *Elderhouse: Planning Your Best Home Ever*. White River Junction, VT: Chelsea Green Publishing.

Carstens, Diane Y. 1993. *Site Planning and Design for the Elderly: Issues, Guidelines, and Alternatives*. Hoboken, NJ: Wiley.

Christenson, Margaret A. 1990. *Aging and the Designed Environment*. New York: The Hawthorn Press.

Conradi, Melissa. 2002. "Iowa Elder-Proofs Its Roads." *Governing* June: 60.

Cockerham, William C. 1997. *This Aging Society*. Englewood Cliffs: Prentice Hall.

Crandall, Richard C. 1991. *Gerontology*. New York: McGraw-Hill.

"Disabled Senior," 2006. *Governing* April: 66.

Dunn, James L. 1994. "For the Elderly, New Ways to Cross the Street and Live." *Governing* May:18–19.

Eitzen, D. Stanley, Maxine Baca Zinn and Kelly Eitzen Smith. 2009. *Social Problems*. Boston: Allyn and Bacon.

Friedsam, Hiram J. 1995. "Professional Education and the Invention of Social Gerontology." *Generations* 19(2): 46–50.

Helal, A., J. King, H. Zabadani and Y. Kaddourah. 2009. "The Gator Tech Smart House: An Assistive Environment for Successful Aging." In H. Hagrass, Ed., "Advanced Intelligent Environments." Springer Verlag. In press.

"Hypothermia-Related Deaths: Georgia, January 1996–December 1997, and United States, 1979–1995." 1998. *Morbidity and Mortality Weekly Report* 47: 1037–1040.

Keen, Kathy. 2003. "UF Study: Elderly Admit Hearing Loss But Not Necessarily Its Effects." Gainesville, FL: University of Florida News. Retrieved January 2, 2009 (http://news.ufl.edu/2003/12/17/elderly-hearing/).

Kovacs, Christopher R. 2005. "Age-Related Changes in Gait and Obstacle Avoidance Capabilities in Older Adults: A Review." *Journal of Applied Gerontology* 24(1) February: 28–34.

Lawton, M. Powell. 1980. *Environment and Aging*. Monterey: Brooks-Cole.

———. 1983. "Environment and Other Determinants of Well-Being in Older People." Robert W. Kleemeier Memorial Lecture. *The Gerontologist* 23: 349–357.

———. 1985. "The Elderly in Context Perspectives from Environmental Psychology and Gerontology." *Environment and Behavior* 17: 501–519.

Lawton, M. P., E. M. Brody, and P. Turner-Massey. 1978. "The Relationships of Environmental Factors to Changes in Well-Being. *The Gerontologist* 18: 133–137.

Leon-Guerrero, Anna. 2008. *Social Problems Community, Policy, and Social Action*. Thousand Oaks, CA: Pine Forge Press.

Mace, Ron. 1998. *Universal Design: Housing for the Lifespan of All People*. U.S. Department of Housing and Urban Development, Washington D.C.

Marcus, Clare Cooper and Carolyn Francis, Eds. 1997. *People Places: Design Guidelines for Urban Open Space*. Hoboken, NJ: Wiley.

Putney, Norella M., Dawn E. Alley and Vern L. Bengston. 2005. "Social Gerontology as Public Sociology in Action." *American Sociologist* 36(3–4): 88–104.

Rhode Island Department of Health. "Extreme Cold and the Elderly." N.D. Retrieved January 11, 2009 (www.health.ri.gov/cold.php).

Roberts, Richard A., Joan Besing and Janet Koehnke. 2002. "Effects of Hearing Loss on Echo Thresholds." *Ear and Hearing* 23(4): 349–357.

Ruchlin, Hirsch S. and Mark S. Lachs. 1999. "Prevalence and Correlates of Exercise Among Older Adults." *Journal of Applied Gerontology* 18(3) September: 341–357.

Sanford, Linda. 1999. "The Importance of Lighting for the Elderly." *Aging & Vision*. Spring. New York: Lighthouse International.

Sykes, Kathy. 2005. "A Healthy Environment for Older Adults: The Aging Initiative of the Environmental Protection Agency." *Generations* 29(2): 65–69.

Suss, Elaine. 1993. *When the Hearing Gets Hard*. New York: Insight Books—Plenum Press.

Swope, Christopher. 2005. "Stranded Seniors: Suburban Life Revolves Around the Car." *Governing* June: 40–42.

U.S. Department of Health and Human Services, Administration on Aging. 2008. "Aging into the 21st century." Retrieved January 8, 2009 (www.aoa.gov/prof/Statistics/future_growth/aging21/summary.aspx).

U.S. Social Security Administration. 2007. OASDI Trustees Report (April 2007), Table V.A.2.

Wahl, Hans Werner. 2001. "Environmental Influences on Aging and Behavior." In J. E. Birren and K. W. Schaie, Eds., *Handbook of the Psychology of Aging*. San Diego: Academic Press.

White, Otis. 2003a. "Welcome Home Grandma." *Governing* January: 12.

———. 2003b. "Dream Town Houses." *Governing* July: 12.

Worfolk, J. B. 2000. "Heat Waves: Their Impact on the Health of Elders." *Geriatric Nursing: American Journal of Care for the Aging* 21(2): 70–77.

CHAPTER 10

Communal Living

INTENTIONALLY RESISTING GLOBAL
WHITE SUPREMACIST CAPITALISM

Johnnie Spraggins, San Antonio
Jammie Price, Appalachian State University
Roger A. Straus, Certified Clinical Sociologist,
Portland

The work of de Tocqueville (2000; original in two volumes 1835 and 1840), *Democracy in America*, is sometimes referenced as initiating community studies in the United States. In this monumental work, de Tocqueville first identified a value that remains a distinctive characteristic of Americans—individualism. The juxtaposition between individualism and achieving community in the United States continues to present challenges for sociologists, anthropologists, and historians. Subsequent community studies have focused on various aspects of community other than values, such as structure, organization, and stratification, to name a few. The tension between individualism and community suggests fertile academic ground as a study in deconstructionism.

In this chapter we explore the nature of intentional communities, otherwise known as communes, by applying sociological theory. We begin by reviewing sociological and cultural explanations of intentional communities. Second, we characterize and describe three such communities drawing on ethnographic data and institutional data. Next, we analyze and discuss how successfully communal living expresses resistance to mainstream society. Particular attention is devoted to locating the communities in their cultural and historical context.

Sociological theory on community (specifically, the area of cultural studies) critiques three broad areas of social life. First, dimensions of power are problematized—that is, treated as challenges that invite transformation of the situations of the people involved (Crotty, 1998). As you will see, there is value in questioning the assumptions used to qualify and justify existing power relations. Second, essentialism, the view that everything, people or phenomena, have an underlying and unchanging essence (Sayer, 1997) is explicitly rejected. We argue that careful consideration of context—political, cultural, historical, economic—is critical for understanding behavioral decisions. Third, sociological theory considers forms of resistance to domination. This dimension is an important part of our argument, namely, that community reconstruction is a form of resistance to the brutalizing effects of globalization.

If "all politics is local," then the focus of this chapter rings true. Interpreting behavioral decisions as resistance is not a new concept. For example, people want control over their lives, and resist when they perceive that as elusive. In their book *Empire*, Hardt and Negri (2001) note that financial and political powers produce commodities and consumers. Following Foucault and others, we know that all wants and desires are dependent upon organizing systems, of language, of culture, of relations, of power. We argue that people's rational choices in matters that most directly affect their lives often represent resistance to these powers and systems. Thus, the reality of life in contemporary society, where control and decisions are increasingly dominated by international, standardized, capital-driven concerns, is met with various types of resistance. The deliberate creation of intentional communities we describe in this chapter is a form of resistance to this domination.

For example, hooks (1994) argues that "white supremist capitalist patriarchy" is the social, political, and cultural reality against which she writes. She contends, further, that understanding action—as operating in this milieu—is necessary to gain purchase on social life. Thus, while one may disagree with her characterization of society, it is necessary to understand her position to further use her analysis. By arguing that our society is so characterized, one gains a perspective that understands action as attempting to gain from, join, or resist the status quo.

Hardt and Negri (2001) argue that the globalization about which we see so much written leads to the commodification of the body, the commodification of desire(s), and the need to systematically interlock production, reproduction, and biopolitical bodies.[1] When we evaluate this position with the stance of hooks we see that operating in this process of globalization is a white supremacist capitalist patriarchy. For example, at this writing, only one person of color has been elected to the highest political position in the country, and as yet no women. In 2007, of the CEOs of Fortune 500 companies, 12 were women (CNN, 2009), a percentage of 0.024 for female representation among one of the more striking indicators of power, prestige, and money in the world. Consequently, the lines in the sand are clear. One may buy into this belief system, unwittingly or not, or opt to resist it. We argue that many of the people we studied and spoke with are actively resisting this hegemonic system with and through their daily lifestyle choices.

One option is to exercise one's free will and break free from the dictum of mainstream society when selecting one's lifestyle. Specifically, we are concerned with those that elect to become an active part of one of the numerous intentional communities present across the country. An intentional community can be defined as "a group of people who have chosen to live together with a common purpose" (Kozeny, 2002). They work cooperatively to create a lifestyle that reflects their shared values. Examples of intentional communities can include land co-ops, co-housing groups, student cooperatives, communes, ecovillages, residential land trusts, urban housing cooperatives, and farming collectives, to name a few. Each seeks to create a sense of community through close proximity, friendship, the formation of support networks, shared philosophy, and lifestyle. It is this phenomenon that remains the authors' focus of examination. We want to turn now to a description of three intentional communities in the Southeast and the methodology used to learn about them.

Ethnography

"Ethnography" refers to a naturalistic research method in which you learn about cultures, groups, and situations by living in communities to gain intimate familiarity with your participants. This allows you to describe the culture and group based on first-hand experience. Intentional communities attracted the first author's attention on a visit to Koinonia Farms in the mid-1970s as part of meeting ethnographic requirements for an anthropology course at Auburn University. Resistance as a means of living characterized the reason for creating this community, specifically resistance to racism and poverty using the ideology of Christianity to justify equality. The fierce opposition from locals when this community was formed mid-twentieth century led to examining local reception to other intentional communities, again largely using ethnographic methods, and considering the meaning of both (community formation and resistance).

Koinonia Farms

Koinonia Farms is comprised of a non-profit corporation (Koinonia Partners, Inc.) and participating community members. Located in rural southwest Georgia, it has facilities for the shelling and processing of pecans and pecan products, a store, a café, a community center, and an office. In addition, there are two neighboring residential areas, Koinonia Village and Forest Park, which provide housing for many of the community members. It is situated on what has grown from 400 to 1,400 acres of rural land, far removed from the (relatively) urban area of Americus, Georgia (with a 2009 population around 8,000—far less when the community was founded).

The word "koinonia" provides some important clues to understanding the community and organization which carries the name. In ancient Greek, the word means community or fellowship, and it was with this in mind that the community was founded in 1942. The founders' goal was to establish an egalitarian Christian community amidst an epidemic of poverty and racism. Their devotion to four principles drove their mission:[2]

1. Treat all human beings with dignity and justice.
2. Choose love over violence (i.e., pacifism).
3. Share all possessions and live simply.
4. Be stewards of the land and its natural resources.

Clarence Jordan came to Americus with his wife and two children from Louisville, Kentucky, where he had been doing missionary work together with Martin England. Jordan and England founded their intentional community on the premises of peace, communal living, and racial tolerance. The reception they received varied considerably as their message did not jibe very well with the dominant culture of rural southern Georgia in the midst of World War II. Accepted by some in the local community, they built friendships, farmed, established youth summer camps, and tried to become part of the larger community. They were greeted with violence by others, however, ranging from death threats to bullets shot from a passing train, firebombs, economic boycotts, excommunication from area congregations, and angry Ku Klux Klan (KKK) rallies. Newspaper clippings in the Koinonia museum recount examples of such acts of terror, which went on for over a decade. The community experienced the burning of its vegetable stands twice in 1956 and 1957, and the KKK proposing a land purchase from Clarence Jordan if he would consent to relocate his community. Despite the KKK's offering a purchase price above market value, the founder of Koinonia refused to accept their offer and relocate.

Perseverance by the members of the community led them to numerous projects involving civil rights, prison ministry, racial reconciliation, peace activism, early childhood education, youth and teen outreach, affordable housing, language training, sustainable agriculture, and economic development. In the 1960s, when only three couples remained, a self-made millionaire businessman from Montgomery, Alabama, Millard Fuller, brought his wife Linda to Koinonia.[3] Following visits to the community and eventually joining it, Fuller offered the group a form of rejuvenation. He did this through the adherence to and the teaching of his own translation of the Bible. It was his intention to live out the ideals of Christ, including the concept of equality. In so doing, Fuller stirred up the locals who were of the opinion that Blacks and Whites were not equal. Fuller, as well as those in the community of Koinonia, disagreed believing that Blacks and Whites should be able to meet and come together, to include living together, on an even playing field. In their search for a vision for the community, Millard and Linda Fuller helped initiate the building of homes for the poverty stricken, with no-interest loans and cooperative building.

Clarence Jordan died at the age of 57 while the community's first house was being built. He would not live to see the realization of his principles that Millard Fuller would achieve by expanding the Koinonia concept of home building. Fuller took the concept of building homes for those in the community and selling them at cost from those being built at Koinonia Village and Forrest Park all the way to Zaire (now the Democratic Republic of the Congo) in Africa. After three years honing his entrepreneurial skills in Africa, Fuller returned to the United States and formed the internationally known Habitat for Humanity. Ruefully, Koinonia now finds itself in stark contrast to its offspring. Corporate headquarters for Habitat for Humanity, located in downtown Americus, is housed in a well-appointed refurbished three- or four-story brick warehouse. The contrast between Habitat for Humanities and Koinonia Partners, Inc. is quite dramatic, the huge disparity in financial resources being most apparent.

What has held the Koinonia Farms community together through daunting adversity? Koinonia Farms is a spiritual community founded on a philosophy of non-violence, racial equality, non-materialism, healthy lifestyle, and collective living. Their emphasis is on peace and providing service to one's neighbor. According to the Koinonia Partners website, the vision of the community is one that stresses "building communities through partnership" (2002).

Another way in which Koinonia lives according to its founding concepts is in striving to meet the needs of its members. One way that this has been done in the past is through the building of homes in which community members and their families, as well as the less-than-well off of the area's residents, live. Koinonia Village was the community's first foray into house building and houses were on small lots, close to the road. Forest Park came later with homes on larger lots, variously placed in relation to the road and each other. Although there are a few domed homes made of concrete, most homes are made of wood. Koinonia builds these homes and sells them at cost, providing non-interest mortgage loans to those who could otherwise not afford to purchase a home of their own (Korban, 1998). The cake and pecan sales support this investment.

The economics of Koinonia are a statement to ingenuity in the face of adversity, resourcefulness with available materials. Koinonia Farms turned to pecans and pecan products after their vegetable stands were repeatedly burned and their produce was, for the most part, spurned by the community at large. Women workers sort pecans and machines crack and dry them prior to their inclusion in baked goods and sweets. Once the fresh, shelled pecans are bagged and the pecan products are prepared, they are placed for sale in the Koinonia Farms store. The pecans and other products are available via mail order (and now through the Internet), thus avoiding local economic boycotts. In addition to pecans and pecan products like pecan stuffed dates and rich peach cakes, the store's inventory also includes tapes of Clarence Jordan, books, coffee, tea, DVDs, and videotapes. A coffee café for visitors is located in the same poured concrete building as the community store.

Koinonia Village opens its community to guests for tours. On one such tour, in addition to the first author, several guests were present for the noon meal prepared by Koinonia residents. Each visitor was asked to stand and introduce themselves. A woman in one couple mentioned having lived in France and Nantucket and a man further down the table mentioned he was from Indiana. By keeping the doors of the community open to visitors, those at Koinonia are able to let the outside world view their way of living as well as recruit new members. Further, Koinonia Farms is, at least partially, dependent on the community-at-large for their financial stability through the sales and purchases of their products. Additionally, the community advertises on their Koinonia Partners website for individuals who might be interested in filling positions, both short-term and long-term (i.e., volunteers, internships, and staff).

Spiral Garden

Spiral Garden, a second intentional community, is considered "the poor person's co-op in Leon County, Florida, the home of Tallahassee" (the state's capital). It is telling that this characterization, by one of the members, suggests that co-ops are a way of life in Tallahassee—an idea not found in most communities. Community members live among locals and with one another in a regular subdivision named Spiral Garden Way. Common amenities include housing assistance, a swimming pool, retreat lodges, a sauna and hot tub, and residential homes. Not all those who reside in the subdivision are members of the Spiral Garden intentional community. Additionally, not all members of the intentional community live in Spiral Garden Way; some individuals live in Tallahassee. The Spiral Garden community is a contract among people, complete with its own Community Directory of phone numbers.

Initially, Spiral Garden was comprised of only a few people and a couple of teepees on some wooded land. The Community Directory describes the evolution of the community with commonly purchased lots, divvied up plots, and like-minded people purchasing nearby land. About 20 years ago, although it was unknown who the landowner was, individuals put a claim on land in the area. Three-acre plots were staked and recruitment occurred by word-of-mouth.

The community was known as the Society for Human Development in the 1970s and has been considered by some, to border on a cult. Membership is both national and international. As members travel, they can consult a Directory of Members in order to find places to stay. The national membership is known as the Seekers and Settlers, while the international membership goes by the name of the Finders. The latter is represented as a type of international travel association, periodically publishing a directory, for purchase, of hosting members. Those connected with this group have been using laptops and a primitive form of Internet as far back as the early 1980s. At one point (according to a 1987/1988 Washington Post article), it was thought there was a connection between Spiral Garden and the U.S. Central Intelligent Agency (CIA) because a number of their community members were once in the CIA (i.e., Marlon David Petty).

Spiral Garden built its community on the premise of shared resources and through a shared view of children. Within Spiral Garden it is felt that children are more intelligent than adults due to the fact they have not yet experienced a lifetime of setbacks. Children see things more logically and are thus treated in such a manner that they are made more independent than their counterparts in the community-at-large. The people of this community live near one another in an effort to create an old-school type community.

Spiral Garden trades goats, milk, and chickens to obtain the things they need. Childcare may be provided by family or community members, and is a community value. Children attend both public or community-based schools or may be home-schooled. Services and goods needed by individuals or families are bartered and this is viewed as preferable to a cash-based economy. Bartering is also not taxable.

People move to Spiral Garden for the feeling of community. However, once there, some largely ignore the community experience. Informants reported not participating in community events due to lack of available time or other reasons. Community-centered and organized events tend to be better attended when in conjunction with culturally-established holidays (e.g., Christmas, Independence Day, and Thanksgiving). Some community members report they need to participate in community activities more than they do, yet the demands of participation in the paid labor force preclude this. Nevertheless, most Spiral Garden members participate in meetings that pertain to such issues as mosquito spraying and flood problems. They get together before dinner to pick up trash and then perhaps participate in potluck desserts. The fact that people felt guilty for not participating in these community-themed opportunities paired with continued organization of community members suggests ongoing support for the value of community.

Grassroots

A third intentional community, Grassroots, was started by a group of parents and future parents in their 30s and 40s with their own resources (i.e., education and jobs), many of whom knew one another through a loosely organized organization, the Tallahassee Peace Coalition. Prior to owning land, the individuals who would come to be part of the Grassroots community had children attending the Grassroots school. The school was in existence for nearly 10 years prior to the founding of the actual community. Historically, Grassroots came indirectly out of another intentional community called Miccosukee Land Co-operative. Founders of Grassroots had investigated membership in Miccosukee Land Co-op but felt that the waiting list was much too long. They started talking about purchasing their own land and creating their own community. It was in this way that casual conversation led to the purchase of a large section of land, purchased as a trust from the state of Florida.

Grassroots was founded on environmentalist and egalitarian values by individuals with a vision of providing private schooling for their children. Since community members knew one another prior to entering into land ownership together, their relationships were built on trust, friendship, and knowledge. They saw this as an alternative community that gave them the opportunity for co-operative learning, complete with a private school and picturesque views. Grassroots' major missions are divided between peace coalitions and alternative schooling. Not only do the individuals of this community want to educate people on a peace vision, they also see a larger educational mission: it is their focus that the larger community be viewed as a classroom.

Emphasis was placed on mistakes they perceived to have been made at Miccosukee. For example, it was felt that when people focused on their own household, broader goals were neglected. For this reason, Grassroots was initially a community purchase. However, when financial decisions became important and questions arose, the trust was later changed to private ownership. At that point, restitution was made on a first priority basis with notice being given to the community. A list of people, in order of preference, was created of potential buyers. Of those on this first list, each had to make a financial commitment to make a down payment for a minimum parcel of 1 acre. There were more people than land, so a dummy corporation, Grassroots Community, Inc., was established as a not-for-profit entity owner of community land. Participating Grassroots members saw this land-related alliance as a way to create their own lifestyle as well as ownership of problems. Once their community was established, they each had the opportunity to live among like-minded individuals in close proximity. The homes are built by individuals for their families on lots they selected from a large plot purchased by Grassroots.

The founders of Grassroots believed that purchasing land meant that they could build, maintain, and run their own community's private school. Educational levels taught at the Grassroots school are based on the current needs of those in the community. Grades typically include preschool or kindergarten though the end of middle school/junior high, although the school could be expanded to include high school students if needed. Most families that send their children to the Grassroots school do so through elementary school or middle school and then move them into the School for the Advanced and Individualized Learning (SAIL), a public school in Tallahassee.

Unique to the Grassroots educational system is their view on teaching. School is rather informal. If children don't want to learn, or chose not to participate, they can sit in a corner, watch the day pass, or clean their fingernails. It is their choice. When they want to learn, and are ready to learn, they can approach a teacher and ask for instruction. The only thing truly expected of the children attending the Grassroots school is that they must to do their chores at the end of the day.

In the Grassroots community, meetings help achieve the value of environmentalism. For example, they have met to fight both mosquito spraying and the actions of a local paper company. Despite community meetings, some lament the lack of community activities like get-togethers to eat, monthly meetings, celebratory events, and softball. There is a need among the members to have regular functions and activities.

Analysis and Discussion

Employing the principles of cultural studies, can we say that these communities offer a realistic form of resistance to the structures of the towns in which they are found? Evidence from Koinonia, the intentional community with a (much) longer history, is strongest. Opposing Jim Crow segregation in the rural south in the 1940s was a direct challenge to the existing structure. The violence with which that was met attests to its reception. The other communities, Spiral Garden and Grassroots, are creative in their resistance yet fail to directly challenge existing structures. Their values are reflected in community behavior expressing their unique values without direct confrontation with larger structures.

Different styles of living and specific cultural practices sharpen the lines between community members and larger society. Community members report strong commitments to unique values as demonstrated by their behavior. Some of the values are not different in content insofar as in degree of commitment by community members. The variation among the communities is significant— Koinonia presents the most fundamental departure, when evaluated in context. Resistance to segregation in the 1940s Jim Crow south was a drastic challenge to the status quo, and the violence suffered by community members attests to it. Adhering to egalitarian principles in the 2000s is not as dramatic a departure from mainstream norms, yet community members in Grassroots and Spiral Garden feel their behavior reflects a closer adherence to their ideals than would be possible with other lifestyles. Commitment to these values by active expression and constant reference to them does support a firmer commitment than occasional reference, as can be seen among non-community members.

The strongest evidence of resistance to global white supremacist capitalism among contemporary intentional communities considered here is the sharing of resources in Spiral Garden. Explicit identification of resources as community resources to be shared is evidence of values reflected in behavior.

The changing nature of social relations among community members and between the community and larger society augment the explicit rejection of essentialism. "Community" as a practice and value must be continually defined. Behavior reflecting values changes over time, as priorities are identified and evaluated. The experience of community members helps them to refine what is important to them, and how this can be achieved via negotiated practices. As communities develop and members explicitly consider the consequences of lived experience, resistance to domination and expression of equality with respect to race, ethnicity, gender, sexuality, and class are clarified.

Going beyond these case studies themselves, what can we learn as sociological practitioners from examining these intentional communities through cultural analysis? At least four lessons can be applied to allow such communities to survive and even prosper in the face of global white supremacist capitalism. These include:

1. Maintaining community boundaries. Another key to their relative success has been to foster communal identity (and differentiation from non-members) through a variety of boundary maintenance strategies. Perhaps the most obvious, and most common among intentional communities, has been to live separately from others, as with Koinonia and Grassroots. Even where, as in the case of Spiral Garden, members live among non-members and there is generally no geographic separation from the external society, boundaries can be maintained. Spiral Garden's alternative to living physically apart from others involves use of a "membership" model, maintaining a directory of members that identifies who is and who is not within the community, and

maintaining a direct communication channel among community members that others cannot access (hence maintaining a boundary) through use of computer technology.

2. Communal activities. In order to express and reinforce community, it appears essential that members engage in activities that express their core values and thus separate them from the world they resist through their lifestyle and behavior. These activities can be part of a total lifestyle, as when engaging in collective agriculture, using barter and trade in opposition to capitalist norms of monetary transactions and private property, or maintaining a separate school system enacting their central theories, as in the case of Grassroots. It seems no less important, however, to frequently bring members together face-to-face in activities that reinforce their sense of sharing an identity, being part of an community of people living according to shared values, whether social get-togethers or task-oriented meetings. It is possible that virtual meetings, through computer networks, may be able to substitute, at least to some degree, although that might not permit enough sense of personal connection to one another and to the community as their reference group. This, for example, seems to be one difference between the Koinonia Community and Habitat for Humanity—one is personal, value-centered, the other has become corporate, pragmatic (even if it engages in genuinely praise-worthy activities).

3. Meeting members' needs. It seems that many communes and other intentional communities, such as those associated with the 1960s and 1970s counterculture movement, have collapsed because they never developed strategies, values, or structures to meet even the most basic needs of members, such as food, shelter, education, and health care on a systematic, long-term basis. In contrast, successful intentional communities that have persisted over time, like Koinonia and newer, yet successful ones like Spiral Garden, both exhibit a commitment to meet members' needs and have generated means to do so. One aspect of this is recognition of the fact that, while the community itself may rest on a rejection of then external capitalist society and its associated values, and may not employ a monetary economy among its membership, they must still find a way to make necessary exchanges with that outer world for food, products, services, etc. Thus, while unable to sell its products to locals, Koinonia used first mail order and now the Internet to exchange what the community creates for the money necessary to meet its member's needs.

4. Openness to Growth and Change. A last success factor appears to be maintaining openness to allowing the community, its structures, values and practices to evolve. Each of these three communities has been able to negotiate changes in values, structures, and behavior enabling them to adapt to internal and external changes. These might be as straightforward as having to relocate

physically, as when the Spiral Garden's original property was flooded, or taking advantage of new technology to spread its message and sell its products, as in the case of Koinonia. As noted a few paragraphs above, "community" as a practice and value must be continually defined—it cannot remain static and survive. Consequently, it would seem essential to incorporate openness to change and growth as one of the central values of the community, and to ensure that structure provides means to reconsider and renegotiate values and practices without giving up those that are central to the community's identity and purpose.

One thing that we have not suggested, it merits note, is the need to stand in direct conflict with the surrounding community, to aggressively assert community boundaries and differences, or to maintain community identity and solidarity by creating an antagonistic us-them situation. All too often, the surrounding community will do that on its own, as in the case of Koinonia—but it appears that the successful intentional community will express its resistance to an oppressive dominant culture by enacting its own values in behavior and ensuring that it establishes the means to meet these five considerations for long-term survival.

To the trained sociologist it will likely seem obvious that all of the above comments could be summarized with one sociological term—praxis. One thread that runs through the success of the three communities discussed here is that each of them not only formed around a central set of theory and values in opposition to the dominant culture, but they continue to enact that comment in their behavior. Their resistance is continually renewed and reenergized by enacting their theory in everyday life.

Works Cited

CNN. 2009. "Women CEOs for FORTUNE 500 Companies." http://money.cnn.com/magazines/fortune/fortune500/2007/womenceos.

Crotty, Michael J. 1998. *Foundations of Social Research: Meaning and Perspective in the Research Process.* Thousand Oaks, CA: Sage

de Tocqueville, Alexis, Harvey C. Mansfield (Editor), and Delba Winthrop (Translator). 2000. *Democracy in America.* Chicago: University of Chicago Press.

Hardt, Michael and Antonio Negri. 2001. *Empire.* New York: Oxford University Press.

hooks, bell. 1994. *Outlaw Culture: Resisting Representations.* New York: Routledge.

Intentional Communities. 2002. "Visions of Utopia: Experiments in Sustainable Culture." http://fic.ic.org.

Interface Group, The. 2002. "Koinonia Partners: Welcome to the Ministry of Koinonia Partners." Minnesota. www.koinoniapartners.org/main.html.

Kozeny, Geoph. 2002. "Intentional Communities: Lifestyles Based on Ideals." www. conscious choice.com/issues.

Sayer, Andrew. 1997. "Essentialism, Social Constructionism, and Beyond." *Sociological Review* 45: 456

Notes

1. As employed by Hardt and Negri, *biopolitics* refers to anti-capitalist insurrection using life and the body as "weapons."

2. www.koinoniapartners.org/History/history.htm.

3. Millard Fuller is socially connected to Morris Dees of the Southern Poverty Law Center (www.splcenter.org), who went on to litigate against the KKK.

CHAPTER 11

Blending Sociology with Federal Funding

THE EXAMPLE OF THE NATIONAL INSTITUTES OF HEALTH SMALL BUSINESS INNOVATIVE RESEARCH PROGRAM

Augusto Diana, The National Institute on Drug Abuse

Sociologists, perhaps more than any other scientific professionals, find themselves most often housed in the university working as professors, either full-time or as adjunct faculty (Spalter-Roth, 2005, 2007; Weinstein and Goldman-Schuyler, 2008). Many sociologists, and virtually all who consider themselves practicing or applied sociologists, hope that their work will have influence outside of the university, and especially in the world of social policy and/or public health.

One area of influence widely associated with sociologists is research. One way to conduct research that can enhance its social policy or public health impact is through federal research grants. This chapter describes some of the reasons sociologists might benefit from a range of research grant opportunities provided by the National Institutes of Health (NIH). NIH consists of 27 Institutes and Centers (ICs); this chapter will focus on the National Institute on Drug Abuse (NIDA).

Funding Opportunities: the World of NIH Grants

Many sociologists do receive federal funds to conduct research and many gain these grant awards through the competitive grant-making process. And many find money to conduct research through a more indirect funding process, by receiving grants from other entities that have received federal funds. For instance, the federal government provides grant funds each year to States, Communities, and Service Agencies, to address particular problems (e.g., substance use or teen pregnancy). Often, the government requires evaluation studies of the use of these funds and the State, Community or Service Agency must contract with groups or individuals to conduct these evaluations. It is not uncommon for sociologists to apply for and win grants of this type. Relative to NIH funding levels, these awards tend to be small and allow for a more limited or less "pure" type of research, because the research setting cannot be controlled (randomized designs are rarely possible in these types of studies).

Although statistics are hard to come by, it appears that relatively few direct federal research funds (i.e., not through an intermediary as described above) go to sociologists, due in part to the relatively low percentage of applications for federal funding that are produced by sociologists. The implication is that sociologists seldom even give themselves the opportunity to receive federal research funds to engage in the work that they love.

Fortunately, there are many types of NIH awards that might appeal to sociologists and to which sociological theory, perspective and methods seem well-suited. As with other ICs, NIDA makes many kinds of funding awards available to potential researchers. From the NIH website (2009), NIDA's mission is to:

> lead the nation in bringing the power of science to bear on drug abuse and addiction. This charge has two critical components. The first is the strategic support and conduct of research across a broad range of disciplines. The second is ensuring the rapid and effective dissemination and use of the results of that research to significantly improve prevention, treatment and policy as it relates to drug abuse and addiction.

An official publication, the *NIH Guide for Grants and Contracts* (2009), lists funding opportunities, grant policies, and guidelines on a weekly basis. Traditional NIH awards, and those considered the most prestigious, are R01s. As described in the *NIH Guide,*

> The Research Project Grant (R01) is an award made to an institution/organization to support a discrete, specified, circumscribed project to be performed by the named investigator(s) in areas representing the specific interests and competencies of the investigator(s) . . . [and] . . . must be related to the stated program interests of one or more of the NIH Institutes and Centers (ICs) based on descriptions of their programs.

Specific ICs will add information about their public health issues to the FOA description, making clear how the research should address that area and, in some cases, specifying areas within the larger public health issue the I/C would like studied. An example from NIDA using the R01 mechanism is provided in the *NIDA Guide for Grants and Contracts* (2008):

> This Funding Opportunity Announcement (FOA) issued by the National Institute on Drug Abuse (NIDA) . . . encourages Research Project Grant (R01) applications on health services research to improve the quality of prevention and treatment services for drug and alcohol abuse. Such research projects might emphasize any of the following subjects: (1) clinical quality improvement; (2) organizational/managerial quality improvement; (3) systems of care and collaborative research; or (4) development or improvement of research methodology, analytic approaches, and measurement instrumentation used in the study of drug and alcohol services.

While the most recognized and prestigious, R01s are also the hardest awards to win. Overall, about 19% were funded in 2007, and the trend has been downward, with lower success rates over the past 10 years. NIDA's R01 success rate is near the average, at 18%, and first time applicants to NIDA have a success rate of 17%. Though the success rate for previous awardees does increase, it averages 26%, hardly a "gimme" even for experienced investigators (*NIH Office of Extramural Research Databook, R01 Equivalent Grants [R01 EQ]*, 2008).

NIH Grants, Besides the R01

The data on success rates may discourage sociologists from seeking NIH funds. In the busy lives of academic and non-academic sociologists, there are less competitive routes to seek research funds. Often, the universities at which sociologists teach offer small amounts of money to faculty for research pursuits. These awards tend to limit the scope and time frame of the research, but the application process is considerably less burdensome and they do offer a great deal of freedom in carrying out the research.

Nonetheless, steering clear of NIH and other sources of federal funding may be a short-sighted response by sociologists. NIH offers numerous alternative grant mechanisms that lend themselves quite well to academic and non-academic careers. Some examples include K awards, early investigator awards and small research awards. Each of these is described briefly below.

K awards, or Mentored Research Scientist Development Awards, "provide support and 'protected time' (three, four, or five years) for an intensive, supervised career development experience." The goal of the K award is to promote independent research careers, often through later application through the R01 program. In some cases, the K award is used to allow individuals to train in a new field, or to reengage in research after an extended absence from it. In other cases, the K funding mechanism is used to promote greater research workforce diversity. From the *NIH Guide for Grants and Contracts* (2009),

> NIH career development (K) awards are intended to support a period of mentored or independent career development in preparation for a role as an independent researcher (mentored K), or to enable and expand the grantee's potential to make significant contributions (independent K) in the biomedical, behavioral, and clinical sciences. Generally, K awards require the candidate to hold a full-time appointment at the applicant organization and devote a minimum of 75% of that appointment to the career award. However, NIH has historically allowed short-term adjustments to the minimum effort requirement under certain circumstances.

For the most recent year of data (2007), K awards (specifically K01s) are made at a roughly 30% rate, which is 50% better than the R01 rate. Over a 10 year period, K01 awards were made to an average of 35% of all K01 applicants (*NIH Office of Extramural Research Databook, Trends in Research Career Development [K Awards]*, 2008).

Often used to support early career investigators, "the R21 mechanism is intended to encourage new, exploratory and developmental research projects by providing support for the early and conceptual stages of their development" (*NIH Guide for Grants and Contracts*, 2009). The NIH Guide provides information on the appropriate uses of the R21 mechanism within NIDA:

> NIDA uses the R21 mechanism to . . . support . . . projects in the early stages of developing or testing innovative ideas in any area relevant to the mission of the Institute. Since this mechanism is intended to . . . support . . . the early and conceptual stages of an innovative research question or approach, preliminary data specific to the proposed project are not expected. Novel scientific ideas, model systems, tools, agents, targets and technologies that have the potential to advance research in substantial ways and relevant to the mission of NIDA are appropriate for this mechanism.

Key to the R21 are its focus on exploratory and developmental research, an appealing option for new or young researchers, and the goal of promoting novel research areas. These characteristics distinguish the R21 from the R01 and suggest that more creative research approaches are desirable.

A third alternative funding mechanism of which many researchers interested in federal grants may not be aware of is the R03. The R03 is known as NIH's Small Grant Program. Thinking back to the strategy commonly used by sociologists, seeking small pots of money for short-term and small projects, the R03 is highly appropriate option. For instance, the NIH Guide suggests that the R03 mechanism is ideal for "projects of limited cost or scope," and those that can be completed in a short period of time, including those that use widely accepted approaches or methods. The *NIH Guide for Grants and Contracts* (2009) provides information about NIDA's approach to the R03:

> NIDA uses the Small Grant (R03) mechanism to provide support for projects requiring minimal funding for limited periods of time in any area relevant to the mission of the Institute as represented by its program areas. Examples of the types of projects supported by NIDA through the small grant mechanism include: Pilot or feasibility studies; development of research methodology; applied research; high risk/high payoff studies; development of new research technology; small-scale, self-contained projects; and analysis of existing datasets.

Success rates are not available from the NIH Databook for the R21 and the R03 mechanisms. However, their appropriateness for prospective research audiences with little or no exposure to NIH grants seems clear.

Making a Case for NIH SBIR Grants

Another NIH funding mechanism not often considered by sociologists, nor by most other researchers, is the Small Business Innovative Research (SBIR) Program. SBIR has a parallel award category called the Small Business Technology Transfer Research (STTR) awards. These two grant award types share one important characteristic: both are restricted to small businesses. As defined by the federal government, a small business is a for-profit entity (individual proprietorship, partnership, limited liability company, corporation, joint venture, association, trust or cooperative) comprised of no more than 500 employees. Large businesses, universities, and public institutions, such as schools and local government agencies, are not eligible to apply for SBIR and STTR funds. (STTR actually requires a partnership with a second institution, often a university. Outside of this distinction, the two mechanisms function in exactly the same way so the remainder of this chapter will only discuss SBIR.) As described in the *NIH Guide for Grants and Contracts* (2009), the SBIR Program is guided by a set of well-defined goals:

- stimulate technological innovation in the private sector;
- strengthen the role of small business in meeting federal research or research and development (R/R&D) needs;

- increase the commercial application of federally supported research results;
- foster and encourage participation by socially and economically disadvantaged small business concerns and women-owned business concerns in the SBIR program; and
- improve the return on investment from federally funded research for economic and social benefits to the nation.

The SBIR Program is structured very differently from other NIH grant mechanisms. As described in the *NIH Guide for Grants and Contracts, Omnibus Solicitation* (2009):

> The SBIR program is structured in three phases, the first two of which are supported using SBIR funds. The objective of Phase I is to establish the technical/scientific merit and feasibility of the proposed R/R&D efforts. The objective of Phase II is to continue the research or R&D efforts initiated in Phase I. An objective of the SBIR program is to increase private sector commercialization of innovations derived from federal R/R&D. The objective of Phase III, where appropriate, is for the SBC to pursue with non-SBIR funds (either federal or non-federal) the commercialization objectives resulting from the results of the R/R&D funded in Phases I and II. In some federal agencies, Phase III may involve follow-on, non-SBIR funded R&D, or production contracts for products or processes intended for use by the U.S. government.

In general terms, the goal of the SBIR/STTR Program is to promote utilization of technological innovation by small businesses as a way to "spread the news" about what works. In the case of NIDA, this has enhanced dissemination opportunities for strategies that have been proven effective for preventing, treating and studying substance use and substance use related problems. The logic behind funding small businesses to accomplish is that the private sector is better situated to create the "applied possibilities," as they are in the business of developing and promoting products for sale and distribution.

Why Might the NIH SBIR Grant Program Appeal to Sociologists?

There are at least two meaningful rationales for considering SBIR funding in the world of sociological practice. First, the project areas that generally comprise the focus of SBIR grant awards cross over very nicely with many areas of sociological research. Perhaps more importantly, applied sociologists who are interested in addressing social problems, one avenue of which is promoting public health, seem better situated in research that seeks to enhance the use of strategies in real-world settings. A number of example areas that are provided in the general funding announcement for the SBIR Program (U.S. Department of Health and Human Services Omnibus Solicitation, PHS 2008-2 SBIR/STTR Program Descriptions and Research Topics for NIH, CDC, and FDA, 2008:66-72) speak to the crossover of SBIR research and sociological principles:

PROGRAM LEVEL AREAS

1. Studies of the underlying mechanisms and effects of various prevention approaches such as persuasive communication (e.g., mass media and print media) as they are affected by and effect drug related cognition, emotion, motivation and behaviors.
2. Development of and testing of environmental change strategies for schools, neighborhoods, communities, etc., to use in reducing substance use initiation and/or progression.
3. Prevention services research on the organization, financing, management, delivery, and utilization of drug abuse programs.
4. Development and testing of adaptations for efficacious prevention research approaches to make these more appropriate for special populations including racial and ethnic minorities, non-English speaking populations, immigrant populations, rural and migrant populations, low literacy populations, or persons with disabilities.
5. New technologies for the reintegration of criminal offenders into the community to help treatment providers in the criminal justice system and in the community coordinate efforts to effectively (a) monitor offenders' recovery once they have been released into the community, (b) prevent relapse, (c) identify relapse early and efficiently reengage released offenders in appropriate treatment, (d) link released offenders with continuing care services in the community, (e) develop social support networks for recently released offenders in recovery, and (f) educate offenders' family members so that they can more effectively support offenders in recovery once they have been released from prison.

STAFF AND PROGRAM SYSTEMS AREAS

1. Prevention intervention dissemination technologies and mechanisms that integrate research with practice; specifically the transfer of drug abuse information to decision makers, funders, and practitioners.

2. Innovative research that develops and validates generic staff selection systems which could be adopted and tailored for use by drug abuse treatment clinics to minimize or address staff turnover issues that affect quality of service to patients and clients.
3. Training modules and ongoing technical assistance for program implementers of research based substance abuse programming strategies.

METHODOLOGICAL AREAS

1. Studies that develop and assess reliability and validity of developmentally appropriate self-report, physiological, and biochemical measures for use in prevention trials in a variety of settings and a variety of audiences.
2. Development of practical and affordable community tools for: needs and resource assessment, selection of appropriate evidence-based programs and strategies, high-quality implementation of identified programs and strategies, evaluation at community, organization and individual levels, and sustainability.
3. Improvement of Reliability and Validity of Reporting of Sensitive Data, including real-time data collection in ecological settings, and studies to minimize the variations of standard survey protocols or computer-assisted self-interview (CASI) and personal interview (CAPI).
4. The development of community diagnostic instruments for psychometrically sound assessment of community characteristics to improve understanding of how community factors affect drug abuse and ensuing behavioral and social consequences.
5. Development and testing of methods and tools to help drug abuse treatment service providers and payers arrive at realistic estimates of the costs of implementing and sustaining new technologies in usual practice settings, and with the ability to identify and estimate costs separately for implementing and for sustaining new technologies.
6. Assessment tools and methodologies for quantifying an organizational culture that promotes and sustains a drug-free workforce, with the ability to a) assess an organization's baseline culture for drug abuse intolerance both on and off the job, b) identify policies and practices that undermine a drug-free culture, c) enable the identification of programs, policies, and practices capable of helping the workforce develop/strengthen an organizational culture of intolerance for drug use, and d) estimate the impact on the organization's quality of work life, job safety, individual and group performance and productivity, and the profitability of the organization itself.

The areas presented in the list above are guided by conceptual areas that are very familiar to sociologists, including:

- organizations, organizational development and organizational management
- mass communication and information dissemination
- family, school, workplace, total institutions and other community settings as service delivery environments
- environmental impacts on individual behavior
- staff training and staff impact on individual behavior
- methodology and tool development
- community adoption of service strategies
- enhancing access to and engagement in effective programs

These areas are not unimportant to other fields; in fact, the most common background of the researchers who pursue these areas in NIDA-funded research is psychology. However, sociology's potential contribution, understandably, is not really addressed by those trained in other fields. And the sociological perspective runs comfortably through these areas, most of which overlay with the NIH priority of translating research findings into practice. Translating research into practice is equivalent to "doing sociology," or the practical application of sociological theory and research.

Beyond the differences in focus of sociology and other disciplines, part of the appeal of SBIR is its non-academic nature. Many of the areas listed above are simply not well-led by academic researchers. By way of example, one common direction for SBIR has been tests of program dissemination. Much research has shown that evidence-based programs are the best ways to change perceptions and behaviors that put people at risk of substance use problems (Hawkins, et al., 2008; Spoth et al., 2007; Glasgow et al., 2006). Basic academic research does not typically allow for expanded tests of programs and strategies on wider populations and settings. Further, university faculty are typically not well-positioned to create marketing and implementation plans for wide-scale dissemination of effective programs and strategies. Those in business settings, like SBIR awardees, can take an existing effective program or strategy and test its application to a wider market and determine the best methods to disseminate the program or strategy to the audience in need of it.

The second meaningful rationale for the contention that SBIR is a good avenue for sociologists and for others as well, in pursuing research funding, is the opportunity for success. As mentioned above, a likely deterrent to the application process, which involves a significant amount of time and expense, is the low success rate for many traditional NIH grants. Comparatively, the *NIH Office of*

Extramural Research Databook, Small Business Innovative Research Grants, 2008 shows a success rate for SBIR applicants well above 20% over a 10-year period, and is nearly double the rate for R01 and most other funding mechanisms.

As mentioned above, the SBIR Program is divided into 3 phases. Phase I and II provide funding to qualified applicants. Data are available on the successful award rates for these two phases. The average success rate for SBIR Phase I applications is 31%; when moving to Phase II, the success rate reaches 44%. (Remember that applicants are only eligible for a Phase II award after successful completion of a Phase I grant).

What Is Involved in Pursuing SBIR Awards?

So far, this chapter has presented some reasons SBIR may make a good avenue for sociologists to apply for federal research funds. Included among these reasons is a wide set of knowledge and skills areas that sociologists commonly address in the research they choose to conduct. If sociologists can be inspired to pursue these awards, they must address a few important additional conditions.

First and foremost, sociologists whose principal work life is housed in the university are not eligible for SBIR awards (they *are* eligible for STTR awards, if they partner with a small business concern that leads the research effort). It is understandable that most sociologists who are housed in the academy will not want to forgo that life for the substantially riskier world of soft money and uncertain economic climates. These sociologist researchers are best-served by considering some of the other opportunities mentioned in this chapter, such as the NIH K, R21, and R03 funding mechanisms.

For sociologists who prefer the applied world outside of the academy, even while they often keep their hands in the teaching world as adjunct faculty, small business incorporation and pursuit of SBIR grant awards may be a viable option. If it is true that sociologists often see themselves as "outliers" or conceptual and methodological "innovators," then SBIR offers a welcome avenue for this innovation. Using Merton's classic model (1949), sociologists are innovators because they are often carving out unique niches for themselves to establish their identity in what they may see as an unwelcoming intellectual world.

Most non-academic practicing sociologists work in traditional workplace settings, including local, state and federal governments, non-profit organizations, private industry and others (Spalter-Roth, 2007). For those with a more entrepreneurial spirit, eligibility for SBIR funding is easier than it may seem. As mentioned earlier, the only organizational requirement for SBIR eligibility is for-profit small business status (see brief description of eligibility criteria above, or the SBIR Omnibus Solicitation referenced here for full details on NIH's SBIR business eligibility requirements).

Small business incorporation is a minor administrative matter that costs relatively little. Ultimately, sociologists who choose this direction are merely conducting research they are interested in, but now with a legal, organizational base in name. In other words, this simple, low cost step allows for the submission of grant applications with a substantially higher opportunity for success, all the while promoting quality research to enhance public health.

Other Opportunities for NIH Funding— Getting in on the Ground Floor

Perhaps the most important reason to consider grant-making opportunities such as SBIR is that sociologists may suddenly find more doors open to them than they previously knew even existed. Calls to participate on review panels, challenging but very rewarding work, would be likely to come. Becoming known in NIH grant circles may also afford sociologists the opportunity to contribute to discussions of new areas of study, as is often done via Science Meetings at NIH. One recent example of such meetings included the convening of experts to discuss the state of the science and, more importantly, the gaps around physical activity as a possible preventive and treatment approach to address substance abuse. This Science Meeting led to the development of a Request for Applications, a special funding opportunity, to solicit grant applications focused on physical activity as a program intervention for substance abuse prevention and treatment. Another Science Meeting was held to assess the quality of current information about the needs of military families and returning veterans of the wars in Afghanistan and Iraq. Sociologists could be among those invited to serve as expert panelists in helping the shape the direction of NIH's science in these and other areas.

Conclusion

Sociologists have a lot to offer. If sociologists are to apply their well-learned content areas, such as social interaction, business relations, research methodology, analytic writing skills, and others, they must engage in the world outside of academia that affords these opportunities. NIH offers a range of grant mechanisms, as outlined in this chapter that are ideal for sociologists. So, sociologists and sociologists in training, consider taking this bull by the horns to help change the world of service, research, and the greater public health.

Works Cited

Glasgow, Russell E., Lawrence W. Green, Lisa M. Klesges, David B. Abrams, Edwin B. Fisher, Michael G. Goldstein, Laura L. Hayman, Judith K. Ockene, and C. Tracy Orleans. 2006. "External Validity: We Need to Do More," *The Society of Behavioral Medicine*, 31(2):105–108.

Hawkins, J. David, Richard Catalano, Michael Arthur, E. Egan, E. Brown, R. Abbott, and D. Murray. 2008. "Testing Communities that Care: The Rationale, Design and Behavioral Baseline Equivalence of the Community Youth Development Study," *Prevention Science*, 9(3):178–190.

Merton, Robert K. 1949. *Social Theory and Social Structure*. New York: The Free Press.

National Institutes of Health. *NIH Guide for Grants and Contracts*, "PHS 2009-02 Omnibus Solicitation of the NIH, CDC, FDA and ACF for Small Business Innovation Research Grant Applications (Parent SBIR [R43/R44])," Program Announcement (PA) Number: PA-09-080, http://grants.nih.gov/grants/guide/pa-files/PA-09-080.html, January 2009.

National Institutes of Health. *NIH Guide for Grants and Contracts*, "Weekly NIH Funding Opportunities and Notices," http://grants.nih.gov/grants/guide/description.htm, February, 2009.

National Institutes of Health. *Office of Extramural Research Databook*, "R01 Equivalent Grants (R01 EQ)," http://report.nih.gov/NIHDatabook/, http://report.nih.gov/NIH_Investment/PDF_sectionwise/NIH_Extramural_DataBook_PDF/NEDB%20R01.pdf, May 2008.

National Institutes of Health. *Office of Extramural Research Databook*, "Small Business Innovation Research (SBIR) Grants," http://report.nih.gov/NIHDatabook/, http://report.nih.gov/NIH_Investment/PDF_sectionwise/NIH_Extramural_DataBook_PDF/NEDB%20SBIR.pdf, May 2008. National Institutes of Health, *Office of Extramural Research Databook*, "Success Rates," http://report.nih.gov/NIHDatabook/, http://report.nih.gov/NIH_Investment/PDF_sectionwise/NIH_Extramural_DataBook_PDF/NEDB_SPECIAL_TOPIC-SUCCESS_RATES.pdf, May 2008.

National Institutes of Health. *Office of Extramural Research Databook*, "Trends in Research Career Development (K Awards)," http://report.nih.gov/NIHDatabook/, http://report.nih.gov/NIH_Investment/PDF_sectionwise/NIH_Extramural_DataBook_PDF/NEDB%20CAREER%20DEVELOPMENT.pdf, May 2008.

National Institute on Drug Abuse Web Site, Home Page, http://www.nida.nih.gov/About/AboutNIDA.html, February, 2009.

National Institute on Drug Abuse. *Drug Abuse Epidemiology and Services Research in Cooperation with the Clinical and Translational Science Awards Consortium (R01), Program Announcement (PA) Number: PAS-09-001*, http://grants.nih.gov/grants/guide/pa-files/PAS-09-001.html, October, 2008.

U.S. Department of Health and Human Services. *Omnibus Solicitation of the National Institutes of Health, Centers for Disease Control and Prevention, and Food and Drug Administration, for Small Business Innovations Research (SBIR) and Small Technology Transfer Research (STTR) Grant Applications,* PHS 2008-2 SBIR/STTR Program Descriptions and Research Topics for NIH, CDC, and FDA, January, 2008.

Spalter-Roth, Roberta. 2007. "Sociologists in Research, Applied, and Policy Settings: Bringing Professionals in from the Cold." *Journal of Applied Social Science,* 1(2): 4–18.

Spalter-Roth, Roberta. 2005. "Increasing the Visibility of Sociology PhDs Outside the Ivory Tower." American Sociological Association. *Footnotes,* November, 33(8).

Spoth, Richard, Cleve Redmond, Chungyeol Shin, Mark Greenberg, Scott Clair, and Mark Feinberg. 2007. "Substance-Use Outcomes at 18 Months Past Baseline," *American Journal of Preventive Medicine,* 32(5):395–402.

Weinstein, Jay and Kathryn Goldman-Schuyler. 2008. "The ASA and Sociological Practice." American Sociological Association. *Footnotes,* September–October, 36(7).

CHAPTER 12

Automating Dillman's Total Design Methodology (TDM) for Mail Questionnaires

AN EXAMPLE OF HOW TO IMPROVE SURVEY RESEARCH METHODOLOGY WHILE DOING APPLIED SOCIOLOGY[1]

Paul T. Melevin, California State Government
Susan Ayres, California State Government

> "When one is responsible for directing research, abstract sociological issues turn into down-to-earth challenges."— Paul F. Lazarsfeld (1962)

The authors of this chapter design and conduct surveys for the State of California's Employment Development Department (EDD), which oversees such programs as Unemployment Insurance and Disability Insurance. We are a small six-person research unit that is housed within a larger auditing division. We mainly survey clients of the various EDD programs and sometimes conduct internal surveys of the department's employees or assess the department's operations.

It is not unusual to find small research units like ours within state, local, or federal government agencies. A considerable amount of applied social research is conducted within government organizations. It must be noted, however, that government researchers are often called upon to justify their methods, especially when using specific research methods that do not easily conform to long-established traditions within a bureaucratic environment.

When one considers the different roles played by the academic and applied sociologist, it would seem that the role of identifying ways to improve research methodology would be most appropriately handled by the academic sociologist. After all, an academic researcher is free to explore the various theoretical models that would dictate the best means for collecting and analyzing data. Additionally, the academic would have the time and means for conducting independent controlled experiments that would be needed to test the validity of these varying models. Unlike the academic, the applied researcher has a primary responsibility to work on research that is directly related and fulfills the needs and objectives of his/her employer or contracting agent. Often, however, in order to meet the needs of a client, one is required to examine existing methods, consider alternatives, and determine whether an alternative methodology can still produce the same quality of data.

Almost fifty years ago, Paul F. Lazarsfeld (1962:27 [6]) made the latter argument in his Presidential Address to the American Sociological Association on September 1, 1962. The title of that address was "The Sociology of Empirical Research." At the time, Lazarsfeld was a member of the faculty at Columbia University and was also the head of the Bureau of Applied Social Research at Columbia University. As both an academic and as someone who had years of experience conducting applied social research, he understood that innovation in research methodology was inspired by the need to collect useful data. Today, one will often hear people refer to this ability to be inspired and innovative as "the need to think out-of-the-box."

It should be recognized that the concept of "thinking out-of-the-box" is really not that new. It is not an invention of the 21st century or even the late 20th century nor is it an invention of individuals who happened to obtain degrees in Business Management. Rather, we would contend that this concept has been an underlying argument for the advancement of research methods for generations.

In 1963, Abraham Kaplan wrote a famous book on research methods. It was entitled *The Conduct of Inquiry.* It is in this book that he characterizes "a human trait of individual scientists." He called this trait "the law of the instrument." He describes it in more detail when he says: "It comes as no surprise to discover that a scientist formulates problems in a way that requires for their solutions just those techniques in which he himself is especially skilled." In other words, they are limiting their ability to conduct research because they are not "thinking out-of-the box."

More recently, in a soon to be published article, Smythe et al. (forthcoming) discusses the problems that researchers are having in obtaining data on the residents of small rural communities. After the 2000 Decennial Census, the U.S. Census Bureau discontinued the use of its long census form and replaced it with the annual American Community Survey (ACS). As he notes, "the Decennial Census long form was one of few sources of data with enough small town and rural respondents to allow analyses of specific towns and geographic areas." While the ACS provides more current data, the sample sizes are too small to make reliable estimates for these areas. Additionally, there have been increasing problems with obtaining response to any survey (whether it is conducted by mail, telephone, or over the Internet). Consequently, this need to identify new methods for obtaining this data has led his team of survey researchers to test new methods for obtaining the data.

From the examples noted above, it would begin to appear that our original assumption about the roles that the academic sociologist and applied sociologist play in advancing research methodology might be valid. The examples presented above do suggest that the practicing sociologist or applied researcher is constantly confronting problems that require innovation. Further, if Kaplan is correct, it would certainly appear easier for the academic sociologist or any academic researcher to fall into the habit of fulfilling "the law of the instrument." If this is valid, then it would imply that a very important part of "Doing Sociology" involves being innovative and creative and requires that the practicing sociologist must be as much involved with testing methods for collecting and analyzing data as they are in conducting the research for their employers and clients. How is this possible? Or more appropriately, you might ask, how is it even practical given the nature of their work, which is usually some sort of client-sponsored research?

Our goal in writing this chapter is to tell you a story that will provide a very good example of how the applied researcher responds to an employer's need for change in the workplace. In this case, our focus was on the *personalization* of surveys—the methods by which one makes a survey seem "personal" to respondents, as will be detailed later in this chapter. The situation required us to change our methods for conducting mail surveys. The methods we had been using had been shown over time to be quite successful. Experiments had shown that the use of several personalization methods increase response to mail surveys by anywhere from three to twelve percentage points (Dillman 2007). Consequently, we were very concerned that, by eliminating some of these procedures, we would be sacrificing response and therein increasing what is commonly referred to as non-response error.

To accomplish this, we will need to provide you with some background information describing the survey research methods that we were using. Primarily, this means that we need to tell you about Dillman's (1978) *Total Design Methodology (TDM) for Mail Questionnaires* and how over the years, it has evolved into what he began calling the *Tailored Design Methodology* (see Dillman 2000 and 2007). He refined this even further with the third edition of his book (Dillman, Smyth and Christian 2009).

After summarizing some of this survey research methodology, we will talk about the challenges that we received in December, 2007 from our division chief who felt that we needed to use more automated methods for mailing our questionnaires in order to reduce the costs associated with the personalization methods that we had been using. To accomplish this request we needed to meet and work with representatives from the Office of Documents, Publication, and Distribution (ODPD) to determine how we could automate our methods and yet, try and keep a certain level of personalization. Upon determining what we could and could not do, we needed to test whether the automation was practical for both the needs of the ODPD as well as for our research.

As mentioned above, we were primarily concerned with the effect that this might have on our rate of response and consequently, the non-response error. We did not have an ability to conduct controlled laboratory experiments. So, we had to devise some method for testing the effect. We were lucky, we had some comparative data from a similar survey conducted in the spring of 2007. So, we will talk about these similarities and present the comparative analysis that we conducted.

By the end of this chapter, we trust you will conclude that we were able to advance our knowledge of survey research methodology. Further, it should not only be apparent that we were able to conduct this analysis in an applied research setting but it should also become obvious that efforts to improve research methodology are very much a part of doing sociology. Last, we will demonstrate some of the practical benefits that may result from such efforts. In this study, for example, we were able to demonstrate cost savings. This has fulfilled the administrative needs of our employer. Additionally, it should become apparent that in automating our methodology, we benefited by having more professional time available to work on other projects. That allows us to spend more time on research and less time on things such as stuffing envelopes and signing cover letters.

Why Do We Need a Specific Research Methodology in Order to Conduct Surveys?

Before we are able to describe the specifics of Dillman's (1978) TDM for mail questionnaires, it is important that we lay the foundation by summarizing the rationale for having a specific research methodology for conducting surveys. There are many books and journal articles that address this issue and we do not need to repeat all of that here. Rather, let's begin with a story. Robert Groves reported the following story in a newsletter published by the American Association for Public Opinion Research (AAPOR) back in the mid-1990s.

Charlie Cannell, a social scientist, had a friend who was a member of an engineering society. The engineering society wanted to conduct a survey of its membership. This friend knew that Charlie had conducted a few surveys, so he asked Charlie for some assistance and expected that he could provide it "in a manner of minutes." Realizing that his friend had the wrong impression, Charlie responded by saying that he would be happy to help if his friend provided him some assistance in return. He requested that his friend, the engineer, come by his house to repair a broken television set. Charlie explained to his friend that obviously he should repair the TV in a manner of minutes, too.

This story illustrates the assumption that to the layperson, writing question-naires and conducting social surveys appear to be simple tasks. After all, everyone has written a question or two. Further, all of us have probably conducted one or more short surveys such as asking our friends where they want to go for lunch or dinner.[2] But, it is important to recognize that when one conducts a survey of a sample of a population in order to make—that is, infer—an accurate conclusion about the opinions of the entire population, it requires a much higher level of knowledge and skill.

Most individuals are familiar with public opinion polls that produced grossly inaccurate results (e.g., the 1936 Literary Digest Poll predicting that that Alf Landon would defeat Franklin Delano Roosevelt or the 1948 Roper and Gallup Polls predicting that Thomas Dewey would defeat Harry S. Truman in a landslide, leading some morning newspapers to publish with headlines to that effect). Many are similarly familiar with polls that produced very accurate results. A very good example of accurate polling can be found in the polls conducted at the end of the 2008 presidential election. Most of the polls that were conducted during fall of 2008 accurately predicted that Barack Obama would defeat John McCain. Not only did they predict the winner, an initial analysis of the 2008 polling data conducted by Mark Blumenthal and Charles Franklin posted on their website, www.pollster.com, indicates that these polls also predicted the point spread.

These recent polls differ from the earlier inaccurate polls in large part because those who conducted the polls controlled for the common sources of survey error. Simply put, there are four potential sources of statistical error that can affect the results obtained from any sample survey. These are non-coverage error (error caused by not properly identifying and covering the population to be surveyed), sampling error (the error caused when surveying only a "sample" or fraction of individuals from the population you want to generalize about), mea-surement error (the error caused by not ensuring that the questions and survey instruments are statistically reliable and valid), and non-response error (the error associated with differences between those who did and did not complete the survey that affect their responses to your questions). For a more complete outline and description of these potential sources of error, see Melevin (1997).

The 1936 Literary Digest Poll failed miserably due to its failure to cover the true population of voters. The 1948 Roper and Gallup Polls failed to predict the true outcome of that presidential election because the sampling methods that were used had a high degree of sampling error. Roper and Gallup used what was known as "quota sampling," selecting predetermined numbers of respondents from specific categories of individuals whose total numbers are already known.

The quotas that were used to derive the sample were based on the 1940 Census. By 1948, the U.S. population had dramatically changed due to such things as World War II, a move from an agrarian society to an urban society, and a more educated population due the G.I. Bill instituted after the war. Additionally, Roper and Gallup conducted their final interviews between October 15th and 25th, several weeks before the 1948 election. Due to all these factors, their measures of the public opinion were neither reliable nor valid predictors of that election.

As survey research was refined in the 1950s and 1960s, those involved in public opinion research focused more closely on the efforts necessary to reduce these potential sources of error. One of the most significant changes came, realization that the quota sampling methods used in the 1940s were limited and prone to error. As computer technology developed, it was far easier to draw random samples from databases that more accurately reflected the population. So, survey researchers began to depend on a different way of selecting respondents, known as probability sampling.

During the same period, the fields of cognitive psychology and cognitive social psychology were also undergoing considerable development. This helped social scientists to have a greater understanding of how respondents interpret verbal and written questions. Research began to focus on the ways in which the order of questions and the order in which response categories were presented affected the responses obtained. This led to an understanding of what is called primacy and recency effects. During this time social and behavioral scientists were also beginning to observe differences in response due to the mode in which the survey was presented (i.e., face-to-face interviews vs. telephone interviews vs. self-administered mail questionnaires). With the advent of Internet technologies and the use of the Internet for collecting survey data, the effort to understand the effects of mixing survey modes continues to be a significant area of research (see Dillman, Smyth and Christian 2009).

As Dillman, Smyth and Christian (2009:3–6) note, prior to the 1960s and 1970s, most surveys and polls were conducted in-person using what is called face-to-face interviews. There were many technical reasons that limited the use of telephone interviews and mail questionnaires. For example, long distance calls were very expensive and the poor quality of the long distance connection made it extremely difficult to conduct telephone interviews. With regard to mail questionnaires, creating the questionnaires on manual typewriters and having limited access to duplication equipment made it difficult to produce the questionnaires—and getting an accurate listing of household addresses from which to sample was nearly impossible.

These hurdles were lessened as technology advanced. Dillman, Smyth and Christian (2009:5) note, "in the late 1960s, area codes made direct dial calls possible, and long distance charges decreased significantly in part because of the development of Wide Area Telecommunication/Telephone Service (WATTS). . . . Moreover, by 1970 about 87% of U.S. Households had telephone service." With regard to mail questionnaires, "the invention and widespread availability in the 1970s of copy machines that could quickly produce quality copies on normal white paper" along with the invention and development of electronic typewriters and better printing methods made mail surveys more efficient.

Nevertheless, as Dillman (2009:5) notes, "yet for some time the perception persisted among surveyors that people would not allow themselves to be interviewed over the telephone." Getting people to respond to a survey sent to them in the mail was thought to be even less likely.

The Advent of TDM

In 1978, Don A. Dillman wrote a book entitled *Mail and Telephone Surveys: The Total Design Method*. As he now describes it (Dillman, Smyth and Christian 2009:11), "the subtitle of the book, 'The Total Design Method,' was chosen to describe the need to give attention to designing every aspect of a survey that in some way touched respondents." More specifically, Dillman (1978:12) noted the two main components of TDM: identifying all survey aspects that affected the quality and/or quantity of response, and administering the survey to adhere to the design intentions.

Dillman (1978:12–16) states,

> "The first step is guided by a theoretical view about why people respond to questionnaires," which is derived from social exchange theory. Basically this theory states that behavior results from weighing the costs of the behavior against future benefits provided by another entity. For surveys, this means reducing costs to respond, maximizing rewards for participation, and establishing trust that the rewards will be provided.

Regarding the second component or administration plan, Dillman (1978:20) identifies four essential elements:

1. Identify all tasks in the process.
2. Determine how each task is interrelated.
3. Outline the order of tasks.
4. Determine how each task will be carried out.

When describing the administrative plan, Dillman provided specific instructions on how to prepare the cover letters and the outgoing envelope, down to the type of postage that should be used on the outgoing and return envelopes and the follow-up postcard, and outlined a schedule of four mailings. These prescriptions are listed below.[3]

PREPARING COVER LETTERS (DILLMAN, 1978:172)

1. Date the letter to reinforce its importance.
2. The respondent's name and address must be placed on the letter consistent with business correspondence practices.
3. Use the sponsoring organization's professional stationery to distinguish it from junk mail.
4. Finally, sign the letter by hand with a blue ink pen that leaves indentations on the paper. This feature is nearly impossible to accomplish by machine, therefore, making it the most important personalization element.

PREPARING THE ENVELOPE (DILLMAN, 1978:175)

1. To attract enough attention to be opened, the envelope should resemble one sent by a business to an individual as opposed to mass mailings from an organization.
2. Names and addresses should be typed onto the envelope itself with the surname placed last according to business correspondence practice.

ADDING POSTAGE (DILLMAN, 1978:175)

1. Always use first-class postage to reinforce the mailing's importance and for better handling by the post office.
2. Use a stamped return envelope rather than a business reply one to increase overall response rates and for quicker returns. Dillman (2000:173) explains that in the social exchange context, respondents view an uncanceled postage stamp as money which encourages importance in the survey and trust in the organization. Further, many people can't throw away something of value, in this case the stamp, which may motivate respondents to complete the survey.

PREPARING THE THANK YOU OR REMINDER POSTCARD

The prescriptions for preparing the postcard are similar to those for the outgoing envelope. It should have the individualized name and address printed on the front of the card, possess a real signature, and have a first-class postage stamp attached. The postcard is mailed to all non-respondents. It serves a dual purpose. It allows the researcher to express appreciation for the respondent's participation as well as to remind those who have not responded that you still want their input.

ASSEMBLING THE MAILING PACKET

With regard to packaging, Dillman's prescription for all items (questionnaire and return envelope) is to be enclosed inside the cover letter so that when the recipient opens the packet, everything is pulled out together.

SCHEDULING THE MAILING OF SURVEY INSTRUMENTS

Week 1: Mail pre-notification letter to let respondent know a questionnaire packet will be arriving in the mail.

Week 2: Mail questionnaire packet with cover letter, questionnaire, and stamped return envelope.

Week 3: Mail thank you / reminder postcard to all respondents.

Week 5: Mail follow-up questionnaire packet to non-respondents with a new cover letter, replacement questionnaire, and another stamped return envelope.

In 2000, Dillman wrote a second edition to his famous book. In updating the book, he changed the subtitle from "The Total Design Method" to the "The Tailored Design Method." Dillman, Smyth and Christian (2009:12) states that "the tailored design strategy involved a significant methodological shift from a one-size-fits-all approach to one in which solutions were tailored to most effectively and efficiently deal with the contingencies of different populations and survey situations."

As noted earlier, at the time of writing this chapter, Dillman just published the third edition of his book. He and his co-authors (2009:13) note that this latest edition "retains the tailored design focus introduced in 2000 but takes the concept further to address some of the difficulties that arise out of increased respondent choice as well as the availability of more survey modes, greater differences in the resources available to survey sponsors, changes in contact possibilities for potential respondents, and differential respondent access to resources."

Meeting Administrative Challenges with TDM

In 2002, the authors of this chapter were able to demonstrate that using Dillman's TDM gave us response rates above 50 percent from Unemployment Insurance recipients. Prior to this, the response rates averaged 25 percent or less. At that time, using Dillman's TDM was complicated by administrative limitations on printing and more importantly, restrictions against obtaining and using real postage stamps.

This led to a formal meeting with our ODPD. We were able to make a convincing argument to manually assemble our questionnaire packets and establish procedures for obtaining real postage stamps to apply to these packets. Our publications and distribution personnel were happy to assist us as long as their personnel were not doing any of the labor, a condition which we readily accepted.

In state government, as in private industry, members of upper management change positions, leave, or retire. In 2007, we gained a new division chief and, soon after, several of our office's laser jet printers began having significant problems. Our use of these machines to print outgoing envelopes and thank you / reminder postcards was alleged to have strained the printers. This caused our new division chief to question our methods of packaging and mailing our questionnaires. Further, since she had missed the demonstration and negotiations that occurred in 2002, she also challenged the rationale for having highly paid researchers sign cover letters, postcards, and apply postage.

In December 2007, despite our presentation of evidence that personalization methods would increase response rates from three to twelve percentage points, we were told that we needed to find alternative methods for packaging and mailing our questionnaires. So once again we met with representatives from ODPD to determine a) whether our questionnaires could be packaged and mailed using their machines and b) the degree to which the automation process could meet the TDM requirements. We agreed to consider alternative methods with the caveat to revisit the issue if our response rates suffered.

When we met with the ODPD, we discovered that they were equally concerned with using the proper methods to conduct our research. Unlike our meeting five years ago, they saw this as a challenge to provide a unique service. Together, the two teams discussed the steps in the TDM personalization process, especially ones we considered vital (i.e., ensuring that the return envelopes were stamped with real postage stamps) and they told us what was possible and feasible.

Over the next few months, we worked together to test how effective their machinery was at applying signatures, stamps, tracking numbers, and inserting materials into a package (i.e., cover letters, questionnaires, and stamped return envelopes).

Initially, their machines could not do two steps. The first was stamping the return envelopes, which was remedied with the purchase of a stamping machine. The second limitation would not be resolved as easily. To match the tracking number on each questionnaire with the name on the printed cover letter for stuffing into the same envelope would require required special optical equipment costing around $80,000. We could not justify spending the additional funds to address this limitation, so we resorted to manually matching these items.

Table 1 displays a list of the personalization elements associated with the TDM prescriptions for packaging mail questionnaires discussed earlier. For each listed element, we identify whether or not it was used with the manual and automated packaging methods and highlight the differences between the methods.

Of the thirteen items listed, three were identical for both methods. These were the printing of dates and the respondents' names and addresses on cover letters and applying real postage samples to return envelopes. Of the remaining ten items, seven automation methods varied slightly from the manual method but met the TDM requirements. One of the automation variations actually enhanced our task. The EDD mailing facility is connected to the U.S. Postal Service (USPS) change of address database. When the mail is processed by our facility, it passes through an optical scanner that reads the address on the cover letter or postcard and checks the USPS database to see if a change has been filed. If so, then the equipment sprays the new information on the envelope or postcard. This feature reduced our receipt of return-to-sender packets.

The last three elements did not meet the TDM recommendations. Instead of hand signing all of the pre-notification letters, cover letters, and postcards with a blue ballpoint pen, the signatures were scanned and printed in blue ink onto these items. Additionally, the letters were z-folded so that the respondent's address is viewable through the window envelope with the return envelope inserted behind the cover letter instead of inside the folds. We were especially concerned that these elements that failed to meet the TDM recommendations would reduce our healthy response rates.

Determining the Effect of Automation on Response Rates

With our new automation system in place, we considered how to test whether our response rates had been affected by the changes. We considered many alternatives for determining whether the changes in methodology might affect the response rate. One possible way for determining this would be by conducting a controlled experiment. However, in spring of 2008, we anticipated conducting a very similar survey to one we conducted in spring of 2007 under the old

Table 12.1.   Recommended Total Design Method (TDM) Personalization Elements Achieved by Method

Elements	Method Manual	Automation
Pre-notice / Cover letter		
Date	X	X
Individual salutation	X	X
Business stationery with letterhead	X (colored paper)	X (white paper)
Real signature	X	**SCANNED, PRINTED WITH BLUE INK**
Questionnaire		
Tracking ID	X (front page top edge)	X (front page L side)
Envelope (return)		
Real stamp	X	X
Envelope (outgoing)		
Businesslike size / color	X	X (with window)
Individualized name, address	X (outside)	X (seen thru window and postal update)
1st-class postage	X (real stamp)	X (presorted, metered)
2nd and 4th Mailing Assembly		
All items enclosed by cover letter	X	**Z-FOLD WITH BOOKLET INSIDE, LOOSE RETURN ENVELOPE**
Postcard		
Individualized name, address	X	X (postal update)
Real signature	X	**SCANNED, PRINTED WITH BLUE INK**
1st-class postage	X (real stamp)	X (metered)

Note: Xs represent TDM elements achieved while descriptions in parentheses note minor differences between the manual and automated methods. Automated element descriptions in all capital letters did not meet the TDM recommendations.

manual method. This enabled us to perform this test by comparing the results of these two surveys.

The population surveyed in both 2007 and 2008 were claimants who had filed claims for Unemployment Insurance Benefits (UIB) during the first quarter of each year using EDD's Internet application called eApply4UI. In both 2007 and 2008, we randomly selected a sample of 400 claimants from each population pool. Further, we used identical questionnaires, cover letters, and postcards. More so, the mailing schedule was the same for each year beginning with the pre-notification letters mailed on the second Friday in April and ending with the final follow-up / replacement questionnaire packets mailed on the second Friday in May.

Consequently, the only differences between these surveys were the year in which the surveys were conducted and the methods used to package and process the mail. There was no reason to believe that the UIB claimants surveyed in 2007 were any more or less likely to respond than were those surveyed in 2008. Therefore, if there were any differences in the rate of response, we would need to conclude that it was due to the method used to package and process the mail.

Results

Figure 1 displays the rate at which we received completed questionnaires for both the 2007 and 2008 surveys. Specifically, it charts the cumulative percent of

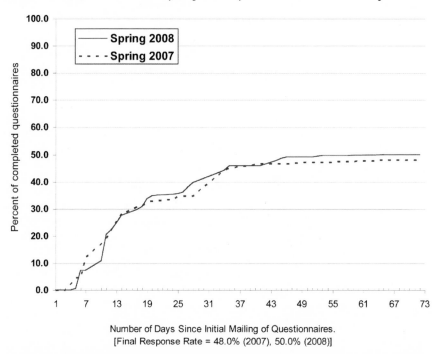

Number of Days Since Initial Mailing of Questionnaires.
[Final Response Rate = 48.0% (2007), 50.0% (2008)]

Figure 1. Cumulative Percent of Completed Questionnaires Received by the Number of Days Since Initial Questionnaire was Mailed (2007 and 2008 eApply4UI Surveys). Note: $Z_{\text{Proportion (2007)-Proportion(2008)}} = -0.57$ **p = .38 (Not Significant)**

completed questionnaires we received during the 73-day data collection period. This figure displays patterns that are almost identical for both 2007 and 2008.

Still, there were some minor differences. In 2007, slightly more respondents returned the questionnaires in the first two weeks of data collection. However, after the initial two-week period, both of the lines in this graph converge. After about seven weeks, we observed a greater rate of response from the 2008 respondents. This difference remained stable for the remaining three weeks of data collection.

At the end of the data collection period, we had a final response rate of 48.0 percent for the 2007 respondents and 50.0 percent for the 2008 respondents. Obviously, the use of the automated methods did not lower the rate of response and technically we obtained a slightly higher response rate in 2008. However, the difference between the two response rates is not statistically different.[4]

COST COMPARISONS

Table 2 displays the estimated number of person hours and the associated labor costs that were needed to print, package, and mail questionnaires to 400 UIB claimants in both 2007 and 2008. In 2007, our research staff provided all of the labor. In 2008, ODPD personnel performed most of the labor. As discussed earlier, our research staff still has to insert the questionnaires into the packets so that the proper questionnaire is matched with its corresponding cover letter.

In order to print, package, and mail the questionnaires in 2007, we estimated that it took a total of 72 person hours. We estimated that the average hourly cost for the researchers involved was $65.50. (NOTE: This is not an hourly wage rate. Rather, it is the rate used for contracting out work. As such, it is inflated to account for benefits and overhead.) Using this average hourly rate of $65.50, we estimated that the 2007 effort cost a total of $4,716.00.

To conduct a similar effort in 2008 using the automation methods, we estimated that it took 25.9 person hours. Of these estimated person hours, 15.9 of them reflect the labor conducted by the ODPD staff at an average hourly rate of $58.50, while the remaining ten hours reflect labor performed by our research staff at an average hourly rate of $65.50. Using these rates, the total cost of the 2008 effort was $1,585.00. These estimates imply a $3,131.00 labor savings (66 percent) by switching to automation without any loss in our rate of response.

Discussion and Conclusions

As noted above, our comparative analysis indicated that our response rate was not harmed due to our automating of the methods used to package and process

Table 12.2.   Estimated Number of Person Hours and Associated Labor Costs Needed to Conduct a Mail Survey with a Beginning Sample of 400

Labor Activity	Manual (2007)	Automation (2008)
Pre-notice (n = 400)		
Print letter / envelope	1.5 hrs	1.6 hrs
Sign letter	4.0 hrs	0.0 hrs
Stamp envelope	2.0 hrs	0.0 hrs
Assembly	8.0 hrs	0.0 hrs
Insert / Seal / Meter	0.0 hrs	1.0 hrs
	15.5 hrs	**2.6 hrs Total Automation**
Initial mailing (n = 400)		
Print letter / envelope / questionnaire	1.5 hrs	3.1 hrs
Sign letter	4.0 hrs	0.0 hrs
ID questionnaire	2.0 hrs	1.0 hrs
Stamp envelopes (outgoing / return)	4.0 hrs	0.5 hrs
Assembly	16.0 hrs	**6.0 hrs**[a]
Insert / Seal / Meter	0.0 hrs	1.0 hrs
	27.5 hrs	**11.6 hrs**
First follow-up (postcard, n = 400)		
Print	1.0 hrs	1.6 hrs
Sign	4.0 hrs	0.0 hrs
Stamp	2.0 hrs	0.5 hrs
	7.0 hrs	**2.1 hrs Total Automation**
Second follow-up (n = 300)		
Print letter/envelope/ questionnaire	1.5 hrs	3.1 hrs
Sign letter	4.0 hrs	0.0 hrs
ID questionnaire	1.5 hrs	1.0 hrs
Stamp envelopes (outgoing / return)	3.0 hrs	0.5 hrs
Assembly	12.0 hrs	**4.0 hrs**[a]
Insert / Seal / Meter	0.0 hrs	1.0 hrs
	22.0 hrs	**9.6 hrs**
Total labor	**72.0 hrs**	**25.9 hrs** $(10^a + 15.9)$
Estimated Labor Costs	**$4,716.00** (72 x $65.50)	**$1,585.00** (10 x $65.50 = $655.00) + (15.9 x $58.50 = $930.00)

[a] Researchers still needed to manually match names and questionnaires.

the mailing of our questionnaires. Additionally, we were able to demonstrate a significant cost savings. However, we have only reported the results obtained from our initial automation effort. Further, this research was conducted by a state government agency that has access to a very high volume mail operations unit.

Since performing this analysis, we have conducted a few more surveys of EDD's claimants using the automation efforts and we have not observed anything that would indicate a drop in response rates due to this use. In spring of 2008, we surveyed 1,000 individuals who had filed claims for State Disability Insurance. Additionally, we conducted a survey of all persons who filed claims for UIB during the third quarter of 2008 (not just those claimants who had used the Internet claim filing process). In both cases, the response rates hovered at or slightly above 49 percent. While we do not have data with which we can make a one-to-one comparison, we can conclude that these response rates are quite similar to those we received when using the manual methods to package and process the mail.

The degree to which other survey researchers will be able to adopt the automation procedures that we use will depend on many factors. The EDD's ODPD is a fairly large operation. Our Mail Operation's Center handles close to ten million pieces of mail each year. As such, this center has some very sophisticated and expensive equipment that require it to be housed in a climate controlled environment. This is done to maintain the proper operation of this equipment and reduce the potential for paper jams.

Additionally, this facility is located near the primary USPS for our region. Since ODPD has a work share and other agreements with the USPS, they are connected to the USPS change of address database. This is a luxury that almost no other survey research organization can access. We strongly suspect that the reduced number of mail pieces that were returned due to inaccurate address information helped us maintain our level of response as well as helped us receive completed questionnaires sooner rather than later.

Nonetheless, even if others are unable to precisely replicate our automation procedures, we believe that the results presented above do advance our knowledgebase and will contribute to advancing the research methods used by practicing sociologists. These results have allowed us to tailor the design of our survey research methods to more appropriately fulfill our unique needs.

When we began telling this story, we noted that it should become obvious that the efforts to improve research methodology are very much a part of doing sociology. There are numerous examples that can be cited (and you will find some of these efforts reported in the other chapters of this book). When one is doing the everyday work of sociology, one needs to be aware of challenges when they present themselves. These challenges may often lead you to identifying improvements in your methodology. Once you recognize the challenge, use your knowledge of research methods along with your creativity to explore methodological changes and potential means for determining the success or failure of changing your methods.

Works Cited

Blumenthal, Mark and Charles Franklin, editors. Pollster.com. www.pollster.com/ blogs/.

Dillman, Don A. 1978. *Mail and Telephone Surveys: The Total Design Method*. New York: John Wiley and Sons.

——. 2000. *Mail and Internet Surveys: The Tailored Design Method. 2nd Edition*. New York: John Wiley and Sons.

——. 2007. *Mail and Internet Surveys: The Tailored Design Method. 2nd Edition. 2007 Update with New Internet, Visual and Mixed-Mode Guide*. New York: John Wiley and Sons.

Dillman, Don A., V. Lesser, R. Mason, J. Carlson, F. Willits, R. Robertson, et al., 2007. "Personalization of Mail Surveys for General Public and Populations with Group Identity: Results from Nine Studies." *Rural Sociology*. 72(4): 632–646.

Dillman, Don A., Jolene D. Smyth, and Leah Melani Christian. 2009. *Internet, Mail, and Mixed-Mode Surveys: The Tailored Design Method. 3rd Edition*. New York: John Wiley and Sons.

Kaplan, Abraham. 1963. *The Conduct of Inquiry: Methodology for Behavioral Science*. New York: Harper and Row, Publishers.

Lazarsfeld, Paul F. 1962. "The Sociology of Empirical Research." *American Sociological Review* 27(6): 757–767. (Originally presented as Presidential Address to the 57th Annual Meeting of the American Sociological Association, September 1, 1962.)

Melevin, Paul T. 1997. "Harder Than It Looks: Four Sources of Error Common to Survey Research." *Social Insight: Knowledge at Work*. 2(1): 38–43.

Smyth, Jolene D., Don A. Dillman, Leah Melani Christian, and Allison O'Neill. (forthcoming). "Using the Internet to Survey Small Towns and Communities: Limitations and Possibilities in the Early 21st Century."

Notes

1. We would like to acknowledge with thanks the contributions made by the following individuals who work in various offices of the State of California Employment Development Department located in Sacramento and West Sacramento, CA: Tonia Lediju, Chief, Audit and Evaluation Division; Michael Greenlow, Chief, Office Of Documents, Publications & Distribution; Karen MacAnneny Sanders, Chief, Publishing & Distribution Services; Sharon Lincoln, Chief, Mail Operations, Cindy Kawano,

Brenda Greenhalgh, Robert Eckman, Philip Pittman, and Mustafa Hasan. The research staff in the Survey and Applied Research Section of the Audit and Evaluation Division provided their support in two special ways. First, they gave us their comments on how we might test these new automation methods. Second, they were extremely supportive of our efforts to present this data and write this chapter. For this, we are very appreciative of the support that we received from Muhammad Akhtar, Ph.D., Research Manager, Chris Cochran, M.B.A., Research Program Specialist II, Keiko Matsushita, M.B.A., Research Program Specialist II, Karene Gamino, Research Program Specialist I, and Onyema Nkwocha, Ed.D., Research Analyst II. Additionally, we would like to acknowledge with thanks the consultation provided by John Tarnai, Ph.D., Director, and Kent Miller, M.A., Mail Survey Manager, of the Social and Economic Sciences Research Center at Washington State University, Pullman, WA.

2. Today this even holds for conducting "survey research." It can be as easy as just going online and putting together a survey from standardized bits and pieces (e.g., using surveymonkey.com), even tabulate and analyze the results (or at least seem to do so) without any knowledge of statistics or research methodology.

3. Of course, some of Dillman's specifications are no longer relevant—for example, there is no longer the option of anything but first-class postage for letter-sized parcels (unless you wish to use more expensive options such as Priority Mail or courier services such as FedEx, which some survey researchers do). However, the underlying principles remain relevant.

4. According to a difference of proportions test, the z-score was -0.57, $p = .38$, which means that the probability that the difference is due to chance is almost four out of ten. We usually look for fewer than five out of one hundred to say that it is not due to chance.

CHAPTER 13

Surveying Health Care Providers

STRATEGIES TO ACHIEVE
HIGH RESPONSE RATES[1]

Jammie Price, Appalachian State University
Christopher J. Mansfield, East Carolina University

Health care providers are surveyed routinely by a variety of means on everything from their attitudes toward complementary and alternative medicines to their practice standards of care (Sikand and Laken, 1998; Hartz, Lucas, Cramm, et al., 2002). Surveys may be administered to providers by an interviewer, face-to-face or by telephone, or they maybe self-administered with respondents engaged by mail, the Internet, or recruitment at professional meetings. Many of these studies are limited by poor response and completion rates, and subsequent sample bias. Further, many of the samples are small and generated by non-random methods.

While these studies may have some descriptive utility, generalization of findings is not scientifically supportable; as these violate assumptions about inferring from a sample to a population (Maisel and Persell, 1996). Surveys are typically of a sample of providers from which the researcher wishes to generalize findings to a larger population. The ability to make this generalization hinges on assumptions about normal distribution of values for variables of interest in the population and sampling procedures. It requires a database (sampling frame) of the provider population of interest, from which a sample can be randomly drawn with known probabilities for individual selection. Inferential statistical procedures then allow researchers to make probabilistic generalizations about the population (i.e., an estimate of a particular value in the population and its statistical significance). Statistical significance then depends on variance and sample size.

A recent extensive review of the literature using physician surveys reported the average response rate from surveying physicians is 54%, far below the minimum 70–80% response rate that methodologists recommend before generalizing from survey data (Field, Cadoret, Brown et al., 2002; Dillman, 1999; Jiwa, Coker, Bagley et al., 2004). Response rates for self-administered surveys are a particular problem, most often ranging from 40% to 60% (Sikand and Laken, 1998; Hartz, Lucas, Cramm et al., 2002; Yedidia, Barr, Berry, 1993; Erickson, Hill, Siegel, 2001; van Walraven, Mahon, Moher et al., 1999).

A few health researchers have studied ways to increase response rates when surveying physicians. One compared the response rates using mail and telephone survey methods on physicians' evaluations of health care plans (Wholey, Christianson, Finch et al., 2003). These authors found that mail surveys with multiple contacts result in reliable, cost effective data with high response rates. Another study contrasted surveying physicians by mail versus during a conference of physicians (Jiwa, Coker, Bagley et al., 2004). The self-administered at-conference survey initially yielded a slightly higher response rate of 86% versus 76% with the mail survey. However, with a follow-up survey on the same sample, the mail survey resulted in a much higher response rate of 88% than the 71% at-conference sample. Additionally, at-conference surveys, though convenient, typically are characterized by selection bias—those who attend a conference differ in many ways from those who do not attend a conference.

Many strategies have been recommended to increase response rates. Personalized, hand-signed cover letters explaining how the survey relates to practice and the providers' interest are effective (Jiwa, Coker, Bagley et al., 2004). Pre-survey notices by mail or telephone, especially from a physician, improve response rates (Field, Cadoret, Brown et al., 2002). Postage costs are always a factor but using first-class stamps to distinguish the mail survey from junk mail is recommended (Dillman, 1999). Always include pre-stamped and pre-addressed return envelopes. The expense of certified mail may be warranted for the last contact attempt. Further, financial incentives may help as may including information useful for practice. In one study, a $50 post response payment increased rates by 9% to 49% (Field, Cadoret, Brown et al., 2002).

Persistence in follow-up is critical to attaining high response rates but it is important to consider high completion rates as well (Tomaskovic-Devey, Leiter, and Thompson, 1995; Shoemaker, Eichholz, and Skewes, 2002). Items with more than 5% nonresponse indicate possible systematic bias (Czaja and Blair, 1996; Kupek, 1998). To achieve high completion rates, surveys need to be perceived as important, short, and easy to complete. For providers surveys must be perceived to have construct and content validity. They should move from general to specific questions, include mostly closed-ended questions, avoid double barreled questions, offer don't-know or no-answer responses only when applicable, and utilize filters and skip patterns to minimize respondent burden (Wholey, Christianson, Finch et al., 2003; De Leeuw, 2001). To improve the validity of survey responses, researchers need to guarantee confidentiality and when possible, anonymity (Yedidia, Barr, and Berry, 1993). This will limit the ideal practice response rather than the real practice response among providers (Hartz, Lucas, Cramm et al., 2002). Further, using more behavioral questions (e.g., Have you observed _____ in your practice in the last month . . .) rather than evaluative (attitudes and belief) questions can increase completion rates (Wholey, Christianson, Finch et al., 2003).

Methods

Our objective with this project was to develop a research design that would attain high response and completion rates, specifically at least a 70% response rate and a 90% completion rate. Adopting many of the suggestions detailed above, we obtained a response rate of 82% for a survey of North Carolina (NC) pediatricians, family physicians, nurse practitioners, and physician assistants on Emergency Medical Services for Children (EMSC). In this paper, we document the research methods used in this project, including pre-test and pilot studies. We describe the full sample survey administration, including information on the sample size determination, telephone contacts, replacements, and non-respondents. Finally, we outline issues for future research.

In 1996, the NC Department of Emergency Services funded an effort to describe and evaluate preparedness of medical practices to provide emergency services for children across NC. A team of pediatric providers at University of North Carolina (UNC) Medical School, Duke Medical School, and East Carolina University (ECU) developed the questionnaire. The team then received revisions from independent consultants at the Sheps Center for Health Services Research at UNC Chapel Hill and the Center for Health Services Research and Development at ECU. The University and Medical Center Institutional Review Board at ECU approved the research protocol.

The survey (see Appendix A) included questions on:

1. Frequency/type of pediatric emergencies occurring in practices;
2. Availability of specific resuscitation and stabilization resources;
3. Provider training in Pediatric Advanced Life Support (PALS);
4. Frequency of office mock pediatric emergencies;
5. Provider perceived importance of providing pediatric emergency care; and,
6. Frequency/type of injury prevention education provided to caregivers.

We designed a cover letter (see Appendix B) and a pocket reference card (see Appendix C) to accompany the survey. The cover letter identified the survey's topic, importance, funding, investigators, and the professional organizations supporting the project. The laminated reference card provided accessible diagnosis and treatment information about pediatric emergencies.

PRE-TEST

We then pre-tested the questionnaire, cover letters, and pocket reference card. We mailed a packet containing these items, along with a pre-addressed and postage-paid return envelope, to three local providers from each of the four professional groups: pediatricians, nurse practitioners, physician assistants, and family physicians. To improve content validity, clarity, simplicity, and flow, we interviewed pre-test respondents concerning question topics, wording, layout, and cover letter content. We also asked about the utility of the pocket reference card.

We received nine returned surveys and conducted interviews with all. The pre-test respondents revealed that some providers in our sampling frame would be ineligible for inclusion because they do not treat children. The pre-test respondents also revealed that providers working in close proximity to emergency departments with pediatric services refer all their pediatric emergencies to the emergency department. The above providers did not have the same need to know about or provide for pediatric emergencies or injury prevention as others. Many of the survey questions were not applicable to them.

Based on the pre-test, we revised the questionnaire wording, sequence, and layout. We added two skip patterns: one for people who provide primary care to few, if any, children, and one for people who work near an Emergency Department. The layout included a front page with the project title and logo and list of investigators and supporters. For the logo, we adopted, with permission, the logo from the EMSC project under the NC Department of Emergency Services. EMSC had previously conducted several statewide mailings with this logo. As such, the logo leant widespread recognition and legitimacy among providers. We then asked two survey methodologists to review the revised 25 item questionnaire.

PILOT

After making minor revisions indicated by the methodologists, we conducted a thorough pilot study to further validate the instrument, determine accuracy of addresses and phone numbers in the sampling frame, refine the sampling strategy, and conduct the power analysis needed to determine sample size. The pilot sample consisted of 48 respondents, with equal numbers of pediatricians, nurse practitioners, physician assistants, and family physicians. The samples were randomly drawn from the NC Medical Board (the state licensing organization) and NC professional association membership lists. The Sheps Center for Health Services Research at UNC Chapel Hill maintained these databases and drew the samples for this project

We mailed reminder cards one week later, followed by a second survey two weeks afterwards to non-respondents. Two weeks later, we attempted telephone contacts with all non-respondents. We attained a 77% response rate in the pilot study (n=37; see Table 1). The sample included 10 pediatricians, 7 family physicians, 9 nurse practitioners, and 11 physician assistants.

We then analyzed the pilot data in the manner intended for the actual study. The pilot study showed no serious problems with question wording or sequencing. However, the pilot study revealed two serious problems with the sampling frame, and two serious problems with the sampling design. First, the sampling frame included many invalid addresses. Second, the sampling frame omitted phone numbers for nurse practitioners and physician assistants.

Third, and most importantly, the pilot survey indicated large differences across provider groups in regard to response rates and eligibility rates (the proportion that regularly treat children; see Table 1). The response and eligibility rates, respectively, were 83% and 100% among the pediatricians; 58% and 71% among the family physicians; 75% and 25% among nurse practitioners; and 92% and 73% among physician assistants. Based on the pilot study findings, we knew that in the full study we needed to improve the sampling design so as to increase the response rate among family physicians and to offset ineligible providers.

Results

A power analysis on two main outcome variables (office preparedness for pediatric emergencies and frequency of patient education on injury prevention) from the pilot data indicated that with samples of 100 in each provider group we would be able to determine whether effect sizes of .5 were statistically different with less than 5% error.[2] In order to attain desired sample sizes of 100 in each provider group we stratified the full sample in proportion to each group's eligibility and response rates in the pilot study. To replace providers who no longer lived or practiced in NC, an issue identified in the pilot study, we drew reserve over-samples of 25 pediatricians, 50 family physicians, 150 nurse practitioners, and 25 physician assistants.

Table 13.1. Research Design Outcomes

	Pediatricians	Family Practice	Nurse Practitioners	Physician Assistants	Total
Estimated response rate from Pilot	0.83	0.58	0.73	0.92	0.77
Estimated eligibility rate from Pilot	1.00	0.71	0.25	0.73	0.67
Sample frame size	1078	2106	838	1238	5260
Sample size needed for analysis	100	100	100	100	400
Size of drawn sample	150	250	400	200	1000
Oversample size	25	50	150	25	250
Replacements from oversample	5	9	9	9	32
Address changes + resends	31	57	9	31	128
Response rate at 4 weeks	43%	31%	43%	36%	39%
Number of 2nd surveys mailed	86	173	227	129	615
Number of non-respondents at 6 weeks (# of phone numbers to call)*	49	123	142	92	406
Phone numbers obtained	37	110	78	69	294
Contacts made**	37	99	70	65	271
Total number of responses (%)	129 (86%)	187 (75%)	322 (81%)	177 (89%)	815 (82%)
Eligible responses (%)	58 (45%)	77 (41%)	97 (30%)	38 (21%)	270 (33%)

* the sampling frame did not include phone numbers for all providers
** includes voice mail messages

In September through December of 1996 we mailed the questionnaire to 1,000 providers randomly selected from a stratified sampling frame containing 5,260 pediatricians, family physicians, nurse practitioners, and physician assistants licensed to practice in NC. Two weeks later we sent out reminder postcards to all providers. At four weeks we had attained a 39% response rate with the following rates among the providers: 43% pediatricians (n=64), 31% family physicians (n=77), 43% nurse practitioners (n=173), and 36% physician assistants (n=71).

We then mailed replacement questionnaires to all non-respondents (see Table 1). If surveys were returned with incorrect addresses we forwarded them when possible. If there was no forwarding address, or if the forwarding address was outside NC, we replaced that provider with one from a respective reserve sample (see Table 1). In total, we replaced 32 providers (see Table 1). By six weeks, the overall response rate improved by 20% (n=594), with the following response rates among the provider groups: 67% pediatricians (n=101), 51% family physicians (n=127), 65% nurse practitioners (n=258), and 54% physician assistants (n=108).

Next we called all remaining non-respondents (n=406), using directory assistance for any missing or incorrect numbers. We asked for both business and residential numbers as many of the physician assistants and nurse practitioners are treated as "practice extenders" and not afforded their own business telephone listing with the physician practice employing them. Only a small number (n=9) of non-respondents contacted by phone refused to cooperate with the survey. Information obtained during this process indicated that most of the non-respondents (90%) were ineligible for the survey because they no longer provided primary care to children in NC.

By the end of the eighth week, we received 815 responses (82% response rate) including 129 pediatricians (86%), 187 family physicians (75%), 322 nurse practitioners (81%), and 177 physician assistants (89%). Many providers did not treat children regularly in community settings, which reduced the sample sizes available for data analysis to 58 pediatricians (45% of responding pediatricians), 77 family physicians (41%), 97 nurse practitioners (30%), and 38 physician assistants (21%). Regarding completion rates, we did not have any items with more than 5% nonresponse.

Discussion

Our research design produced an overall response rate of 82%, much higher than many recently published studies. Our item nonresponse was less than 5%. We believe three strategies were critical in achieving these response rates. First, we developed a well designed, pre-tested questionnaire, perceived by providers to be valid and important, which focused on behavioral questions related to everyday practice. Our experience confirms recommendations of several other health researchers (Sikand and Laken, 1998; Jiwa, Coker, Bagley et al., 2004; Wholey, Christianson, Finch et al., 2003). Second, following Dillman's Tailored Design Method, we made up to 10 contact attempts to each provider, primarily via the mail but supplemented with telephone calls to non-respondents at six weeks post initial mailing (Field, Cadoret, and Brown, 2002; Dillman, 1999). Third, one of the physician PIs (principal investigators) on the project hand signed all the cover letters with each mailing.

In conclusion, we identify and test survey methods resulting in high response rates with a mail survey of North Carolina pediatric providers on emergencies encountered in their practices. The research design obtained an overall 82% response rate (815/1,000) with an 86% response rate among pediatricians, 82% family physicians, 81% nurse practitioners, and 89% physician. We recommend the use of mail questionnaires when surveying health care providers. Specific recommendations include using up to 10 contact attempts; a well designed, pre-tested questionnaire focusing on behavioral questions that relate to everyday practice; a personalized cover letter hand-signed by a physician; and contacting non-respondents by telephone. We recommend that health researchers adopt these methods in future surveys of health care providers. With a strong sampling frame, these methods could result in response rates as high as 90%. Further, our findings reinforce the recommendation to use mail questionnaires over telephone or Internet methods when surveying health care providers. Personalization is key to high response rates; the researcher(s) needs to convey how important the responses of health care providers are to advances in public health.

Appendix A. Survey, Formatting Differed in Actual Administration

Childhood Emergencies In the Primary Care Office:
A Survey of North Carolina Physician Assistants, Nurse Practitioners, Family Practice Physicians, and Pediatricians

Sponsored by:

NC Office of Emergency Medical Services

Duke University, Division of Emergency Medicine

Eastern Carolina Injury Prevention Program

East Carolina University, Center for Health Services Research and Development

Emergency Medical Services for Children Project

Statement of Confidentiality

All your comments will be confidential. The information you provide will be reported only in aggregate form. Identifying information will not be disclosed for any reason.

PLEASE CIRCLE ONE ANSWER CODE FOR EACH QUESTION.

1. To what extent did your training emphasize childhood injury prevention?
Not at all 1
Only a little 2
Moderately 3
A great deal 4

2. Did your training emphasize the capabilities and training of prehospital providers (Emergency Medical Services)?
Yes 1
No 2

3. What proportion of your practice involves the care of children (< 18 years)?
Almost none .... 1 (Go to Question 23)
Some 2
Half 3
Most 4
Nearly all 5

4. In what proportion of routine (sick, well child, or follow-up) pediatric visits do you incorporate injury prevention counseling?
Almost none... 1
Some.. 2
Half... 3
Most.. 4
Nearly all... 5

5. To what extent do you agree with the following statements about injury prevention?

	Strongly Disagree	Disagree	Agree	Strongly Agree
a) I am satisfied with the amount of time I spend teaching children and their families about injury prevention	1	2	3	4
b) I usually just mention a point relating to injury prevention when it is appropriate during the visit	1	2	3	4

c) I rarely discuss any injury prevention subject in detail during a routine (sick, well child, or follow-up) office visit	1	2	3	4
d) It is an important part of my job as a clinician to teach injury prevention to children	1	2	3	4
e) I spend more time discussing injury prevention with first-time parents	1	2	3	4
f) I spend more time discussing injury prevention during well child visits	1	2	3	4
g) With my training and experience, I am capable of effectively teaching parents and children about injury prevention	1	2	3	4
h) I don't have time in my busy day to do all of the childhood injury prevention teaching that I would like to do	1	2	3	4
i) With some patients I do a better job teaching injury prevention than with others	1	2	3	4
j) Health care educators (e.g. public health professional, teaching nurse) should counsel patients and their families about injury prevention, not physicians, NPs or PAs	1	2	3	4
k) I spend about the same amount of time discussing injury prevention with each of my patients	1	2	3	4
l) I am not reimbursed enough for my time to do all the childhood injury prevention teaching I would like to do	1	2	3	4
m) Teaching injury prevention to school-age children and teenagers should be done in school	1	2	3	4
n) The amount of injury prevention teaching I do with the parents of a young child depends on the education level of the parents	1	2	3	4
o) I do about as much injury prevention counseling as other				

clinicians who see children in
their practice   1   2   3   4

p) I have a good working
knowledge of injury prevention
issues for all childhood age
groups   1   2   3   4

6. In what proportion of your routine (sick, well child, or follow-up) pediatric visits is injury prevention not discussed?

Almost none 1
Some 2
Half 3
Most 4
Nearly all... 5

7. To what extent are you familiar with the injury prevention teaching materials below?

	I've never heard of it	I've heard of it	It's in my office	I use it
a) IPP (The Injury Prevention Program)	1	2	3	4
b) "Make the Right Call"	1	2	3	4
c) SAFE KIDS program	1	2	3	4
d) Medic Alert program	1	2	3	4

8a. Does your practice use a reminder system for childhood injury prevention teaching (e.g. check list, reminder "flag" attached to chart)?

Yes .... 1 (Go to Question 9)
No 2

8b. If no, would you like one?
Yes...................1
No 2

9. For the following age categories, in what proportion of routine (sick, well child, or follow-up) office visits do you incorporate injury prevention counseling?

	Almost None	Some	Half	Most	Nearly All
a) Infant (< 1 year)......................	1	2	3	4	5
b) Toddler (1-2 years).................	1	2	3	4	5
c) Pre-school (3-5 years).............	1	2	3	4	5
d) School age (6-12 years)	1	2	3	4	5
e) Teens (13-17 years)................	1	2	3	4	5

10. Do you work directly adjacent or in the same building as a hospital emergency department?

Yes... 1 (Go to Question 15)
No... 2

11. In the last 12 months, how many times have prehospital providers (EMS) come to your office?

None... 1
1-2... 2
3 or more..3
EMS is not available in my area.................   4 (Go to Question 15)
Don't know...................................9

12. On average, how long do you think it takes an EMS unit to arrive in your office?

2-3 minutes................................. 1
5 minutes or more................................. 2
10 minutes or more................................. 3
Don't know.................................9

13. To what extent do you agree with the following statements about the skill level of EMS personnel in your community?

	Strongly Disagree	Disagree	Agree	Strongly Agree	Don't Know
a) The EMS personnel are skilled and know-ledgeable enough to help me in the event of a true office emergency	1	2	3	4	9
b) The EMS personnel are trained to provide adequate care during the transport of an ill or injured child to the hospital	1	2	3	4	9

14. In order to work with EMS personnel during an office emergency, how important is it for you to know about their levels of skill (e.g. Paramedic, EMT-B, First Responder)?

Not at all important..................................... 1
Only a little important................................. 2
Moderately important................................. 3
Very important... 4

15. Please indicate which of the following pediatric emergencies have presented to you in your practice setting during the last 12 months.

	Yes	No
a) Moderate to severe croup..	1	2
b) Asthma flare...	1	2
c) Allergic reaction...	1	2
d) Foreign body in airway	1	2
e) Seizure...	1	2
f) Dehydration..	1	2
g) Serious febrile illness.................................	1	2
h) Respiratory or cardiac arrest................................	1	2

16. How important is it to you that your office or practice setting be prepared to stabilize a true pediatric emergency?

Not at all important..................................... 1
Only a little important................................. 2
Moderately important................................. 3
Very important... 4

17. Which child resuscitation items are immediately available to you in your office?

	Yes	No	Don't Know
a) Oxygen (wall or tank)...	1	2	8
b) Continuous pulse oximetry....................................	1	2	8
c) Pediatric-sized Bag-Valve-Mask Device..............	1	2	8
d) Suction and pediatric catheters............................	1	2	8
e) Oral/nasal pediatric airway....................................	1	2	8
f) Pediatric laryngoscope and ET tube......................	1	2	8
g) Braeslow® tape...	1	2	8
h) Child-sized IV catheter (24G,22G).......................	1	2	8
i) Intraosseous needle (IO)..	1	2	8
j) IV fluids..	1	2	8
k) Resuscitation drugs (Epi, Bicarb, D25W).............	1	2	8

18. How important is it to you that your practice provide the following services?

	Not at all important	Not very important	Somewhat important	Very important
a) Provide emergency care to critically ill children in my office.	1	2	3	4
b) Educate families and children about "911" and the EMS system	1	2	3	4
c) Provide special instructions for my patients at "high risk" for childhood emergencies (e.g. asthmatics, seizure patients)	1	2	3	4

19a. Has your office ever conducted a "mock" or practice pediatric emergency?

Yes.. 1

No.. 2 (Go to Question 20)

19b. If yes, how many months ago was your last exercise? _____

20. Have you taken a PALS (Pediatric Advanced Life Support) or APLS (Advanced Pediatric Life Support) certification or instructor course in the last 2 years?

Yes.. 1

No.. 2

21. What proportion of the clinical providers in your office (e.g. physicians, PA's, NP's, and nurses) have taken a PALS or APLS course in the last 2 years?

Almost none... 1

Some... 2

Half.. 3

Most... 4

Nearly all... 5
Don't know..................................... 9

22. How many continuing medical education (CME) hours related to pediatric emergency care did you complete during the last 12 months?

None... 1
1-2.. 2
3-10.. 3
More than 10................................. 4

23. In your practice, do you see patients........

Full-time... 1
Part-time.. 2

24. Please describe your practice. (Circle all that apply)

	Yes	No
a) Private practice..................................	1	2
b) Academic.......................................	1	2
c) HMO or Managed Care........................	1	2
d) Government....................................	1	2
e) Health Department.............................	1	2
f) Urgent Care....................................	1	2
g) Other (specify) _____		

25. Where do most of your patients live? (Circle One)

Rural areas.................................... 1
Suburban areas............................. 2
Urban areas.................................. 3
All of the above............................ 4
Don't Know.................................. 9

Please write any comments you have below.

_____
_____
_____
_____

Thank you for your help.

Please return the completed survey in the enclosed postage-paid envelope to:

Center for Health Services Research and Development
East Carolina University
Physicians Quadrangle, Building N
Greenville, NC 27858-4354

❏ Check here if you want a summary of the survey results.

Appendix B. Cover Letter

Date

«Title» «Name»
«Company»
«Address1»
«Address2»

Dear «Title» «Name»,

The North Carolina Emergency Medical Services for Children (EMSC) project is conducting a survey on office preparation for childhood emergencies and injury prevention counseling. You were selected from a random sample of all the family practice and pediatric physicians, physician assistants, and nurse practitioners licensed in North Carolina. Your participation will help improve the quality of medical care for children across the state.

Please take 10 minutes to complete the enclosed questionnaire. Your answers will be kept confidential. You can return the completed questionnaire in the enclosed self-addressed envelope. You can receive a summary of the survey findings by checking the box on the first sheet of the survey. If you have any questions, please contact at xxx or Jammie Price, our project director at East Carolina University, Center for Health Services Research and Development, xxx.

In addition to the survey, we have enclosed a pocket reference card on pediatric emergencies in the primary care office. Thank you in advance for your help.

Sincerely,

Name, MD
Affiliation
North Carolina Academy of Family Physician

Pediatric Emergencies in the Primary Care Office—Info on Both Sides of Card
CALL "911" FOR ASSISTANCE AND TRANSPORT
Have Ready for EMS: age, how sick, equipment needed (eg., IV, O2),
meds given
USE BRAESLOW® TAPE FOR RESUSCITATIONS IF AVAILABLE

Age	ET Tube	Weight Estimate	Epi (1:10,000)	HC03	Dextrose (D 25W)	Fluid Bolus (For Shock Only)
Premee	2.5–3.0	1.5–2.0 kg	0.2 ml	1–2 ml	3–5 ml	15–20 ml
Newborn	3.5	3 kg	1/3 ml	3 ml	6–12 ml	30–60 ml
5 mo	4.0	6 kg	1/2 ml	6 ml	15 ml	60–120 ml
1 yr	4.5	10 kg	1 ml	10 ml	30 ml	100–200 ml
Toddler	5.0	13–15 kg	1.5 ml	15 ml		
5 yr	5.5	20 kg	2 ml	20 ml	50 ml	200–400 ml
10 yr	6.0 cuff	30 kg	3 ml	30 ml		
Teen	7.0 – 8.0 cuff	50–70 kg	5–10 ml	1 amp (50 ml)	1 amp D50W	500+ ml

	Dose	Route	Supplied	Conc.
Epinephrine (1:10,000)	0.01 mg/kg	IV, ET,) Intraosseous (IO	1 amp = 1 mg = 10 ml	0.1 mg/ml
HCO3	1 mEq/kg	IV, IO	1 amp = 50 m Eq = 50 mll	1 mEq/m
Atropine (*Min 0.2mg)	0.02 mg/kg	IV, ET, IO	1 amp = 1 mg = 10 ml	0.1 mg/ml
Dextrose (D25W)	1–2 ml/kg	IV, IO	1 amp D50W	0.25 gm/ml

ET tube distance (teeth or gum to mid-trachea distance) = 3 X ET tube size or "just through" vocal cords

Drugs down ET tube = "LEAN": Lidocaine, Epi, Atropine, Narcan

Pediatric Emergencies in the Primary Care
Office—Info on Both Sides of Card

Airway Emergencies		Seizures	
Croup	Racemic Epinephrine 0.5 ml/3ml NS	Valium®	0.5 mg/kg per rectum
	Decadron® 0.25 – 0.5 mg/kg IV		0.1–0.3 mg/kg IV, IO
Asthma/	Albuterol Nebulizer/Inhaler	Ativan®	0.05–0.1 mg/kg IV, IO
Bronchiolitis	Solumedrol® 1–2 mg/kg IV	Dilantin®	10 mg/kg IV Bolus,
Allergic	Epinephrine (1:1000) 0.01 ml/kg SC,		repeat x1 for
Reactions	max 0.3 ml		continued seizing
Foreign Body		Phenobarbital	10–20 mg/kg IV Bolus

Age<1	Back blows X5, then chest thrusts X5+ finger sweep (repeat)
Older and alert	Heimlich maneuver
Older and max 0.3 ml	Abdominal thrusts x 4

Fever/Dehydration/Shock		Pain/Sedation, Miscellaneous	
Fluid Bolus	10–20 ml/kg NS or Lactated Ringers, IV or Intraosseous (IO), repeat as needed	Versed®	0.05–0.1 mg/kg IV, IO
		Morphine	0.1 mg/kg IV, IO
Febrile Illness	Ceftriaxone® 50–100 mg/ kg IV/IM	Cardioversion	0.5–1.0 Joules/kg
		Defibrillation	2–4 Joules/kg
"r/o Sepsis"	Ampicillin 100 mg/kg IV/IM	DKA Fluid Bolus, followed by 0.1 U/kg	
age<4–6 wks	Gentamycin 2.5 mg/kg IV/IM	Regular Insulin IV	

Works Cited

Czaja, R. and J. Blair. 1996. *Designing Surveys: A Guide to Decisions and Procedures.* Thousand Oaks, CA: Pine Forge.

De Leeuw, E. D. 2001. Reducing missing data in surveys: an overview of methods. *Quality and Quantity* 35: 147–160.

Dillman, DA. 1999. *Mail and Internet Surveys: Tailored Design Method.* New York: Wiley.

Erickson, M. J., T. D. Hill, and R. M. Siegel. 2001. Barriers to domestic violence screening in the pediatric setting. *Pediatrics* 108(1): 98–102.

Field, T. S., C. A. Cadoret, M. L. Brown, L. Martin, M. Ford, S. M. Greene, D. Hill, M. C. Hornbrook, R. T. Meenan, M. J. White, and J. M. Zapka. 2002. Surveying physicians: do components of the total design approach to optimizing survey response rates apply to physicians? *Medical Care* 40(7): 596–605.

Hartz, A., J. Lucas, T. Cramm, M. Green, S. Bentler, J. Ely, S. Wolfe, and P. James. 2002. Physician surveys to assess customary care in medical malpractice cases. *Journal of General Internal Medicine* 17(7): 546–555.

Jiwa M., A. E. Coker, J. Bagley, J. Freeman, and M. Coleman. 2004. Surveying general practitioners: a new avenue. *Current Medical Research and Opinion* 20(3): 319–324.

Kupek, E. 1998. Determinants of item nonresponse in a large national sex survey. *Archives of Sexual Behavior* 27(6): 581–594.

Maisel R. and C. H. Persell. 1996. *How Sampling Works.* Thousand Oaks, CA: Pine Forge Press.

Shoemaker, P. J., M. Eichholz, and E. A. Skewes. 2002. Item nonresponse: distinguishing between don't know and refuse. *International Journal of Public Opinion Research* 14(2): 193–201.

Sikand A. and M. Laken. 1998. Pediatricians' experience with and attitudes toward complementary/alternative medicine. *Archives of Pediatric and Adolescent Medicine* 152(11): 1059–1064.

Tomaskovic-Devey, D., J. Leiter J, and S. Thompson. 1995. Item nonresponse in organizational surveys. *Sociological Methodology* 25: 77–110.

van Walraven, C., J. L. Mahon, D. Moher, C. Bohm, and A. Laupacis. 1999. Surveying physicians to determine the minimal important difference: implications for sample-size calculation. *Journal of Clinical Epidemiology* 52(8): 717–723.

Wholey, D. R., J. B. Christianson, M. Finch, D. Knutson, T. Rockwood, and L. War-
rick. 2003. Physicians Evaluating Health Plans Research Team. Evaluating health plan
quality 2: survey design principles for measuring health plan quality. *American Journal
of Managed Care* 9 Spec No 2: SP65–75.
Yedidia M. J., J. K. Barr, and C. A. Berry. 1993. Physician's attitudes toward aids at
different career stages: a comparison of internists and surgeons. *Journal of Health and
Social Behavior* 34(3): 272–284.

Notes

1. This project received funding support from the North Carolina Office of Emergency Medical Services and was approved by the IRB at East Carolina University.

2. This means that differences of .5 between the groups could be detected with less than 5% error.

CHAPTER 14

Ethics and Values in Sociological Practice

Harry Perlstadt, Michigan State University

Sociological practice raises a set of ethical issues and values that differ somewhat for clinicians who conduct interventions and applied researchers who carry out assessments and evaluations of programs or analyze policies. This chapter will review the history of human research protections, examine portions of Title 45, Part 46 of the *Code of Federal Regulations* referred to as *45 CFR 46* or the "Common Rule" that governs federally funded research, and discuss issues confronting sociological practitioners in obtaining approval for research activities.

A Brief History of Human Research Protection

The issue of the ethical responsibilities of researchers emerged after World War II with the realization that Nazi physicians had conducted experiments in concentration and prisoner of war camps. The physicians were brought to trial and the verdicts against them included ten points that became known as the Nuremberg Code. The points included obtaining voluntary consent to participate in experiments, avoiding all unnecessary physical and mental suffering and injury, the ability of a person to end their participation at any time and the willingness of scientists to terminate the experiment at any stage if its continuation will result in harm to the participant.

In February 1966, U.S. Surgeon General William Stewart issued a statement on clinical research and investigations involving human beings (see Schrag, 2009). It required that in order to receive a Public Health Service (PHS) grant, all studies, including those in the behavioral and social sciences would have to undergo the same vetting as medical experiments. This meant prior review by institutional associates to assure an independent determination of the protection of the rights and welfare of the participants. As a result universities began to establish what are now known as Institutional Review Boards (IRBs).

While the original focus had been medical and clinical research, the social and behavioral sciences were included because of concerns over invasions of privacy. In 1965 Congressman Cornelius Gallagher (D-NJ) and a House Government Operations subcommittee held hearings on the use of psychological tests such as the Minnesota Multiphasic Personality Inventory (the MMPI) on federal employees and job applicants. During the hearings a witness mentioned that some mental health research sponsored by the PHS contained questions of a personal or intimate nature, but that participation was entirely voluntary and that invasion of privacy did not arise. Gallagher and three other congressmen requested that the PHS make sure that protecting personal privacy was a paramount concern. In turn, James Shannon, director of the National Institutes of Health assured the congressmen that this was the policy and later stated "It's not the scientist who puts the needle in the bloodstream who causes trouble. It's the behavioral scientist who probes into the sex life of an insecure person who really raises hell." (Schrag, 2009, 3).

A 1972 article by reporter Jean Heller about the Tuskegee Syphilis Experiment propelled the protection of human research participants onto the front pages of most major newspapers. In 1932 the PHS and the Tuskegee Institute enrolled 400 poor black men in a longitudinal study of syphilis. The men were not told they had syphilis, but were given free medical exams, free meals and free burial insurance. At the time, no proven treatment existed, but by 1947 penicillin was recognized as being effective. Nevertheless the men were not treated, and as a result many of their wives and children were infected (Tuskegee, 2002). The Department of Health, Education and Welfare (DHEW) appointed the Tuskegee Syphilis Study Ad Hoc Panel to review the study as well as the department's existing policies and procedures for the protection of human subjects. The panel recommended that Congress establish a permanent body with the authority to regulate all federally supported research involving human subjects (Advisory Committee on Human Radiation Experiments (ACHRE), 1995).

The US Senate held hearings in February 1973 on the issue and identified a wide range of abuses in medical research and the field of human experimentation, which included psychology and by extension, other social and behavior sciences. At the end of May 1974, DHEW published regulations for the use of human subjects requiring the formation of an IRB to approve all research proposals before they submitted to DHEW for funding consideration. These committees were to review, among other things, the safety (risks and potential benefits) of the proposed research and the adequacy of the informed consent obtained from each subject prior to participation in the research. Two months later, in July 1974, the National Research Act was passed, officially giving DHEW the authority to establish regulations in this area (ACHRE, 1995). The law specifically limited the scope to biomedical and behavioral research.

The National Research Act also established the National Commission for the Protection of Human Subjects of Biomedical and Behavioral Research. Congress charged the National Commission with the task of identifying the basic ethical principles that affect the decision to use, or to not use, human research subjects. The Commission was to then develop guidelines to assure that research involving human subjects would adhere to the ethical principles, that is, it was asked to link norms with values. Specifically, the Commission was to address issues that had been raised in the Tuskegee Syphilis Experiment: informed consent, assessment of risks and benefits, and selection of subjects. The eleven member Commission consisted of three physicians, three attorneys, a bioethicist, a Christian ethicist, a behavioral-biologist, a physiological-psychologist and the president of the National Council of Negro Women, Inc. Noticeably missing were members representing the main line social science research disciplines such as social and clinical psychology, sociology, and anthropology. In February 1976, the Commission held a four-day meeting at the Smithsonian Institution's Belmont Conference Center. Its 1979 final statement, "Ethical Principles and Guidelines for the Protection of Human Subjects of Research," would be known as *The Belmont Report* (1979).

The Belmont Report begins by distinguishing between the practice of accepted therapy and biomedical/behavioral research. "Practice" was defined as interventions designed solely to enhance the well being of an individual patient or client and that have a reasonable expectation of success. "Research" involved activities intended to test hypotheses, permit conclusions to be drawn, and thereby to develop or contribute to generalizable knowledge. The Report recognized that the boundary between research and practice is often blurred because both may occur together, for example when research is designed to evaluate a therapy. Furthermore, while a clinician may develop new or untested procedures that could be considered experimental, this did not automatically place it in the category of research. Rather, the Commission expected that at an early stage such experiments would be made the object of formal research in order to determine whether they are safe and effective. The Report concluded that if an activity included any element of research, that activity should undergo review for the protection of human subjects.

The Commission declined to make any policy determination regarding the research problems related to social experimentation because such problems may differ substantially from those of biomedical and behavioral research. The Commission, naïvely it turns out, stated that such problems ought to be addressed by one of its successor bodies. As a result all research efforts—biomedical, behavioral, and social—were essentially treated alike when it came to writing legislation and regulations. But by the time the Commission was finishing its report; two social science research studies had become highly controversial for their methods and findings, raising new ethical issues regarding social and behavioral research.

Stanley Milgram's (1974) *Obedience to Authority* investigated the conditions under which naïve individuals would follow the direction of an authority figure even when it was apparent that they would injure another person. Milgram deceived subjects into believing they were administering ever increasing electrical shocks to a learner every time he gave an incorrect answer. The last ten shock levels were clearly marked as "extreme intensity shock," "danger: severe shock" and finally between 435 and 450 volts as "X X X." It is obvious from Milgram's pictures and film that many subjects exhibited signs of intense stress as they decided whether to administer the next higher level of shock or stand up to authority and refuse to continue. At one point Milgram likened the stress to the temporary scare one experiences riding a roller coaster. Milgram debriefed all subjects after the experiment was over and conducted a follow-up survey to identify any long-term effects. The survey revealed that only one percent reported feeling sorry or very sorry to have participated in the experiment. But critics claimed that the realization of what they had done had a lasting impact on the subject's own personality and that the subjects told Milgram what they thought he wanted to hear during the debriefing and in the follow-up survey.

Around the same time, in the field research reported in *Tearoom Trade*, Laud Humphrey (1975) observed homosexual encounters at a men's restroom in a public park. A few men at the restroom questioned why he was hanging around, and advised him to function as a "watch queen," that is a voyeur who also served to warn of any approaching police. To gain more information about some of the men, he copied their license plates and was able to obtain home addresses with the assistance of someone in the local police department. He then included 50 of them as a comparison group in an ongoing survey he was conducting of men's social health. He interviewed them in their homes, explaining that they had been randomly chosen to participate in the survey. But none of those interviewed knew the true reason they were selected or that he had previously observed them as the watch queen at the restroom. In his dissertation and subsequent publications, Humphreys hid the identity of the men he observed and interviewed, knowing the consequences if they were "outed." He later burned all identifying materials. Nevertheless, some claim that the level of detail was such that a few individuals could be identified.

To accomplish its main task, the Commission looked at writings and discussions that had taken place to date and asked, "What are the basic ethical principles that are used to judge the ethics of human subject research?" *The Belmont Report* identified three principals relevant to the ethics of research involving human subjects: respect of persons, beneficence and justice. The principle of *respect for persons* concerned the moral requirements to acknowledge the autonomy of individuals to make informed decisions and to protect those with diminished autonomy, specifically children, and prisoners. The principle of *beneficence* was the obligation not to harm, which reflected the Hippocratic Oath. It also considered the consequences of action by focusing on maximizing possible benefits while minimizing possible harms. The third principle, *justice*, asked, "Who ought to receive the benefits of research and bear its burdens?" It required that the selection of research subjects be fair and directly related to the problem being studied. Subjects should not be recruited on the basis of convenience or manipulability. Further, the resulting therapeutic devices and treatments should not be provided to only those who can afford them and denied to those who had participated in the research.

The Commission then applied the three principles to the three major charges set by Congress: informed consent, assessment of risks and benefits and the selection of subjects. While these already existed in semi formal research practices, the Commission took what might be called scientific folkways and developed an ethics of responsibility by identifying a corresponding moral requirement. *The Belmont Report* retrospectively provided a rationale for title 45, part 46 of the *45 CFR 46* that was published just before creation of the Commission. The Report became the basic document that underpinned the implementation and interpretation of the federal regulations as well as future amendments.

The Common Rule—Review Categories and Waivers

In 1981 the President's Commission for the Study of Ethical Principles and Guidelines for the Protection of Human Subjects of Biomedical and Behavioral Research recommend that all federal agencies adopt a "Common Rule" for research protections. By 1991, 16 federal agencies had adopted *45 CFR 46* as governing the research they sponsored. Of interest to most social and behavioral clinicians and researchers are the definition of research, the categories for exemption from review and expedited review, as well as conditions for waiving consent and documentation of consent.

Research is defined as a systematic investigation, including the development, testing and evaluation of hypotheses designed to develop or contribute to generalizable knowledge. In addition some demonstration and service programs may include research activities. This means that, if supported by federal funds, sociological practitioners involved with the development, assessment or evaluation of various programs and groups are subject to an IRB. An IRB is the administrative body of a university, hospital or research institution established to protect the rights and welfare of subjects recruited to participate in biomedical or behavioral research. It has the authority to approve, require modifications or disapprove all research activities as specified by both federal regulations and the institutions own research policies (Office of Human Protections, 1993). Private foundations that fund programs and initiatives involving assessment or evaluation generally require IRB review and many universities and hospitals require that all researchers submit their proposals for IRB review.

Some research activities conducted by sociological practitioners such as political polling, market research and program evaluation may not fall under the definition of research in *45 CFR 46*. In most cases the results will only be used by the sponsoring entity and are not intended for external reporting. Similar activities conducted by journalists and the media are not covered because they are not federally funded and their findings are widely distributed and contribute to public knowledge of events and issues.

45 CFR 46 contains provisions that exempt some activities from review. These include (a) research conducted in established or commonly accepted educational settings, involving normal educational practices, (b) research involving the use of educational tests (cognitive, diagnostic, aptitude, achievement), survey procedures, interview procedures or observation of public behavior as long as the subjects cannot be identified and any disclosure of their responses outside the research could not reasonably place them at risk of criminal or civic liability or damage their financial standing, employability or reputation, (c) research involving the collection or study of existing data, documents, records, pathological specimens, or diagnostic specimens, if these sources are publicly available or if the information is recorded by the previous investigator in such a manner that subjects cannot be identified, (d) research and demonstration projects which are conducted by or subject to the approval of department or agency heads, and which are designed to study, evaluate, or otherwise examine public benefit or service programs, and (e) taste and food quality evaluation and consumer acceptance studies.

What Does this Mean for the Practicing Sociologist?

A prudent sociological practitioner employed by or under contract with a university, health care facility or social service agency should submit a research application or proposal to an appropriate IRB requesting recognition of exempt status. This protects both the practitioner and the institution by assuring that human research protections are followed although the activities will not be monitored by the IRB.

Research involving no more than minimal risk may undergo an expedited rather than full review. Minimal risk means that the probability and magnitude of harm or discomfort anticipated in the research are not greater in and of themselves than those ordinarily encountered in daily life or during the performance of routine physical or psychological examinations or tests. The following types of research are eligible for expedited review if they involve no more than minimal risk:

- Research involving data, documents or records that have previously been collected for either research or non-research purposes or will be collected solely for non-research purposes,
- Collection of data from voice, video, digital or image recordings already made for research purposes,
- Research on individual or group characteristics, attitudes or behavior including interpersonal relationships and cultural beliefs or practices,
- Research employing methods commonly used in social, behavioral, epidemiological, health services and educational research such as survey, interview, oral history, participant observation, ethnography, focus group, program evaluation, human factors evaluation or quality assurance methods.

While some of the above listed research may already be exempt, it is the responsibility of the researcher to check with the appropriate IRB on the correct review category for their research and to explain how the proposed research would not exceed minimal risks.

Researchers may also request a waiver from the requirement to obtain informed consent. Research conducted by or for state or local government officials to study, evaluate or examine public benefits or service programs may be eligible for a waiver if the research could not practicably be carried out without the waiver. But more generally, informed consent may be waived if the research involved no more than minimal risk, the waiver will not adversely affect the rights and welfare of the subjects, the research could not practicably be carried out without the waiver and subjects will be provided with pertinent information about the research after participation whenever appropriate.

In general IRBs are reluctant to waive informed consent for subjects who are likely to be vulnerable to coercion or undue influence, such as children, prisoners, pregnant women, mentally disabled persons, or economically or educationally disadvantaged persons. However, some IRBs have waived parental consent or permission for a minor child to participate in research, as well as the assent of the child. For example, Youth Risk Behavior Surveys (YRBS) are administered to middle and high school students about the use of alcohol, tobacco and other drugs or dietary and sexual behaviors. The survey is entirely anonymous, standardized, and administered nationwide through state and local public health agencies. The survey design selects classrooms not individual students to participate. Each local school district approves the survey, the decision to participate in it, and the mechanism for active or passive parental consent. The IRB at the Centers for Disease Control, which oversees and partially funds these national surveys, determined that the surveys were not research but rather part of public health practice. Therefore, IRB review and approval was unnecessary, and by extension individual or guardian informed consent under the Common Rule was likely unnecessary (Hodge 2004:44).

Nevertheless some state and local health departments and their university partners that conduct the YRBS research require that all federally funded research be locally reviewed. This complicates matters. For instance, one university IRB denied approval because parental consent was passive. In passive consent a form and detailed information about the study was distributed to parents and if the parents did not return the form, the parents were deemed to have granted passive consent. Some parents will send the form back indicating they do not want their child to participate, and those children will not be included in the study or given the survey.

The request for a waiver from documented informed consent began by pointing out that the survey was being carried out on behalf of state or local public health officials. It then argued that the study could not be practicably carried out using active consent. The purpose of the study was to identify and assess risky behavior among students and having a highly biased sample of only those children whose parents returned a signed consent form would not suffice. In addition the children received an assent form with the survey that they did not have to sign. The assent form clearly stated that they did not have to complete the survey and should quietly sit at their desks until time was up. The questionnaire was anonymous, the completed surveys and data would be securely kept by the university based survey research center, and all reports would contain aggregate data. The rights and welfare of the children were protected through the sampling procedure of classrooms rather than individuals and the anonymity of the surveys. Finally the children were told that if, after the survey, they had any questions or problems they could contact a trusted guidance counselor in their school. After some negotiation with the university IRB the waiver was approved.

Documented informed consent may be waived in cases where the data is collected and recorded anonymously and subjects would be better protected without the existence of a signed document. Waivers may also be granted for secondary data about human subjects where no possible personal identifiers are transferred to the researcher. Finally in some cultures and organizations individuals are wary of signing a consent form but are willing to verbally consent to an interview, survey or observation. Again it is the responsibility of the researcher to fully document the waiver request by addressing each of the four waiver criteria whether they seem to apply or not.

Obtaining Approval for Research Activities

All researchers and practitioners should act ethically and adhere to the principles and regulations covering human research protections, but problems arise in dealing with the system. A good deal of *45 CFR 46* pertains to the establishment and functioning of Institutional Review Boards. As we have discussed, the system is decentralized and the government has, in effect, entrusted human research protections to individual educational, health and research institutions (Seligson, 2008). The idea was to avoid a federal level review board that would not be able to handle the hundreds of thousands of proposals and could not take into account local research conditions and contexts. Decentralized review had developed during the middle of the twentieth century when organizations sponsoring medical research created scientific advisory panels to monitor the hazards of clinical trials. The scientific community was seen as the carrier of informal morality, or research mores, which rested on networks of researchers sharing a sense of collective responsibility. Their expertise and investigation of common questions enabled them to provide informal oversight and evaluate potential hazards (Halpern, 2004).

Decentralized review has its drawbacks, especially if an appeals procedure is absent. In modern society most governmentally established bodies have limited powers of decision making for which they can be held accountable (Nobles and Schiff, 2002), but each IRB is an autonomous entity and is not required to follow precedent. Each case is decided on how well it meets the seven criteria listed at *45 CFR 46.111*. This means that an IRB may reach different decisions in what appear to be similar circumstances. Furthermore, research approved by one IRB may not be approved by another. While IRBs may be accredited by the Association for the Accreditation of Human Research Protection Programs (AAHRPP) for having and following standard policies and procedures, this does not replace an appeals process in which decisions can be reviewed and overturned by a higher level administrator, independent mediator, or a law court. Researchers do not enjoy a right of appeal of IRB decisions (Perlstadt, 2004). An appeal of an IRB decision cannot be made to an official of the institution such as a Vice President for Research. Rather, the appeal is to the chair of that IRB who may then ask other members of the IRB to review or reconsider the decision. This means a researcher who strongly disagrees with an IRB decision must find a way to finesse the system.

In one case a university researcher working with a community based organization received IRB approval for an observational study of tobacco sales to minors (Malone, Yerger et al., 2007). The study would include mapping all convenience and liquor stores in the community, a survey of tobacco advertising in the community, observed smoking activity of minors in public places and store sales practices including single cigarette sales. No individuals, stores or sales clerks would be identifiable from the data and findings would be reported in the aggregate. After a short time, the community based organization wanted to have minors attempt to purchase single cigarettes. This modification was submitted to the IRB which rejected it, arguing that the minors were being asked to commit an illegal act and that trying to buy single cigarettes constituted entrapment of store personnel.

The decision was appealed and the researcher submitted documents including a grant of immunity signed by the local district attorney, a section of the state penal code that buying a single cigarette was not illegal, a written opinion from the state attorney general that such research activity was not entrapment, and citations to other studies using identical procedures. The IRB turned down the appeal on the grounds that the anticipated benefits of the study did not justify the risks. Perhaps it believed that the modification had become an experimental intervention involving deception of clerks and was no longer a research project that it could approve and monitor. In response the community based organization broke off from the research project and carried out the activities independently as a community action project, knowing that any results could not be published or reported as findings of the university based research project. It could, however, post its findings on its own website and present them at city or county council meetings on tobacco control.

In another case, one component of a federal program required the provision and evaluation of mental health services to teen parents who were referred to the agency by child protective services for child abuse or neglect. The mental health agency used a standardized and verified intake and exit instrument that could be used to assess the success of treatment. The evaluator made arrangements to obtain de-identified data on the cases that included only summary measures of attitudinal and behavioral change. Because these were mental health records, the IRB insisted that the evaluator obtain documented informed consent from each parent. But the research could not practicably be carried out without the waiver because if the evaluator were to contact the families to obtain consent it would mean their confidentiality, and from the evaluators perspective their anonymity had been compromised. Further, parents were given a booklet at the time of their intake containing the state law governing mental health services that informed them that their cases could be used for research or evaluative purposes provided that their identities were protected. When the IRB rejected the appeal, the evaluator drafted a report to the sponsoring federal agency explaining the above situation, inserted a blank page and stated that as a result, the following blank page was the total evaluation report for this component of the program. The draft was sent to the chair of the IRB who quickly set up an appointment and negotiated a procedure to access the data without requiring the documented informed consent.

Of greater interests to sociological practitioners is when a project starts out as non-research but slowly evolves into research. *The Belmont Report* recognized that the boundary between practice and research is often blurred because both may occur together or that research may evolve out of non-research activities. The Report believed that in such situations, the activities would become research and adhere to the basic principles. However, *45 CFR 46.119* only deals with this issue in terms of research that was undertaken without the intention of involving human subjects. In such circumstances, the research is first reviewed and approved by an IRB followed by a certification submitted by the institution to the federal department or agency that can grant final approval for the proposed change. This appears to be a rather high hurdle and one that might be appropriate for drug trials moving from laboratory or animal testing to human subjects.

Activities carried out by sociological practitioners usually begin with individuals or groups as human clients, not as human subjects. At some point the practitioner realizes that the activities and results should be systematically recorded as they could contribute to generalizable knowledge and be treated as research. The prudent sociological practitioner should be following the code of ethics of the Association of Applied and Clinical Sociologists (AACS) or the American Sociological Association (ASA). The AACS principle on responsibility notes that in their practice, sociological practitioners bear a heavy responsibility because their recommendations and professional actions may alter the lives of others. Sociological practitioners recognize that they must not do harm to clients or research subjects. In addition, sociological practitioners are alert to personal, social, organizational, financial, and political situations or pressures that might lead to the misuse of their influence.

Concerning unanticipated research opportunities, the ASA's ethical standards state that if during the course of teaching, practice, service, or non-professional activities, a sociologist decides to undertake research that was not previously anticipated, steps should be taken to announce this intention and to ensure that the research can be undertaken consonant with ethical principles, especially those relating to confidentiality and informed consent. The sociologist should seek the approval of an Institutional Review Board or, in the absence of such review processes, another authoritative body with expertise on the ethics of research.

If some aspect of research has already been started such as recruiting subjects or data collection, the practitioner-turned-researcher now has the tricky task of applying for retrospective approval. Clearly the regulations call for review prior to starting a study in order to protect participants, and the very concept of retrospective review is considered anathema. Almost all university based IRBs explicitly state that they do not have the option of granting retroactive approval after research is completed, and most professional journals state that they will not publish manuscripts that lack prior IRB approval.

Michigan State University's IRB offers a training program that features a series of scenarios that deal with the problem of emerging or unanticipated research (Vasilenko, 2007). The scenarios state: "You are the IRB Administrator and must decide if the following research needs to be reviewed by the IRB." Three scenarios are presented and discussed below.

In the first scenario, a Foundation contracts with a faculty member to do an evaluation of its teen pregnancy prevention programs, which include interviews with grant recipients and teen clients. The evaluation report will (a) be given only to the Foundation or (b) the Foundation has given the faculty member the right to publish any interesting data. Here the IRB administrator will probably decide that the project is exempt if the report is to be given only to the Foundation for its internal purposes (a), but that if permission has been granted to publish (b), an expedited or full review may be necessary depending on the nature of the questions asked of the teen clients who are considered doubly vulnerable as minors and possibly pregnant females.

In the second scenario, a professor is subcontracted from another institution to perform an analysis on de-identified data. The professor is paid merely to provide statistical analysis and a statistical report to the investigator from the other university, but (a) is not to be a co-investigator or co-author, or (b) will be listed as a co-author on papers. In this case one assumes that the collection of the de-identified data was previously reviewed and approved. The preparation of a report on de-identified secondary data would not require review (a). The request to include the subcontracted professor as a co-author (b) could be exempted under the subcontracting institution's IRB approval, yet require an expedited review at the subcontracted professor's home institution.

In the third scenario, a teacher developed and used a novel approach to teaching science to elementary students. After three years, she has compared students' knowledge and performance (using students' work and grades) and finds the new approach is much superior. She wishes to present her method and data to a national teachers' convention. Clearly the teacher began this project for the benefit of her own students to improve teaching techniques and learning skills that would be exempt under *45 CFR 46*. It is her intent to present her findings at a national teachers' conference that apparently triggered the submission for IRB review. On the surface, this appears to be a request for retroactive approval and the IRB administrator could recommend that the IRB reject the proposal without any review. The teacher should have realized early on that, certainly by the end of the first year, the results were presentable or publishable and requested a review. When practice activities have evolved into research, Tufts University, for example, recommends that the research be put on hold and an application submitted to the IRB. By coming to the IRB "as soon as you realize that you have made the mistake of not getting IRB approval in advance, you may be able to salvage some of your project" (Tufts, 2005). Often the cost of retrospective approval is the destruction of all data collected up to the point of approval.

Another issue facing the teacher in this scenario is finding an appropriate entity to review her research proposal. In general, school districts do not have formal IRBs, but they have committees that review and approve research. In fact, IRB is a generic term used by federal agencies to refer to a group whose function is to review research to assure the protection of the rights and welfare of the human subjects (FDA, 2008). Although not the case in this scenario, if federal support is involved, such an entity is required to follow federal regulations.

Similarly, independent sociological practitioners should try to find an IRB to review their proposal if they are being funded in some degree by federal funds or intend to publish their findings. Besides universities and hospitals, the AAHRPP accredits commercial and independent IRBs that provide reviews for a fee. But many specialize in biomedical clinical trials, so it is important to find a commercial or independent IRB that has experience in social and behavioral research.

Lessons Learned

The last half of the twentieth century has witnessed the emergence of research ethics. The basic principle of beneficence, or do no harm, was extended from the realm of practice to the realm of research. Compared to practice, research imposes a rather impersonal and systematic relationship between investigator and subject. Therefore, the principles of respect for person or individual autonomy and justice or being treated fairly and uniformly were added. Sociological practitioners must learn to deal with the boundary between practice and research.

Research ethics are reinforced through a decentralized system based at institutions providing administrative support and facilities for researchers. Each IRB interprets and enforces the federal regulations, which leads to inconsistencies within and across IRBs. Since the IRB system reviews each proposal on its own merits, researchers perceive the decision as a private trouble requiring a private solution (Mills, 1959) that they must individually deal with if they wish to carry out and publish their research. They must learn to navigate and work the system. Unfortunately, training and tutorials for human research protection concentrate on exemplars of research misconduct that lead to the development of research ethics, and the key requirements of documented informed consent, protection of vulnerable populations, and fairness in recruitment of subjects. What is largely omitted from trainings and tutorials are the provisions for waivers from these requirements and how to build a case for those waivers.

It is, therefore, necessary from the start for sociological practitioners to properly identify the nature of their research and its potential risks in order to apply for an appropriate review whether exempt, expedited or full. Since IRB members will interpret the regulations somewhat differently and take into account local research conditions and contexts, researchers should be prepared for requests to revise and resubmit their proposal. Usually this involves rewording the informed consent document or adding details on how the data will be securely maintained to protect confidentiality. But occasionally a proposal will be rejected for reasons that can be appealed through a waiver. The regulations are fairly clear on the four grounds for requesting a waiver and the researcher should address each of them in their appeal whether they seem to apply or not.

More problematic, however, is when a sociological practitioner realizes that a project not previously regarded as research now has research potential. The regulations at *45 CFR 46.119* dealing with research undertaken without the intention of involving human subjects appear to be based on biomedical and pharmaceutical research. They do not address situations that arise in social and behavioral research or the question of research that may evolve out of non-research activities. The reluctance of IRBs to consider retrospective review is understandable, but, nevertheless, some IRBs have done it. The best advice for a sociological practitioner at the point where the project is perceived to be researchable is to temporarily suspend all activities that could be construed as research and apply to an IRB for review. It helps if the practitioner already has a working relationship or at least contacts with an IRB. Both practice and research ethics demand the protection of clients and subjects.

Works Cited

ACHRE. 1995. *Final Report of the Advisory Committee on Human Radiation Experiments*, Chapter 3: The Development of Human Subject Research Policy at DHEW. Washington DC: Superintendent of Documents, U.S. Government Printing Office. www.hss.energy.gov/healthsafety/ohre/roadmap/achre/chap3_2.html.

The Belmont Report. 1979. *The Belmont Report: Ethical Principles and Guidelines for the Protection of Human Subjects of Research, Report of the National Commission for the Protection of Human Subjects of Biomedical and Behavioral Research.* Washington, DC: Department of Health, Education and Welfare. www.emerson.edu/graduate_studies/upload/belmontreport.pdf.

FDA. 2008. "Information Q&A." www.fda.gov/oc/ohrt/IRBS/faqs.html.

Halpern, Sydney A. 2004. *Lesser Harms: The Morality of Risk in Medical Research.* Chicago: Univ. of Chicago Press.

Hodge JG, Gostin LO. 2004. "Public Health Practice vs Research: A Report For Public Health Practitioners Including Cases and Guidance For Making Decisions." *Council of State and Territorial Epidemiologists*: Feb. 10, 2004. www.cste.org/pdffiles/new pdffiles/CSTEPHResRptHodgeFinal.5.24.04.pdf.

Humphreys, Laud. 1975. *Tearoom Trade: Impersonal Sex in Public Places.* Enlarged Edition with a retrospective on Ethical Issues. Chicago: Aldine Publishing Co.

Malone, Ruth E, Yerger, Valerie B, McGruder, Carol and Froelicher, Erika. 2007. "Ethical Tensions in IRB Review of Community Participatory Research." http://depts.washington.edu/ccph/pdf_files/Malone.pdf.

Milgram, Stanley. 1974. *Obedience to Authority: An Experimental View.* New York: Harper and Row.

Mills, C. Wright. 1959. *The Sociological Imagination.* New York: Oxford University Press.

Nobles, Richard and Schiff, David N. 2002. "The Right to Appeal and Workable Systems of Justice." *Modern Law Review,* 65: 676–701.

Office of Human Protections. 1993. *Protecting Human Research Subjects: Institutional Review Board Guidebook.* Washington, DC: DHHS. www.hhs.gov/ohrp/irb/irb_guidebook.htm.

Perlstadt, Harry. 2004. "The Researcher's Bill of Rights." *Medical Humanities Report,* 25:2 (Winter). http://bioethics.msu.edu/newsletter.

Schrag, Zachary M. 2009. "How Talking Became Human Subjects Research: The Federal Regulation of the Social Sciences, 1965–1991." *Journal of Policy History,* forthcoming (accepted April 2008).

Seligson, Mitchell A. 2008. "Human Subjects Protection and Large-N Research: When Exempt Is Non-Exempt and Research Is Non-Research." *PS: Political Science & Politics* 41: 477–482.

Tufts. 2005. "Frequently Asked Questions: What Do I Do if I've Already Started Research That Might Need IRB Approval?" *Social, Behavioral and Educational Research.* www.tufts.edu/central/research/ResearchNews/Administrations/MIRBIssue4.htm.

Tuskegee. www.npr.org/programs/morning/features/2002/jul/tuskegee.

Vasilenko, Peter. 2007. "Are They Human Subjects? Is it Research? What is Your View?" Handout at Fall IRB Conference, Michigan State University.

Index

Page numbers in italic represent figures and tables.